telling tales
out of school

**Also available by Kevin Jennings
from Alyson Books**

One Teacher in Ten: Gay and Lesbian
Educators Tell Their Stories

Becoming Visible: A Reader in Gay and Lesbian History
for High School and College Students

telling tales out of school

gays, lesbians, and bisexuals
revisit their school days

edited by kevin jennings

alyson
books

LOS ANGELES • NEW YORK

MANUFACTURED IN THE UNITED STATES OF AMERICA.
PRINTED ON ACID-FREE PAPER.

THIS TRADE PAPERBACK ORIGINAL IS PUBLISHED BY ALYSON PUBLICATIONS INC.,
P.O. BOX 4371, LOS ANGELES, CALIFORNIA 90078-4371.
DISTRIBUTION IN THE UNITED KINGDOM BY TURNAROUND PUBLISHER SERVICES LTD.,
UNIT 3 OLYMPIA TRADING ESTATE, COBURG ROAD, WOOD GREEN,
LONDON N22 6TZ, ENGLAND.

FIRST EDITION: AUGUST 1998

02 01 00 99   10 9 8 7 6 5 4 3 2

ISBN 1-55583-418-3

LIBRARY OF CONGRESS CATALOGING-IN-PUBLICATION DATA
    TELLING TALES OUT OF SCHOOL : GAYS, LESBIANS, AND BISEXUALS REVISIT THEIR
    SCHOOL DAYS / EDITED BY KEVIN JENNINGS.—1ST ED.
        ISBN 1-55583-418-3
        1. GAY STUDENTS—UNITED STATES—BIOGRAPHY. 2. LESBIAN STUDENTS—UNITED
    STATES—BIOGRAPHY. 3. BISEXUAL STUDENTS—UNITED STATES—BIOGRAPHY.
    I. JENNIGS, KEVIN, 1963–   .
    LC2575.T45 1998
    371.826'64'0922—DCB   98-20717 CIP
    [21]

It's my book, so I can do as many of these as I want.

For:

— Nan Dunham —

who always manages to be there, even

when she's Down Under;

— John Spear —

the absolute bestest person I have ever worked with;

and, of course,

— Jeff Davis —

good gorilla!

Contents

Acknowledgments

Since publishing *One Teacher in Ten* in 1994, my life has been completely absorbed by the process of building the Gay, Lesbian, and Straight Education Network into a national organization. This book, in fact, was inspired by our Back-to-School Campaign, in which we encourage lesbian, gay, bisexual, and transgendered adults[1] and their allies to write their former teachers, explain what antigay bias did to them during their own school years, and ask what they are doing to make it better for today's youth. Given that GLSEN has become my entire life and has inspired this book, I'd like to thank a number of folks who have played an important role in making that organization happen:

—a wonderfully dedicated staff, and I am delighted to have had the pleasure to work with the following people at some point over the last three years: Jenn Carriere, Shih Chang, Deidre Cuffee-Gray, Michael Finkle, Janice Goldfarb, Phoebe Hanshew, Asha Leong, Sara Marcus, Leif Mitchell, Stéphane Riethauser, and (last but certainly not least) John Spear. Special thanks go to Jenn Carriere and Stéphane Riethauser, without whose help I could never have done this book;

—a hard-working board of directors, blessed with an extraordinary president in one Charles E. Todd;

—literally hundreds of chapter leaders and board members,

whom I will not dare to mention by name because I'd leave some deserving soul off in my dotage;

—extraordinary volunteers who give unstintingly of their time and energy, among whom are: Mary Bonauto of Gay and Lesbian Advocates and Defenders and David Buckel of Lambda Legal Defense and Education Fund (real heroes of mine); Doug Livingston, Brock Waldron, and everyone at the Rabid Design Group; Rich Carson, Willis Emmons, Mary Gentile, and Jonathan Rotenberg, who have all been critical parts of our Leadership Training Institute; Joel Heller, who has given so much in so many ways; and undoubtedly many others whom I do not have space to name but to whom I give thanks;

—and wonderfully generous individual and institutional supporters, including: Ron Ansin; Vic Basile; Terry Bean; Beth Behar and the Streisand Foundation; Susan Clark and the Columbia Foundation; Bob Crane, Moy Eng, and the Joyce Mertz-Gilmore Foundation; David Dechman; Tim Gill and Katherine Pease of the Gill Foundation; Brook Glaefke; Stuart Harrison and David Ring; Jim Hormel and Ray Mulliner of Equidex; Billie Jean King; David Mixner; Michael Palm and Craig Anderson of the Michael Palm Foundation; Andy Spahn, Porter White, and the David Geffen Foundation; Arnold Schwab; Andy Tobias and Charles Nolan; Michael Sporn; everyone at Tzabaco; Henry van Ameringen; and Terry Watanabe.

My family (which for me includes some folks who are biologically related to me and many who are not) has been a constant source of love and support for the past three years. I know I'll leave somebody out, but hey, here goes: David Beck and Greg van Boven (for the editing help on the Fourth of July weekend!); Frank Burnes and John Geheran; Greg and Mary Lou Davis (personifications of that overused term "family values"); Tom DiMaria; Scott Ellis; Anne Gable; Alan and Claudette Jennings (an inspiration that we can all overcome the limitations with which we were raised); Fred Koch; Rod Oneglia; and Ben Stilp. A few special thanks go to: John Di

Carlo, who gets mentioned here because nobody gets *two* books dedicated to him; Jeff Dupre, for making one of my dreams come true; Philip Lovejoy and Jim Moses, who are as much fun as you can have without breaking the law; and Luke, the world's best poopalah and one with unerring aim.

And, of course, there's Mom. You continue to inspire me.

Kevin Jennings
New York City
July 1997

NOTES

[1] From this point forward, I will use "gay" only, which I intend to be inclusive of all of these different groups. I would use queer, but I hate that word.

thought as kids would compensate for being faggots. Some obliterate their minds with K or X or alcohol, to forget themselves. Most never, ever want their contemporaries to know that they were not always fabulous. Maybe they don't even remember that themselves anymore.

I believe that the roots of virtually all of our community's problems go back to what we experienced as kids, especially in school. It is in our school years that we learn the lesson which our education system imparts best to young gay people: Hate yourself. We spend most of our lives trying to unlearn that lesson. We often think that if we can just get far enough away from what happened then, we might be OK.

I was inspired to do this book by GLSEN's Back-to-School Campaign, in which adults write their former schools and tell the teachers there what it was like to be gay. People started sending me copies of their letters, and the stories were so incredible, so moving, that I knew there was a book crying out to be made from them. Our stories are our best weapons in the fight against homophobia: I believe deeply that most people don't mean to hurt and, that if people knew what they were doing to those of us who are gay, they'd change. In spite of everything, I still believe people are good at heart, even though I know what happened to the person who became famous for writing those words.[2]

But most important, I saw what the letters did for the writers. By going back and confronting the demons of their pasts, the writers emerged as new people, somehow freer of the burden of self-hatred, empowered to move beyond the lessons they were taught as kids, able to reclaim their whole selves. And I thought, what if our whole community did this? Maybe we'd all be a little more whole, a little more able to love ourselves, a little more kind to each other. Maybe we'd grow up.

My real hope for this book is that it will teach two distinct lessons to its potential readers. For any nongay readers, I hope you'll emerge from these stories with a deeper sense of exactly how horrible it is for most people to grow up gay in this country, and a strong enough sense of outrage that you actually try to do something about it. For my gay readers, I hope that these stories will help you in your own process of unlearning what we were all taught in school, and that you'll be moved enough to think of the generation growing up today, a generation experiencing much the same pain we experienced in our youth, and that you will resolve, once and for all: Never again.

A lot to ask of a little book. But the impossible always starts with the absurd, doesn't it?

Notes on the Editing and Structure of this Book

Editing this book presented numerous challenges that I would like to briefly share with the reader. First is the issue of gender imbalance in the collection. I received over four times as many submissions from men as from women, resulting in an anthology that is slightly over 60% male. Why is this? Was there something flawed in my outreach and recruitment of writers? Or was the school experience somehow more traumatic for men, so that they felt compelled to write about it? I don't have an answer to these or any of the dozens of questions that occurred to me when I thought about this disparity. I'd love to hear your opinions.

Second, I had a real struggle around the issue and the role of sexuality in these pieces. Some essays use explicit language and describe scenes that might startle some readers. Part of me wanted to sanitize these pieces, in hopes of making the book somehow more "acceptable" (whatever that means) to the "mainstream" (whatever that is). But, in the end, I felt that to do so would be both dishonest to the writers and a misrepresentation of the experience of many in our community. For many, these experiences were critical components of their coming of age as gay people, and it would be wrong for me as an editor to declare them off-limits in hopes of getting the book into a few more school libraries. I decided to let them stand, as I am an editor, not a censor.

Finally, I found certain themes came through the many disparate voices found here, and I have structured the book along those lines. The reasons behind the groupings are as follows: "The Good Old Days(?)" includes contributors from the pre-Stonewall era; "Misfits and Rebels" includes selections from those who somehow chafed against the norms of their communities; "Sissies and Tomboys" deals specifically with those who found the restrictions of gender to be the most burdensome (an overwhelming theme in the book—I never fully appreciated how the issue of sexual identity is often first expressed as an issue of gender nonconformity before editing this anthology); "Youngsters" features essays that focus on pre–high school experiences; "Love Stories (Of a Sort)" centers on those for whom romantic and/or sexual interludes were the key events of their narrative; and "Survivor Stories" focuses on those who overcame violence, harassment, and isolation (as if we all didn't!). Some pieces could easily be moved into two, three, or even four of these categories but, by breaking it down in this way, I hoped to help readers focus on the themes that most interested them. With that in mind, I encourage you to "skip around" rather than read the book cover to cover.

NOTES

[1] To repeat a footnote from the acknowledgments, for stylistic purposes, I use *gay* to mean *gay, lesbian, bisexual, and transgendered.* I know I should use *queer,* but I hate that word.

[2] These words are taken from *The Diary of Anne Frank.*

telling tales
out of school

Prologue

Revelation

by Irene Zahava

My teacher, one nylon-encased leg neatly crossed over the other, allowed a delicate ankle to swing slightly, and I caught a sudden glimpse of slip, the color of melted caramel, a scallop of silky hem against seam, which promised so much more, and in that instant the mysteries of grammar were revealed.

The Good Old Days(?)

Occasional Angels

by Sally Miller Gearhart

– *1946* –

– *1997* –

Rampant hormones, I now figure. That's what must have been going on in my junior year of high school (1946) when my boyfriend and I couldn't keep our hands off each other. My favorite teacher called me to her desk in the English room between classes and sternly admonished me for "smooching in the halls."

Now in my tiny high school in the mountains of southwestern Virginia, it was sort of a badge of honor to have a boyfriend (particularly if he played football, which mine did) and sort of risqué to indulge in "public displays of affection." It was also sort of courageous to be so blatant about such behavior as to have it commented on, and sort of heroic to endure chastisement for it.

But I was mortified. Miss Arraga McNeil was my mentor, my role model, my champion; she was the woman who had told me when I came to school in male drag—complete with hat, vest, tie, watch, and watch chain—that I looked "quite dapper"; she was the teacher who would have let me play Macbeth if Richard Gilmore hadn't gotten well in time to croak his way through the immortal lines. She ended her scolding of me that day with a sentence that made me feel like I had cheapened southern womanhood for all time: "You can do better than give yourself to boys."

Four years later, when I awoke in the arms of my first woman lover, Miss McNeil's words pounded in my head, this time with a heavy emphasis on the word "boys." I grinned. Had that wonderful woman on that dreadful day really intended that emphasis? Had she been bestowing a coded blessing on my giving myself to girls? I would never know. But I did realize at that moment that throughout my childhood and adolescence there had been several teachers like Arraga McNeil. They had suspected that, in spite of my loving family, I felt out of place in my hometown, and they had reached out to help me at crucial times. They had been my "occasional angels," precious chaperons of my soul.

I was born not just into a family but also into a Tribe—a Tribe of white Protestant Anglo-Germans who resided among the oaks and sugar maples that footed Angel's Rest, one of the Appalachians' most picturesque mountains. There, in a town that had been given its latitude and longitude by a young surveyor named George Washington, I learned my tribal lessons: loyalty to one's own, mistrust of outsiders, fear of all who were not like us. I also learned how girls and boys were expected to behave, how they were to preserve tribal customs and bear the children who would do things tomorrow exactly as their grandparents had done them yesterday. We were a salt-of-the-earth people, farmers-moved-to-town. We believed in a threefold god and in the everlasting virtue of hard work, a clean house, and strong drink.

Six unmarried women supervised my first years of school: Miss Ethel St. Clair, Miss Aileen Walker, Miss Doris Miller, Miss Lila Guthrie, Miss Josephine Miller, and Miss Nancy Pearson—though as for that every woman in town was called "miss" except when she was sporting her husband's name; then she was, for instance, "Miz Deward Walker" or "Miz C.A. Hoilman." (It was my piano teacher, Miss Sue Phillips, who once told me with a wink, "You'd better not put 'miss' on my tombstone, because I haven't missed as much as you think I have!")

I remember some gift of personal support from several of these women and from a number of my high school teachers. I'm now sure that most such gifts went beyond the ordinary validation that good teachers give their students.

For instance, I think of Miss Lila Guthrie, who knew how desperately I wanted to go on the 4-H camp-out to the top of Angel's Rest; I wasn't yet ten, the requisite age for 4-H membership, but she conferred with the club sponsor and two days later I stood mountaintop-high above New River, watching its northward progress toward the Ohio. And of Coach George Surber, who encouraged me in my determination to dribble like the boys—after-practice exercise far beyond the single bounce we frail girls were allowed on the half-court.

And there was Miss Lucille Fizer, young and brand-new to the high school faculty. Like several other teachers, she lived at my grandmother's rooming house, and it was she who pleaded The Grapevine Case in my behalf. I was an inveterate grapevine rider, always trying to perfect my Tarzan style, sometimes swinging out over the river or the railroad tracks. I'm not sure whether it was the danger or my comparative nudity that most upset my family, but Miss Fizer defended me for both offenses. I was in love with Miss Fizer for a very long time.

Then there was Mr. Joe Meredith, who knew something of what it means to be different. He never allowed his "deformed" right hand out of his pocket, and he once saved me some embarrassment (probably the judges some too) by asking casually, "Do you really want to enter that beauty pageant?" He also assured me that the C he had given me in chemistry could not stop me from being a doctor.

In retrospect I'm struck by how ardently these teachers supported the dominant culture and yet found it possible to encourage my small acts of rebellion. They were for me sort of ground and figure, the guardians of my Tribe's sacred myths and at the same time my protectors, magically present just when I needed them.

Miss Macie (Miz C.L.) McClaugherty is a case in point. She was a pillar of the church, a member of the DAR, and one of the town's most highly respected citizens. She was the formidable principal of grades one through seven, dispensing a relentless justice to the tardy, the disruptive, and the disobedient. We heard about her whippings when we entered the first grade, and we prayed daily that we would never in our school years run afoul of her paddle. She was a legend in her own time and a worthy priestess of the Tribe. All of us had to pass through her seventh grade classroom if we were ever to achieve the status of high school student.

I was a fifth grader when the "war" between the boys and the girls was most constant and intense. It wasn't all the girls, of course, for sure not the ones who never got their dresses dirty. But there were eight or nine of us who had a fort, a large outcropping of rocks in the field adjoining the school grounds, which we had roofed over with tree branches and grass. Before and after school, at recesses, and at lunch time, we defended it against the boys who regularly raided and vandalized it. Ordinarily we dodged their rocks and dirt clogs and then retaliated by sailing stickweeds into their midst—wonderful yard-long stalks that made awesome spears. We had perfected the Camelot Volley, which we executed with spine-chilling Valkyrie battle cries and derisive laughter. It was extremely effective.

But on one fateful day, having just been warned that another stickweed fight would be grounds for expulsion for all of us, we had no recourse but to fling our bodies at the attackers. I was rolling down to the bottom of the sinkhole in full body clinch with Jesse Trout—both of us choking, scratching, poking, pounding, and hollering—when we were rudely pulled apart. I looked into the face of Miss Nancy Pearson, the vice-principal, and knew the jig was up.

Miss Macie interviewed us one by one, all 15 or so of the miscreants who had bruised and cut each other beyond any previous damage, and then blessedly decided on a group punishment instead of individual whippings. But while we each waited our turn outside her office, we suffered far more in fear and anticipation than we did in the following weeks of detention. I sat there bargaining with God, promising him everything from regular Prayer Meeting attendance to my mumblety-peg knife if he'd just get me out of this one. Miss Macie's conversation with me was brief.

"So you're the one who rassled Jesse Trout."

"Yes, ma'am."

"He's big."

"Yes, ma'am."

"Are you about to try that again?"

"No, ma'am."

"Good. You can go now. You'll probably be staying after school for a month with the others. Go on. No paddle this time."

"Yes, ma'am!" I lunged for the door.

"Sally!"

"Yes, ma'am?"

She was writing something as she spoke. "Did you lick him?" Then she looked up at me over her glasses.

I stammered a little. "Yes, m-m-ma'am, I think I was about to."

Miss Macie smiled. "Good." She went back to her papers.

I left feeling properly chastened. And like I had just found a friend.

When I got into Miss Macie's seventh grade I felt even more that she was my ally. She never favored me above others but she made it clear that my "crazy" ideas were OK. I once contended that the United States shouldn't bomb Rome because of all the ancient buildings and artwork there. The whole class, patriots one and all, laughed and booed and hissed. Miss Macie took up my cause, made a big lesson out of it, and had us all looking at pictures of St. Peter's and the Sistine Chapel.

During that year another girl and I debated two boys on the proposition, "Women Are As Intelligent As Men." (Believe it.) We took it before a joint meeting of the PTA and the Lions Club. By the final rebuttal, logic was in tatters and there were no holds barred. I got so riled up that with a burst of totally unconscious lesbian separatism I announced that women could do very well without men, thank you very much, and that in fact the world didn't need men at all, since men couldn't even have babies. The audience roared, we lost the debate, and I wallowed in an agony of confusion and distress.

Miss Macie sat with me afterward in the empty auditorium. She gave me a long-overdue lecture on human reproduction that served only to show me the enormity of my naïveté and to deepen my embarrassment. But then she reminded me that bees reproduce all the time without fertilization, and that a good bit of the plant kingdom does, too. And didn't I know that lots of ordinary things once seemed foolish—like airplanes and radio communication? Maybe in a hundred years my idea wouldn't seem foolish at all.

I sat there scraping my feet around on the heavily oiled wooden floor of the auditorium, listening hard to this tough woman, keeping my upper lip unwaveringly stiff and my chin very high. I could take the humiliation. Any good tomboy knew how to manage that one without letting on how much it hurt. What I couldn't handle was her kindness and her obvious respect for me. So it was finally tears of gratitude that broke free from my brave little heart. They fell on the greasy floor and scattered like crystal BBs all around my saddle oxfords and her medium-heeled black kid pumps. I think she hugged me. I know she unwadded a Kleenex and handed it to me. And she gave me a beautiful smile. I was of course in love with Miss Macie.

*   *   *

For the past 28 years, ever since I became a blatant and very vocal lesbian-feminist, I've been asking queer people—all of us sexual outlaws who tumble up and down and around the scales and parameters of sexual identification—what their childhood was like, specifically how they related to the culture or subculture they were raised in. A huge majority describe themselves as misfits or "kooks," painfully restricted or repressed children/adolescents who seemed constantly to be going against the grain. Many of us suspected that we were adopted, so out of step did we feel.

Lately I've expanded my sample, asking almost everyone I know the same question. Not surprisingly, queers are not alone in feeling that we never wholly bought the culture we were expected to embrace. Artists (like painters, poets, actors) and dreamers (dropouts, mystics, "crazies"), of whatever sexual identification, frequently describe childhoods of disharmony or displacement.

I've come to believe that the queers, artists, and dreamers (categories which of course overlap) are the trailblazers in the new way of thinking that characterizes this end of the millennium. We're sort of the vanguard of the changes that everyone, maybe even our old Tribe, will be undergoing in these next few decades.

Maybe my occasional angels—and teachers like them all over this country—had some special mission, some divine charge to reach out to misfits and to help us survive. I know that I got the message loud and clear from somewhere that my pain was temporary, that I was simply undergoing some necessary period of indenture. I now suspect that the Arraga McNeils and the Macie McClaughertys of the world gave us room and opportunity to imagine the unspeakable, to entertain the notion that the perceptions of our Tribe were limited and even disabling. I think they were helping us to remember—at least the artists and dreamers among us—that intuition and not reason is the true gift of the human animal, that we are spirits having a human experience, and that Love is the universal truth from which we all come. For sure the Tribe would have considered all this sheer balderdash, and probably our occasional angels did not themselves know consciously what they were helping us to remember. But there they were, those angels; and, in a sense, because of them, here we are.

I think that even beyond what artists and dreamers suffered in childhood and adolescence, we queers experienced our misfit-dom in a special way. Since time runs backward as well as forward, we were different then because of what we have become now, as if we knew in our young bones that we would be a part of a powerful political force. As I sat in Miss Macie's seventh grade classroom there dwelt in me the whole of the Stonewall rebellion, the increasing gay glory of the 1970s, and every struggle and sweet victory that we have participated in since that time.

If I could have spoken up from the best (and most unknown) part of myself that day when I rolled down the hill with Jesse Trout, I could have petrified him by informing him that he was rassling with a social movement that was scheduled to escalate the entire planet's appreciation of diversity by demonstrating for that world a few more patterns in the 9 million faces of love. I could have told Joe Meredith that in saving me from that beauty pageant he was tempering the steel of the queer sword that would cut clean through the dichotomy of sex-role ideology. And I could have told Miss Arraga McNeil that she didn't need to worry any longer about the purity of southern womanhood, that in touching my life she was contributing to a whole new design for relationship for which queer people would someday be the operative definition—that is, partners or comrades of whatever age or sex and in whatever number, not husbands and wives one-on-one with the requisite 2.5 children.

If I had known of and could have spoken about the Queer Nation that was rumbling inside me 50-odd years ago, I could have assured all those occasional angels of mine that I shall always be in their debt. Moreover, I could have assured them that I shall always honor the Tribe for the gifts and the lessons it afforded me. I could have told them that the Tribe is not and has never been "wrong"; it has simply outlived its usefulness.

In fact, I figure my task now at this millennium's end will be to return to my Tribe, and to take back to it in the form of my own life the message of love, gratitude, and forgiveness. There's a good chance that, at least in this incarnation, my Tribe members will choose not to join me in the global changes that are now underway. They may still fail to understand my message. They may deliberately misunderstand it.

But I'm betting that some of them will remember that they really are stardust and not just muscles and bones toiling in this vale of tears. If any of my occasional angels are still around—it's possible!—maybe I can find them and thank them. I'm pretty sure Miss Lucille Fizer would be glad to dance with me out here on this edge between chaos and order where queer people live our lives. She was always up for a good time.

The Gay Kids and The Johns Committee: 1956

by Merril Mushroom

– 1956 –

In 1956, when I was in my third year of high school, the terrors of McCarthyism came home to Miami Beach, where I lived. Back then, Miami Beach had a small-town ambiance. The population was low, and lots of folks knew lots of other folks. The warm climate made life seem easier. There was not much personal crime against individual citizens, but there was a good bit of organized crime activity that included gambling and gay bars.

Miami Beach was a gay paradise in the '50s. I say "gay," not "gay and lesbian," because in those days, "lesbian" was a word spoken only in whispers, like "vagina." We all were "gay"—gay guys, gay girls, gay life, gay parties, gay restaurants, gay bars, gay beach. Homosexuality was not mysterious. Even when I was in grade school, we'd often overhear adults talking about the "homos," and by the time I entered high school, the fact that there were lots of homos living in our community was taken for granted by us kids. So I was not at all surprised to learn that several of my friends had been hanging out at the gay beach, and that two of them decided to see if two girls together could get as much of a thrill as a girl and a guy. They did, and they liked it enough that they concluded they were gay, too. After that, coming out became a common event for those of us who were tending in that direction.

But in 1954 a gay man was murdered in Miami by a teenage hustler, and the case became sensational. Because of this, the extent of the gay subculture in Dade County was publicized as scandalous. The media demanded that something be done to purge the county of this pestilence. An anticrime commission was set up to investigate perversion and gambling, and two years later, the state legislature appointed the Johns Committee to investigate "freedom riders, communists, and homosexuals" throughout Florida. These investigations continued for the next eight years, and countless gay people had their lives destroyed as a result.

Amid all this, my friends and I were coming out in high school—realizing that we were gay, learning to camp and carry on, engaging in same-sex passion, weaseling our juvenile selves into the adult gay subculture by going to the gay bars and beach, and discovering a new set of reasons for covertness and secrecy. With these particular interests in common, seven of us, ages 14 to 17, hung out together. We formed a "gay crowd" apart from the other cliques—the rich kids, the working class kids, the bikers or "rough trade," the goyim—but we didn't say that "G" word except among ourselves. We didn't do anything open or political or consciousness raising or socially changing. We knew that we had to be silent about our proclivities. Being gay was not safe. We read the newspapers, listened to the radio, and overheard discussions among our parents. We knew there was an investigation going on. We knew that a few of our teachers had given notice or been terminated. We heard from the bar dykes that adult gays were being arrested, incarcerated, given electroshock treatments, and lobotomized; were losing their jobs and families and freedom; were committing suicide. While we felt the nearness of the threat, the immortality of our youth made what happened to the grown-ups seem far away compared to our own immediate fears, which were that our parents would *find out* or that we'd be kicked out of school because someone *knew*. So we didn't say the *G* word very openly in high school, but we knew who were, and, although it wasn't spoken, so did a lot of other folks.

Gay kids who were over 18 usually didn't hang out with us "jail bait." It was too risky. Eighteen-year-old gay kids might not be adult enough to legally drink in the bars, but they were adult enough under the law to be arrested and jailed for "contributing to the delinquency of a minor" and "crimes against nature" if caught in a compromising position with someone a few months younger than themselves. There were a few gay adults who'd associate with us, who even would allow some of us kids to come to their homes; but this was very brave of them, because if ever we were followed or if there was any surveillance of the adult, the adult could get busted. Such surveillance, wiretapping, and entrapment were common police activities during the investigations.

Because it was so dangerous to be outed, especially if one was a teacher, we tried not to speculate too openly about any of the faculty at school, but we did suspect that several of our teachers might be gay, and a few of those were covertly supportive of us. My English teacher, Mr. Robin, was a dashing, handsome fellow, somewhat reserved in his manner, rather effete, and I KNEW he just HAD to be gay. I adored him. I also adored the girl who sat in front of me one row over. I connived in every way I could to get to be in groups with her, worked my brain to the bone so that I could impress her in class, stared at her while my heart fluttered and my belly clenched. Mr. Robin, bless him, must have noticed my crush because I was sure that he contrived to place us together whenever possible, often on the school publications he sponsored. I always will love him for that.

Of course no discussion of teachers by a lesbian would be complete without mentioning the gym teachers. I recall a succession of unmarried, butchy women throughout junior high and into high school, but every year we had new ones. I wonder now, in retrospect, if this rapid turnover was a consequence of the investigation. In any event, by 1956 unmarried women no longer were hired to teach girls' physical education, and two very safely married women were installed in those positions. My buddy Jess was going through a traumatic breakup with her girlfriend, and she immediately confided in the cute butchy new gym teacher, hoping for some support and adult wisdom. To her dismay, the teacher lectured poor Jess quite sternly on the wrongs of homosexuality and told Jess that she was never to raise the issue again. But the other dear teacher, as straight as she looked and behaved, turned out to be warm, open, and available as a friend and mentor. To several of the girls she gave good advice about the perils of being a gay person in our society.

Except for one very blatant young queen, all the gay kids I knew in high school were girls; and most of us were involved in high school sports—that haven for young lesbians. We were required to take three years of PE for credit and could opt for a fourth year if we wanted to. Our high school also offered a rich after-school intramural program which, of course, all us gay girls went out for. The few role models we had as young lesbians in those days were women athletes, and being that the only pattern for our own behavior was based on the heterosexual stereotypes of the day, we as lesbians were "supposed to" act like boys, and that meant playing sports. We also were able to make contact with other gay girls our own age through county-wide high school intramural, and, besides all this, we all really enjoyed physical activities and playing games.

After-school sports was very different from our daily required PE class. After school, only girls who wanted to be there were, and the teachers were much more relaxed, laid back, and informal. And we didn't have to take showers. Part of in-school required PE was that we changed from school clothes into gym suits, then showered before we put our school clothes on again, so we wouldn't go smelly into our next class. Taking showers was mandatory, and the teacher checked off on a chart that we did so. The girls in junior high all had to undress together in a big locker room and shower together in an open shower room; but in high school, our older adolescent dignity was considered, so that in addition to the communal shower room, there also were a few partitioned semiprivate cubicles that would accommodate only three girls at a time, thus giving an illusion of privacy.

One would think that we gay girls would be in our heaven, with so many other naked females surrounding us, but most of the time, the opposite was the case. We felt vulnerable in our youth, in the newness of our sexuality. We were terrified that we might inadvertently look at another girl's body and be caught as a queer and kicked out of school. If one of us were known or even suspected to be gay, there were girls who'd make as much an issue over showering with us as they would if they had to shower with boys. And if we should be so unfortunate as to find ourselves in the shower room with a girl we had a crush on, the conflict of the deliciousness of the opportunity to look at her with the threat of giving our secret away by *looking* at her would have us completely undone by the time we arrived at our next class.

The reality of our situation was that there was not yet even a dream of support systems or recreational activities for gay youth. The only places for gays to hang out were the gay bars, the gay beach, and a very swank gay coffeehouse in Coconut Grove. It was especially difficult to find a place to make love when you both are in high school and living with your parents (who never would understand). Even the few of us who had the opportunity to spend the night together always were afraid that if we did more than just kiss a little and maybe grope one another, *someone* might *walk in* on us. The hetero kids always could go "parking," do it in their cars, and run not much more of a risk than to have the police give them a warning and make them move on, were they to be discovered. We gay girls would never dare to do that. We'd heard too many stories from bar dykes who were caught together necking in a car and had to give the police blow jobs to not get beat up, and maybe they got beat up anyway.

As normal teenagers, we also wanted to be with adults who were like ourselves, adults we could admire and emulate. Most of us aspired to be bar dykes, and our greatest goal was to attend the gay bars by the time we rounded our 16th birthday. The bars were places where we could feel safe, where we could be our gay selves openly. We'd muster all our ingenuity in order to obtain phony identification to prove that we were 21, which was the legal age for drinking. Photocopy machines were very new in those days, and it was a real skill to be able to alter documents like birth certificates and driver's licenses well enough for them to pass inspection.

I opted to get a real voter's registration for my own proof of age. I went down to the local office and told them I wanted to register to vote. With small-town trust, the registrar gave me a form to fill out, never asking me for any verification. I wrote in all my information correctly except the date of my birth, which I made five years earlier. Soon, I was on the street with voter's registration safely tucked away in my wallet ready to be my passport into the bars that very weekend.

All went well until the next election. One day when I came home from school, Mom was waiting for me.

"Did you register to vote?" she asked.

My belly dropped into my toes. *Omigod,* I thought, *how did she find out? She must know I'm going to the bars. She must know I'm gay. Omigod, am I in trouble? What if she puts me in the hospital?*

"Did you?" Mom asked again.

"Um, uh-huh," I nodded.

"Why?" demanded Mom.

"I dunno," I shrugged.

"Why?" Mom insisted.

"Just wanted to, I guess," I mumbled.

"Just wanted to? Do you know you've perjured yourself?" Mom started to yell. "Amy's mother called me up. She was working for the elections and saw your name on the register. She said she didn't know you were 21—she thought you were the same age as Amy. I told her you *were* the same age as Amy, 16, and that this must be some mistake, but she said your name, address, and phone number all were right there on the register. Now you call down there this minute and tell them you want to be stricken from the record. Do you know you could be put in jail for perjury?" I didn't, but I was so relieved that this whole incident had nothing to do with revealing my gayness I almost peed in my pants. I picked up the telephone and did as Mom had ordered. The following week I went to Miami and got a driver's license with a made-up name and address and a birth date that confirmed I was over 21.

Getting into bars required ingenuity and daring, but one could go to the gay beach no matter what one's age. That beach was wonderful—a block-long stretch of sand and surf teeming with gay girls and gay guys, bounded by a small hotel on one side and a long pavilion with a snack bar on the other. There was a jukebox on the pavilion, and we'd dance to its music down the length of the pavilion, out over the Atlantic, to six plays for a quarter. We'd dance to Johnny Mathis, Ella Fitzgerald, Roy Hamilton, Etta James, Edith Piaf, Perez Prado. We'd dance to "Tico Tico," "Only You," "Unchained Melody," "C.C. Rider," "Poco Pelo." We'd dance lindy, bop, fox-trot, samba, hully-gully, and cha-cha-cha. We'd dance mixed sex, gay girls with gay guys, so that we wouldn't be arrested and charged with "crimes against nature" by any of the undercover police who haunted the gay beach like vultures.

Because of the investigations, the beach, like the gay bars, was fair game for police raids. Sometimes, as we danced on the long pavilion in the sun, we'd suddenly, unexpectedly be approached by these officers of the law, grabbed by them and pushed roughly toward the sidewalk. Sometimes, as we lay our towels and blankets, sat on our chairs and chaises, floated on our rafts and inner tubes, we'd suddenly be assaulted by an onslaught of uniformed and plainclothes agents, ordered to our feet, marched from the beach. We'd be loaded into a line of paddy wagons and taken to the local police station. There we'd be fingerprinted, booked, thrown into a cell, and sometimes beaten, humiliated, sexually assaulted. If we were found to be underage, we'd be sent to the juvenile detention center, and our parents would be called. Everyone over 18 would have their names, address, telephone numbers, and places of employment listed in the local newspapers beneath headlines proclaiming the latest arrests for perversion. And I never will forget when Eddie, a young Latino fairy without immigration papers, was taken along with others during one of these raids. In his fear over being discovered, he attempted to escape by leaping through the glass of a second-story window in the police station. He landed belly first on the decorative spikes atop the iron fence that surrounded the building, impaling himself to death.

Julie was another casualty of this climate of persecution and homophobia. She was a year behind me in high school. She played after-school sports with us, but she didn't socialize with us gay girls much otherwise. Even though she dated boys, we all were sure that she was gay but just didn't admit it to herself yet. One Sunday we finally convinced her to come to the gay beach with us, not telling her what kind of people went there. When she noticed all the queers, she was shocked and horrified. She left immediately, and ever after that, she avoided us gay girls in school.

After I graduated one of the other seniors told me that Julie, in spite of herself, had fallen in love with her best friend Sophie that year. They were inseparable for months and finally went to bed together. Julie could not handle the fact of her gayness, and there were no counselors, no therapists, no support systems to help her. All treatment was geared toward "normalizing" the gay individual back into heterosexuality through invasive, violent, destructive "cures." Julie hung herself from a tree in her backyard with the sash of a terry cloth bathrobe. Afraid of what her future might hold, she died for being a queer in 1959, three months before her 18th birthday.

From Farm to Fulfillment

by Grant F. Peterson

- 1937 -

- 1997 -

I remember as if it were yesterday: my mother making it very clear that she didn't want me messing around with girls. I never disappointed her.

It was in 1935 when, at age seven, she caught me playing doctor with a girl who was visiting from a nearby farm and the dictum came down. It also put a damper on any aspirations I may have had for a medical career.

Actually, it was one of the easier admonitions, of which there were many, for me to deal with. I was raised on a farm in North Dakota where every other living creature was running, flying, or crawling in pursuit of an opposite-sex liaison. My urges in that direction never seemed to materialize. Strange. I wondered why.

Both my parents were socially responsible individuals with a strong sense of conscience and justice. We were regulars at church, and I spent much of my young life with my two younger brothers in the front pew of the Maria (named after my paternal grandmother) Lutheran Church. There were very few enjoyable activities that were not sins. Dancing was right up there at the top of the list with drinking and mayhem of any sort. An exasperated minister, tiring of my whining "Why can't we dance?" routine, rebuked me with, "If you want to dance so much, why don't you dance with boys?" Not such an unreasonable alternative, I concluded, and certainly an excellent introduction to understanding the concept of compromise and its potentially positive results. Unfortunately, there seemed to be no other boy who shared my enthusiasm for this solution. It was not until many years later in a Seattle dance club that I was able to put this advice into practice.

North Dakota is not your typical gay mecca. The Castro just isn't there. So you make do with what is at hand. And so I did, in the back of the house, around the corner of the barn, in the outhouse at the one-room rural school, behind a tree. Any obstacle to block vision was in itself an invitation beckoning. I stayed occupied.

My father employed some hired hands who were magnificent specimens, and at an early age I became adept at creating rationales why I should share their beds. That accomplished, a routine developed. It was just a matter of time before their breathing would become heavy and my explorations could begin. I don't recall any of these men, aged 18 to 23, ever awakening during my ministrations, nor was it ever suggested that I sleep elsewhere. They intrigued me no end and provided the only effective motivation to do farm work. Milking cows, haying, shocking grain, driving tractors—none of them turned me on. I had been born into an alien land.

School was a one-mile hike down a graveled road or a ride in a horse-drawn sled in the winter, a six-month period that began and ended with summer. I liked the one-room school. There were people there. Not many. The number of students in the entire school never varied from a low of five to a high of eight during those first eight years of my formal education, and while they were at different grade levels, the teachers had time to offer considerable individual attention and encouragement. Describing the school's "library" as sparse gives increased definition to that adjective, but the "basics" were drilled into all of us until we could diagram the most complex of compound sentences and manage "arithmetic" with the best. It was at this rather early age that the possibility of teaching crossed my mind, and when I retired from education in 1990, things seemed to have come full circle when my second- and third-grade teacher, one of my favorites, came to San Francisco from Southern California and spoke at my retirement dinner, a gala affair on a magnificently refurbished ferry with the lights of the Bay Bridge twinkling above us. We both agreed that the scene was a bit of a change from the one-room schoolhouse and the view from its windows.

Democracy was at work in the little school on the prairie. Weekly meetings of the Young Citizens League were conducted by the elected officers (I preferred being president). The YCL was a statewide organization, so there were meetings at the county and state level. It was considered a great honor when in the eighth grade I was elected president of the state organization, and I admit to being rather taken with myself as this media personality. The annual state YCL Convention was held in the legislative chambers of North Dakota's Capitol in Bismarck and I was really looking forward to sitting in that big chair in the ornate chamber, the Big Man himself, but those dreams went down the tube when the U.S. entered World War II in 1941 and the state meeting was canceled, the victim of war-related restrictions.

My parents were very active in the North Dakota Farmers Union, which had numerous activities for youth. There were camps around the state, and the activities included folk dancing, songfests, campfires and a goodly amount of free time. One youth camp in the Bad Lands found me successfully wheedling my way into the bed of an adult male dance instructor. I had already had some successful experiences in the art of seduction, and this experience was more of a skill-building exercise.

The 4-H Club, on the other hand, was a disaster. I don't know whose idea it was that I become a member, but it couldn't have been mine. I haven't the faintest recollection what any of the "aitches" stand for, but one of them certainly must have been "hell." I was the only boy totally lacking enthusiasm for what had to be accomplished and was seldom able to perform the tasks as well as the other boys. This once again caused me to stand out, and it was in this group that I was often the object of derision. Not a happy experience but certainly one that established in my mind that I was different from the rest of the group. I must have been, for other guys didn't get called "sissy." I was two to four years younger than most, and I'm sure I attributed some of the unkind remarks to our age difference.

Fitting in. Being part of the group. These were of the utmost importance to me, but probably no more so than for any other youngster. Knowing that I didn't really fit in, I had to try harder. The ninth grade meant high school in Braddock, N.D. (it's easier to find on the map than to see it when driving through). There were perhaps 35 students, grades 9-12. I was tall and skinny, 6 feet 2 inches and 140 pounds, so by North Dakota standards I was certainly meant to be all-state center on the basketball team. Wrong. Varsity marbles or hopscotch, perhaps, but team sports were activities where I stood out primarily in a negative sense.

So how do you become part of the "in" group? I used what wit I had, but that wasn't enough. Getting good grades was not yet out of fashion, but while I gained respect for doing well, it still wasn't enough. I hasten to add that a high school of 35 students instructed by a full-time teaching superintendent and full-time teaching principal hardly assured stimulating course offerings. I did hone my typing skills to over 80 words per minute on a relic Underwood typewriter, and while I didn't realize it at the time, that skill would become a lifesaver when I joined the Army years later.

If I were to belong, I would have to do anything that would make others want me around. I learned to party at an early age and became extraordinarily adept at it. My behavioral antics, all designed to gain approval, would have cost most of my peers a heavy penalty, but manipulation was the name of the game. My parents were highly respected in the community, and I survived.

I left Braddock at the conclusion of the second year of high school and went to school in Napoleon, some 17 miles away. My parents didn't feel I was getting a proper education in Braddock, and I'm sure they tired of my constant whining, "I want to go to Napoleon!" Gee! A big high school of 100 students! And during the week I got to live in a room my parents rented for me. I also had a beautiful, newly painted black Model A Ford sedan with bright yellow wheels.

What does a 16-year old boy do 17 miles away from home with no supervision? Put "study" toward the bottom of the list. My grades were fine with little effort put forth. No problem there. The name of the game was "fun." And I had wheels! It was 1944, and there was a war. Not a lot of gas available, but one learns to be resourceful. I ate in a restaurant in Napoleon, and the owner always sold me two packs of cigarettes each Monday. No other high school student had commercially made cigarettes. Score another one for "how to win friends."

There were dances in Napoleon and in neighboring towns. Up to eight of my friends would pile into my Model A, and off we'd go for a night of dancing and partying. I really dreaded having to go home to the farm on weekends. My friends were my life. Yet these escapades seldom translated into sexual activity. On one occasion, proclaiming my expertise in the art of French kissing, a skill unknown to the other boys, I willingly agreed to share my knowledge and provide lessons to a few handsome fellow students. On a particularly noteworthy evening, I was paired with a popular sophomore whose eagerness to learn propelled him to a quite a frenzy. At one point he gasped the obvious: "Gosh, this is really crazy! I've got a hard-on!" A memorable evening, yet one that I never heard discussed again in any venue.

With my 1946 graduation from Napoleon High School, it was college time, but first, courtesy of the Farmers Union again, a six-week trip to New York for the first Encampment for Citizenship. It was not the catalyst that would propel me from my roots (I've always said that I knew at age three I had to get my ass out of North Dakota!), but it did provide increased motivation to plan for a move. Minnesota's Gustavus Adolphus College was not only 500 miles from home, but it was a Lutheran college, and how could my parents say no? I was on my way to being on my own, and teaching became the vehicle for movement. My first real job, teaching English in Astoria, Ore., was sealed when the school district responded positively to my written inquiry. Then came a year of graduate school at the University of Washington followed by enlistment in the Army and assignment to Tokyo. At age 23 I fell into the arms of an Army sergeant, and that's when I finally said, "I know who I am." The last piece of the puzzle had fallen into place.

California beckoned when I returned to teaching in 1956, first in Los Angeles County and then the San Francisco Bay Area where classroom teaching assignments segued into the area of counseling and from there to administration at both the site and the district level. When I signed a contract in Union City's New Haven Unified School District, a fortuitous move that lasted until my retirement 29 years later, it seemed only a few short years before the "faggot" classification took hold ("Mister Faggot to you, child."). A gay teacher speaking out in the '60s was a particularly juicy target for the district's reactionary elements opposed to integration and other social and political movements that were "right," but right prevailed. I was no different from the vast numbers of my gay brothers and sisters who worked twice as hard to prove their value, always wondering if indeed the ax would fall.

As I thought back on my rewarding career in education following my retirement, I still could not help feeling a certain lack of fulfillment. I had worked with numerous oppressed minorities over the years, but what had I really done to help gay youth, many of whom were suffering far more than I did at their age? If this were to be addressed, now was the time. And so my days became (and remain!) longer than ever as I work with school districts assisting them to put in place staff development programs that address the needs of sexual minority youth. One result is experiencing an increased level of personal satisfaction.

In August of 1996, when I returned to North Dakota for my 50th class reunion (where is my false ID when I need it?), I considered it important that my former classmates and friends know "the real me." I completed and mailed the requested questionnaire detailing my activities and accomplishments during the past half century, proudly proclaiming to have done it all as a gay man, and now even more proudly committed to playing a part in righting the wrongs being perpetrated on gay, lesbian, bisexual and transgendered students in our schools.

Walking into that room full of people, most of whom I'd not seen in 50 years, was in and of itself a satisfying experience, made more so by the warmth with which I was welcomed. I was no longer a stranger.

Miss O'Grady! Old Shep! Where Are You Now?

by Patricia Pomerleau Chávez

– 1939 –   *– 1994–*

I did not fall in love with my gym teacher. Never. The first love of my life was my second grade teacher, Miss O'Grady. She was plump and red-haired, with crinkly blue eyes in a crinkly pink face. Her arms were soft and plump and she smiled a lot. I don't remember learning anything academically in the second grade and, in retrospect, I think it is possible that my idol was not a very good teacher.

But I did learn some things in her class! I learned to avoid Elwood, who teased me because I wore glasses. Glasses were definitely *out* in the second grade in 1938 in Taft, Calif.

Elwood, at the age of seven, was a diminutive Rocky Balboa, and as might be expected, his name calling was unimaginative: *Four Eyes! Hey,*

Four Eyes! Elwood and his band of smelly, rough followers singled me out. They were obviously frustrated and baffled, because I could throw a ball as well as any of them could. Although I was too nearsighted to know where the ball was going, I could crank up and really zing it. I could hear the boys muttering: *Hey, that girl can THROW!* I did not, however, wow them with my batting ability, but I did put on a show. I would stride up to the plate scowling, knocking imaginary mud out of my imaginary cleats with the butt end of the bat. I spat in my palms and hunkered low over the plate, squinting at the pitcher. Ruse, pretense, and bravado—coupled with my extraordinary throwing skill—got me through.

Learning to cope with Elwood would prove to be extremely useful because the world, I discovered later, was rampant with Elwoods, who could sometimes be dangerous rather than simply annoying.

More important, I discovered that Miss O'Grady stirred unfathomable urges within me. I learned years later that those urges were sexual in nature but, at the time, I though they were feelings of pure love and admiration. I did my lessons well in order to receive Miss O'Grady's praise and not for the joy of learning. And I *divined* rather than learned that it would be unacceptable for me to express any of my thoughts about that most wonderful of all persons. My attachment to the marvelous Miss O'Grady carried a whiff of danger.

The confusion and frustration that entered my mind, if not my psyche, when I struggled with parallel feelings of love, with its soft glow and excitement, and the attendant sense of guilt and danger, set the stage for the next 25 years of my life.

Miss O'Grady was my one love until I reached high school, where I began a succession of unrequited loves with a fascinating variety of English teachers. There was Miss Lacey, Mrs. Moran, and, finally, the glorious and enigmatic Miss Gellato of raven hair and deep-set eyes that held me transfixed. I had no interest in gym teachers. But, ah! The teachers of English! The subtleties! The innuendoes! The compound sentences that left room for delectable varieties of interpretation! The imagined dangling propositions! And the trips to the darkened supply closet, where I might stand, if only for a few seconds, beside the provocative Miss Gellato until one of us found the elusive piece of string that would jerk life into an obscene, naked light bulb.

By this time, my family had moved to a remote part of Oregon, and many of the students had difficulty getting to school since it was often necessary to cross rivers and travel through storms and over rough dirt roads. I remember watching the light of a kerosene lantern as it bobbed in the bow of a small skiff on the Umpqua River one dark, stormy morning while we waited in the school bus for our classmate, Angelina, to row across with her two little brothers. Angelina, with her Mona Lisa face and her gold earrings, in hip boots and sou'wester, was a dream of androgyny.

But I did not fall in love with Angelina despite her charisma and her obvious strength and determination to get an education. At that time I was heavily involved, in my fantasy life, with the sophisticated Mrs. Moran.

Mrs. Moran, who had no apparent husband, bicycled every summer with a woman friend in the south of France. She often wore a fresh red carnation in the lapel of her tailored suit jacket. I imagined her life was filled with intrigue. I supposed she was familiar with all the little twisted streets of Montmartre. I speculated about the source of the red carnations. Were they shipped on ice from Paris?

Mrs. Moran was from "The Outside" as natives of our area referred to that part of the world lying beyond the four or five neighboring counties. Mrs. Moran's sophistication made her alluring to me, but at the end of that school year, she left for other places. I stifled my grief and wondered who would replace her.

Sometime during my junior year I became aware of Bud. My acquaintance with Bud suddenly propelled me beyond fantasy, and I began to grapple, though reluctantly, with the unknown and unnamed dimensions of my inner self.

Bud wore hip boots too, even when it wasn't raining. She was large and messy, and strands of limp orange hair hung before her face. I noticed a Miss O'Grady crinkle at the corner of one eye.

Bud lived on a secluded ranch with a mysterious family. Her mother was missing, it seemed, or at least, she was never mentioned. There were a great number of brothers and sisters who came and went and whose names were reminiscent of characters I had encountered in stories of the southern hills: Jeremiah, Fletch, Ella Mae. Bud was not popular. Maybe it was the slightly grimy clothing or the mysterious home life that made people feel uneasy. *I* thought it was the look in her eye: defiant, remote, lonely. That look was something to which I could relate. Bud interested me, even if she didn't know any poems.

She was popular with the other kids in one regard. She could sing a song. Only one song, as I recall, but that one was enough. It was called "Old Shep," and it had something to do with a faithful dog who had grown old and infirm and had to be shot. (I grew up in a place and a time when a rifle was said to be the best veterinarian.) We often called on Bud to sing "Old Shep," which she did in a heartfelt way that expressed so much more than the apparent meaning of the words. Her rendition of "Old Shep" always affected us, but it seemed to touch Bud even more deeply. She would lift her face and gaze into the distance, and then a tear would appear at the inner corner of each eye and begin a slow, glistening course down the length of her nose and to the corner of her mouth. No matter how many times she sang the song, that faithful old sheepdog each time became as vivid and as alive in his last few moments as any dog any of us had ever known. I came to realize that Old Shep was a metaphor for Bud herself.

One day one of my classmates, a girl who had recently moved to the area from the Great Outside World, suggested to me that I ought to get to know Bud better and others of my kind, as she put it. I looked at her in terror. I said nothing. I went home and nursed my suspicions. Could it be that my natural place was with a class of people who were set apart and alien? That was an almost incomprehensible suggestion to me and yet there was a ring of truth to it that I could not ignore. I dodged, feinted, told lies, and managed to avoid that student, and we had no further conversation.

As my high school years wound down, I felt that my life too was entering its last stages. I had great difficulty forcing myself to think of marriage and children, the inevitable and desired state of life, as I had been raised to believe. While I had no idea of how one conceived a child, the thought of childbirth itself frightened me. Furthermore, while sex with a boy or a man might have been an intriguing idea, to have gone through with such an act would seem to be a mark of disloyalty, if only theoretically, to Miss O'Grady, Mrs. Moran, and Miss Gellato. Only years later did I realize that forcing myself into a relationship with a man would have been a profound act of disloyalty to myself.

Nothing in my school experience helped me overcome my fears. Sex education in our high school had consisted of a film that was shown one afternoon to the entire student body of 200 at the town movie house. Great fanfare accompanied the proposal to show the film. Each student was required to have written permission from his or her parents to see the film. I suppose many parents regarded the film as an opportunity to dodge having a face-to-face talk about sex with their children. I think mine did. At least, the topic was never discussed in my home.

The film opened with images of men and women in their 20s or older, dancing and murmuring in darkened rooms. Suddenly a great pale penis wavered before us. We were raptly attentive. I heard a few nervous giggles from some boys in the audience. The huge penis was grossly infected. A nurse in uniform stood at the back of the theater, presumably ready to render aid to any student who collapsed. Following several full-screen depictions of a variety of badly damaged penises, we were treated to a lecture on the evils of what was then called "The Social Disease." I hung perilously between feelings of hilarity, and indignation at being subjected to such absurdity. I could not find anything in the film that had anything to do with me!

Finally the film came to an end with a dramatic crescendo of music typical of the Hollywood of the 1940s. That concluded the sex education of my formative years.

School had provided me with a certain educational package, but in no way was I prepared for the particular dangers and confusions I would soon encounter.

I graduated from high school and decided to enter college, thus putting off the future that seemed to hold nothing but doom regardless of my choices. I could not marry, and I did not yet understand what my love for women meant or where it would lead me.

I stumbled on, hoping that something would happen to save me. I hoped for deliverance—deliverance from confusion, uncertainty, fearfulness, and anger that came when I thought about the possibility of expressing my still undefined but true self and the future of punishment and condemnation it would bring. I had no idea what hope for happiness and fulfillment lay in that outside world. I entered that world with a great sense of foreboding. The 1940s were coming to an end and I was thrust, unwittingly, into the turmoil of the 1950s. It did not seem to be *my* world!

The memory of Miss O'Grady with her kind eyes and her soft, enfolding arms receded into the past. The faithful Old Shep was not to be found.

Gay Students Graduate,
But Our Memories Don't

by John R. Selig

– *1959* – – *1997* –

I ts amazes me that it took the crisis of my 13-year marriage being thrown into its final death knell in 1990 for me to face the fact that I was gay. My wife had moved out, and I had become the full-time cus-todial parent of our 12-year old son, Nathaniel. My life, as I knew it, was collapsing around me. Amidst the chaos, I finally began facing my sexual orientation head-on. I admitted to myself that I had been living a lie for most of my 37 years, even though all of the signs had been there since the age of five or six.

In order to survive I learned to live a lie in school. My isolation was more subtle than that of those who came out during their school years. Often the sting of being different was no more than a look of disgust from another kid or a nasty quip. I felt assured that all kids suffered such treatment from time to time. It was only after coming out that all the pieces finally fell into place.

Growing up during the 1950s and '60s in Huntington, a suburban bedroom community on Long Island's north shore, I only knew of two gay people in the world. One was an effeminate salesclerk in the local camera store. The other was a flamboyant florist. My parents, liberal people in their distaste for prejudice towards most other groups, would make derogatory comments about the "fairies." I grew up an hour and a half from one of the world's major gay meccas, New York City, and just 45 minutes from the renowned gay playground Fire Island, but I thought that there were only two "fairies" in the world!

Who could blame me? In the '50s and '60s being gay was never mentioned in the media. Families strove to become clones of the model American families portrayed on *Leave It To Beaver, Father Knows Best,* and *The Donna Reed Show.* Parents slept in separate twin beds, wearing enough clothes to survive an Arctic winter. If double beds were considered too risqué to be seen in America's living rooms, mentioning homosexuality was beyond imagination.

Looking back, it is obvious that my sexual attraction toward and fantasies about other males started at a young age. I had crushes on boys as early as the first and second grade. I developed a strong longing for a classmate named Billy. I tried to find opportunities in school to be around Billy, to gain his attention and his friendship. I didn't understand my feelings. On the one hand, they were so strong. On the other, none of my friends seemed to have such feelings. I never was able to make it into Billy's inner circle, as most of his friends lived nearer his home than I did, but that didn't stop me from lying in bed at night dreaming about his alluring personality and his dark hair and eyes.

Many of my memories of Nathan Hale Elementary School involve not fitting in during recess. Recess was a time of hell. I dreaded time spent on the playground, away from the protective safety of the classroom. I hated ball, no matter the game, so I usually hung out with the girls and the other unathletic boys. I was often ridiculed, even by the girls. I had the unique talent of being able to attract the attention of every bully in the school. Teachers were never nearby when I needed them. Usually I just bided my time until the recess bell finally rang. I was too embarrassed to tell my parents about my daily humiliation. I knew that my mom and dad would tell me to be more like the other boys; that by being meek, I was inviting others to pick on me. But I couldn't deny my feelings, and I couldn't change my core being to become more masculine. I hated letting down my parents, so I tried to keep my frequent teasing by classmates to myself.

I entered Simpson Junior High School in the fall of 1964 with much anticipation. I was excited at the prospect of having different classes, each with a different teacher. I also had a fresh start, meeting many new kids I hadn't been in school with before, so I thought my life could only improve. During eighth grade I developed a crush on a preacher's son who was one year ahead of me. God, he was so gorgeous—straight blond hair, blue eyes, tall and thin. I would spend hours in class and at home dreaming about his contagious smile. Of course, he never knew anything about his role in my fantasies.

But one junior high experience would stay with me. It occurred when I went on a school trip to Washington, D.C. in the eighth grade. Four of us shared a room for five days, and each room had only two beds. So it was two of us guys in a bed together. My first time in bed with another guy, and I was both scared to death and thrilled. I touched my bed partner's penis in the middle of the night. He jumped out of bed and accused me in front of the other roommates of touching him sexually. I was so embarrassed, mainly because it was true. I spent the rest of the trip denying it. Though the story of my embarrassing nighttime adventure surprisingly didn't spread throughout the school, I lived in constant fear for months that it would. The desire to be sexual with other boys never lessened, but I learned the hard way not to act on my longings.

High school was somewhat better than junior high. I focused on academics and began to experience some success with my social skills. Several clubs captured my fancy, and I was able to develop a few meaningful friendships. What really bothered me was that support within my school for gay people, such as myself, was nowhere to be found. Even though I made a few friends, I knew I was different from my classmates and I felt isolated. I did not admit to myself or anybody else that I was gay. During school such topics as racism, sexism, drug abuse, alcoholism, and premarital sex were discussed. But the topic of homosexuality was avoided at all costs. So I suffered my feelings in silence, frightened that somebody might discover my hidden thoughts. I subscribed to *The New York Times* and read it daily in homeroom. I secretly looked at the ads for the all-male cinemas in New York City (a short train ride away). After fantasizing about sneaking in to watch the movies, I felt so dirty and developed immense shame and remorse for having such feelings. I looked up homosexuality in the dictionary and encyclopedias in the school's library and found gays referred to as suffering a psychological disorder. I had been the apple of my parents' eyes and was considered a model son. How could I have a psychological disorder? Since I was determined to be the outstanding son that my parents told me I was, I couldn't fail my parents. Therefore, I couldn't have a psychological disorder. Ergo, I obviously wasn't a deviant—a homosexual.

I decided to try to live the life that my parents, society and my schools had scripted for me. Six years after graduating from high school, after graduation from college and halfway through my graduate studies, I fell in love with a special friend I had met during my college freshman year. I married her because I truly did love her. But I could not be in love with her, not the way a heterosexual man would love his wife. I could not be intimate with her and provide her the love that she deserved. The sexual feelings simply were not there.

As my marriage disintegrated and the dreams of my lifetime turned to sand, I finally came out first to myself, then to my wife, my son, family, friends, and even coworkers. As I traveled the road of self-confrontation, I grew to become happy and proud of myself.

After coming out I blossomed. In my own way, I really have made a difference. My marriage produced a son, Nathaniel, who is a unique, loving person. After my divorce, I raised him as a parent who happens to be gay. My son is 110% straight, so if gays recruit, I have been a total failure. Nathaniel has never had to question his dad's unconditional love. He is comfortable with his own heterosexuality but is a proponent of gay rights. He chose to write his high school senior research paper about difficulties faced by gay teens.

But my greatest satisfaction has come from writing about what I have seen within the gay community. I was fortunate to become involved as a writer, photographer, and editorial consultant on an important book that was the brainchild and life dream of a visionary, Phillip Sherman. The wonderful book, *Uncommon Heroes,* was about lesbian and gay role models. After meeting many of the heroes in the book, my anger increased at the lack of gay role models when I grew up. Had such a book been available when I was a child, just maybe I would have been spared so many years of despair.

After *Uncommon Heroes* was published, I realized I had a unique opportunity to confront the high school I attended. I donated a copy of the book to my high school and challenged the local school authorities to support their gay and lesbian students. I sent the book along with letters to both the principal of Huntington High School and the school district's superintendent, writing:

"You might ask why a gay parent who has custody of his 16-year-old son would take the time to donate such a book to his high school. After all, I now live half way across the country, and I graduated over 20 years ago. The answer to this question is quite simple. I don't want the current generation of gay and lesbian youth to go through the inner turmoil that I had to suffer growing up in Huntington. You have the power to turn the tide and make a difference. I am sure that such a move will not be an easy one, and there will be those in Huntington who will oppose your assistance of gay youth. I ask you the following questions. What is Huntington High School doing to ensure that students who are lesbian or gay can come to terms with their sexual orientation in a safe environment? How many gay boys are still being beaten up after gym class? How many young lesbians are being ostracized for not being feminine enough? What is the school doing about the self-esteem of its gay teenagers? What materials and counseling are available through your guidance office? How many more gay and lesbian teenagers have to needlessly kill themselves or put themselves through many unnecessary years of self-hatred before the schools of this country care enough to do something about this pressing issue?"

By sending letters to both the principal and the superintendent with carbon copies of each letter to the recipient of the other, I felt assured that the book and the subject of the difficulties gay students faced in school could not be so easily ignored. To be sure I mailed the book and copies of the letters to my hometown newspaper. Fortunately, the newspaper decided to run a story on my involvement with the book and included quotes from the letters. The challenges facing gay youth would finally receive some attention in my own hometown.

It is sad, but not surprising, that I never received a reply to my letters from either the Huntington High School principal or the Huntington superintendent of schools. As an alumnus of Huntington High, I deserved the respect and courtesy of a reply, even if the book ended up in the trash rather than the library or guidance office per my request. But it seems my old school is no more ready to support its gay students today than it was in 1970.

My painful years in school seem so distant. Yet, reading a story about gay youth facing problems at school today brings memories crashing back down upon me like a ton of bricks. I can still feel the emotions of the young child inside of me feeling so much alone with nowhere to turn. Though I am now in a good place and proud to be gay, the child inside still hurts when such memories bare themselves.

Misfits and Rebels

My Sex Education

by John Di Carlo

– 1983 –

– 1997 –

I cried when I first heard what happened to lobsters. I was almost 13, and it was the Fourth of July weekend, 1977. My father was choosing our clambake lobsters from their glass encased tank at Benedetti's Fish Shop in Cranston, R.I. At intervals he described, to my increasing horror, the underwater gulag established by lobstermen. (At 12, I still whispered to my lunch box apple, "I'm sorry, but I have to eat you. I hope it doesn't hurt too much.") My father explained, with lusty enthusiasm, how the lobsters were lured into their pots with bait through a funnel shaped hole. The pots were designed so the animals could fold their claws enough to get through on the way in, but then their copious claws opened up and they were trapped. "That one, Gino, *quello, là!*"

For my little brother Tony's entertainment, Dad began teasing the crustaceans with his car keys, causing the stunned but still fierce animals to rear forward impotently, their powerful claws bound. I walked out of the store tried to compose myself by saying a prayer to Saint Francis, the patron of animals. On the way home I was sullen, my brother couldn't wait to get home to "boil 'em UP, boil 'em UP!" The scene in my grandmother's kitchen was worthy of the Inquisition: boiling pots, innocents waiting their turn for torture, the dead, and smiling, smug, busy Catholics all around. I have never tasted lobster sumptuous enough to erase this memory.

I went out into the blazing hot backyard and decided to go to one of my thinking places, but everywhere I went, the grapevine, the hammock, the far garden, there were uncles or cousins. To the emergency think tank, then: in the pool, underwater. The problem was that my older cousins, high school age, were already splashing plumes of water that peeped over the seven-foot stockade fence, squeals and yells accompanying. In stark contrast, my grandfather and the great-uncles sat quietly under the grapevine nearby, sipping their bitter homemade wine and speaking in hushed Italian. I wanted to go and sit at their feet like many times before. I envied their irrelevance, but I was, as everyone said in the same annoying tone, "a big boy now." I saw the frantic activity through the opened pool door and went in to face my responsibilities as a fellow teenager.

By this time I knew I liked boys more than I should. I had already had a torrid, if one-sided, affair with Montgomery Clift and several other actors I saw in late-night movies on TV. My cousin Danny, though, was never an object of love. It was pure lust. When I walked in and he was poised on the edge of the diving board, posing with his 15-year-old wrestler's body and goose-bumpy olive skin, flashing his cocky smile, I almost gasped. Liz and Mary, his sisters, and all their high school girlfriends were in the pool. They all looked like overfed seals waiting for their meal to drop in the water. He was accurately considered my opposite by the family: I the good scholar, the sullen altar boy, *lo santo*. He, the gigolo, the dummy, *il diavolo*. I changed into my too-large swimtrunks and emerged, but the scene had changed only in its particulars; the girls were still trying to be close to Danny, now using the pretense of Marco Polo. I put on my snorkel and flippers. I was painfully aware of my ungainly height, my pasty skin, but thankfully I was invisible to the adherents of Danny's cult.

I slipped into the pool and underwater. Beneath I was alone, powerful, silent: a shark. Into the stillness, punctuated only with the unearthly distant thuds of the swimmers kicks. Now I could think. I could also look at Danny, his body, his grace, without fear. I imagined that the water was a kind of bed we two shared alone. I could even get excited, beyond the scope of prying eyes. I sometimes lay at the bottom of the pool as he, sunlight streaming about him like Apollo, swam over me. The distorted sky framed his compact beauty nicely, his muscles, the dark hair under his arms, all bathed in the sky-blue reflection of the pool bottom. As I skulked under the rancor, occasionally dragging one of the girls under, like in the opening scene in *Jaws,* a thought came to me: *I am no shark, I am a lobster. Danny is a shark, and I am a lobster, and at this rate I will be stuck under here forever.* Tears added to the water under my mask. I resurfaced.

The boring games went on, and I walked toward the pool house, knowing something tumultuous, something very new was happening. I sat down on the bench and latched the door. Shivering and looking in the murky mirror of the changing room, I started to say to my reflection "I am gay, I am gay, I am gay…" I repeated it perhaps 30 times before the call for lunch drew us all together.

*　　*　　*

I was a paperboy in the late '70s and early '80s, and I read my free copy of the *Providence Journal-Bulletin* with solemn interest. I knew the *Journal* was the truth and that everyone important read it. The headlines of the *Journal* were my first brush with what it meant to be part of a larger gay community. Whereas the library provided a scant and clinical treatment of the subject and the rest was silence, the *Jour-*

nal reported and I learned. In between stops on my bike I learned about Anita Bryant's hate-mongering. In those years I learned that an older gay man was murdered in Providence by fag bashers who were upperclassmen at my school. I learned that the movie *Cruising*, a neat cocktail of murder and hatred, premiered. As I delivered the papers I was wondering which one of my neighbors (maybe Mr. Clancy; his wife left him, he listens to show tunes, and he always invites me in to collect) was queer and if anyone could tell I was. I read that the No-Name, a gay bar in Providence, was firebombed. I stared longingly at the postage-stamp ad of a muscled torso from the Apollo Theater in downtown Providence. Finally, when I was 16 I found out about a gay cancer that was spreading among homosexuals in New York and San Francisco. This little information was poisoned by the homophobic opinions of my peers, family, teachers, and pastor. The rest of what I knew about these mysterious homosexuals was framed in thundering silence. Still I wondered. They went to bars and theaters, and they lived despite murder and hatred and disease. In fact, I was convinced that simply because I was gay I would develop HIV, since it seemed to be genetic.

I felt the noose firmly around my neck. My childhood was a taste of Stalinist Russia. To be oppressed along with others is one thing, but my cell was invisible; I was a child, solitary and sealed with silence. It was a bitter irony for me that at the same time sexual freedom was being celebrated everywhere, along with the Bicentennial, I was using most of my energy to remain underground.

Since my life was placed outside the realm of human development by my school's curriculum and my family's concerns, I became an autodidact in matters of "the life." I am happy that I adopted the very adaptive Boy Scout attitude: "OK, so I am doomed to hell, but I must set some course, live as best I can, and find out about the dimensions of this Prison City where I am incarcerated. I need to know its customs and rules, because being wretched together must be better than being wretched alone." I certainly was not going to come out. I broadcast a strictly straight appearance, and every action in this middle-school totalitarian terror state was self-monitored and mutually checked by my peers. I was not too homophobic, nor was I the least bit understanding: an accomplished collaborator. In my eighth-grade year a poor boy, Matt Grassi, was unfortunate enough to get an erection in the middle of the common shower room. He was beaten up several times soon afterward and would never again shower after gym. He became more and more of a pariah, and the story plagued him through high school. The irony was, I was checking him and the rest of the boys out: Matt was straight, and he was scarred for life by homophobia.

The metaphor of the closet did not make sense to me. "Come out, come out, wherever you are! It's easy!" Do you forget, in your gay enclaves, all of us behind the barbed wire ties that bind us to parents and friends? Why didn't the Jews just "come out" to the Nazis? Would that would have made every goddamn thing better? This was my attitude, a sort of Anne Frank model of waiting for things to force action. I was trapped, immobile, far from shore, behind enemy lines; all metaphors fail. I did have a chilling insight when I was visiting Germany a year after I graduated college. Walking around the streets of Munich, with its pleasant beer gardens and friendly population, I was trying to understand how this place could be the birthplace of Nazism. I stopped dead in my tracks, and I thought of my own hometown experiences. I struggled against the thought, "But they are good people, and my hometown is not capable of that." That indicted Munich, Bavaria, and Warwick, R.I. on the same count. True, on the surface I grew up in postwar full-refrigerator, country club, split-level suburban bliss, but I had seen below the surface.

One small affirmation in the midst of all this negation did make a profound impact on me. Aaron Frick, a senior at Cumberland High School, a half hour's drive from my school, made national headlines when he took a male date to the prom. This caused protestations from all the apes at my school: "I'd kill the fucking faggot if he did it here." That one act of "social disobedience" by someone my age caused me to doubt that all was lost. Hearing one small "yes" in that riot of "no's" gave me pause.

With this distorted and short geography of the gay world, I slouched toward Providence to see "my people" first hand.

*　　*　　*

As soon as I could get away from home I went to explore "the life" for myself. My map was, for the most part, from stories about vice in the city. But where else would you learn about places for underage gay youth out for an evening in the family car in Rhode Island, 1981? I would like to take this opportunity to thank the parks department of the city of Providence as well as the transportation and police departments for being my faithful guardians in my sex education. I would also like to thank my teachers, the anonymous closeted gay men of the city and its environs, for their skilled instructions and valuable insights in Public Sex 101. Thank you for doing what my parents, teachers, and clergy could not and would not do. At this time I had overdosed on Whitman:

Stranger, if you passing see me and desire to speak to me,
Why should I not speak to you? And why should you not speak to me?

I fancied myself a sleepwalker who would, when awakened by Love, spring into His arms. I hummed or whistled to fight the terror and excitement. Many nights I walked through grove after grove of beautifully landscaped tress in Roger Williams Park, often bathed in moonlight. Ghostly figures moved in the trees, their faces shadowed, their dicks out, beckoning in slow motion. The stage, the ritual, was as conventional as opera or kabuki; it was a constant in the midst of chaos. I understand now this was a very male way of organizing a reality: rules of the game, winners, losers, spectators. Memories of these evenings seem to be unfolding in a sunken wreck.

There was something curiously alluring about all this, the least of which was sex. Beauty and fear slowly exchanging secrets in the dark. I never indulged myself in the parks, I was there as a voyeur cum anthropologist. I eagerly learned the language: *tea room…trade…trick.* I was shocked at the amount of unwanted attention I got. In retrospect, the dark-Irish, hollow-cheeked 15-year-old I was must have been a fantasy for those trapped in cruising limbo. There was something more enticing here than I could explain, something Genet understood: the barren and marginal spaces where power was not, the thrill of the hunt and its arcane rules, the addictive and forbidden qualities of the ever-receding prey. But what Genet did not understand was that these things became fetishes precisely because love was an impossibility there. Anonymous gay public sex is a direct result of the degradations of homophobia that deny we are lovable, that we deserve homes. I felt tough (*How many of my straight friends could do this?*) and strangely proud of my double-agent status. A self-administered coming-of-age ritual? Perhaps. I know now all this was dangerous, as no one knew I was there and the surrounding neighborhood had the highest crime rate in the city. I still enjoy brinkmanship.

These men showed me they were ashamed and fearful. I learned from them that love between men was sex: fast, brute, unsatisfying, and anonymous sex. Youth was given great weight, and my teachers taught me that I was attractive and could be cruel to them without reprimand. They looked on me and on each other as if they were starving, but I don't think they were hungry for another unsatisfying encounter. At the time I did not credit that these people were prisoners, that they were trapped in a labyrinth not of their own making, but by the daylight prohibitions, silences, and stares that drove them to seek some comfort in that more forgiving kindly whore, night.

*   *   *

After about a year of searching for Him in the parks and malls I was dejected. In late June I found myself downtown, downcast. I made my way up the short, steep, beautiful climb that is College Hill to Prospect Park, a small park surrounded by beautifully maintained colonial and Federalist period homes. The late afternoon had begun to get a great deal sunnier after a brief shower, and I could smell a hint of the sea as the sidewalk steamed in the reemerging sunlight. This place is magic at sundown; even today, coming down from the Cape or Boston, if I'm in the area I sometimes wait an hour to see the wonderful vista of the sunset over Providence. How could the ideal of *cameraderos* be so sublime and the reality I found so tawdry?

I sat down in the park and began writing in my journal. I had no idea I was being watched. David was a sophomore at Brown, a wiry, handsome, Jewish self-proclaimed poet from New York City. I was so gloomy I didn't even notice him, but no one needed to notice David if he noticed you. He had an irresistible energy and prep-school confidence. I was flattered and embarrassed. In five minutes he had me doubled laughing at solemn Robert Frost, whom I had mentioned as my favorite poet. "What a boring idiot! A block of stone would have more passion!" he said, breaking into an exaggerated New England accent, " 'Good *fahn*-ces make good *nay*-bahs?' " His little round glasses glinted in the streetlamp, and I fell in love.

We were in his room (Jerry Garcia, decorator) in Hope College within fifteen minutes. Along the way my heart, I noticed, increased its pounding until it scared me. I was shaking and sweating. He was nervous too, probably wondering what the penalty in Rhode Island was for sodomy (30 years, I think). He sat me down on his bed and offered me a Bass. I walked over to him and clumsily grabbed him; we kissed and fell on his squeaky little bed. It was fun. I loved David's hairy chest and quick wit. He taught me how to kiss and how to be cool, but affectionate. Neither of us could get enough of each other in the next three weeks.

He took me out, my first real date, to an Indian restaurant, something I found wildly exotic at the time. More important for me was that after dinner we went out dancing at a place called the Rocket. I instantly found a home, albeit a halfway house.

The Rocket had a "mixed" night. In this place boys looked like me. I was introduced to a network but they were all boys, all on the Island of Lost Boys sealed by silence and death. The gay generation before was dead or busy dying, at least that was my perception, and anyone over 25 probably "had it." Intimacy and mortality were fused for us. But a generation, despite this, was being born. Around this little bar I began to build my new little life. So much happened, so much was happening in this rich little vein of queerness. These were heady times for me. My feelings of alienation and dread probably increased, but I learned that I had company.

This downtown dive played new wave and hard core. Music that sang with my voice, romantic and despairing and alternatively virile and raging. In this music Love was the dancer, Death the dance: Joy Division, New Order, the Smiths, Minutemen, and Black Flag all sang what we were feeling. When I heard Morrissey's thin, distant Birmingham voice, I began to realize that there were many ways of being who I was. Like the faint sounds of rescuers getting closer to buried victims, this music prepared me for a series of events that would define our community's future and mine.

The community responded, reaching out to the dying, battling Reagan's thoughtless evil. People were outed, rage was incited. ACT UP crescendoed. There was certainly enough outrage waiting for a catalyst. Distant battles were engaged. I entered a world, albeit a small one, that was openly and proudly gay. Often offensive and bumbling, but inherently subversive and defiant. Aaron Frick's simple act of civil disobedience would accelerate with ACT UP's dynamism. I discovered two things in the course of this part of my sex education: that I was lovable and that I was going to have to fight hard to have the life I wanted.

All the summer of 1983, I was ecstatic and David seemed happy, but we were from different worlds and were at very different stages, probably doomed as a couple. Suddenly he stopped answering my calls. I was heartbroken, but that is not my point. From his point of view this is understandable. I thought, what would he say? "Hi Mom, Dad, I know you had a hard day at the law firm, Dad, but this is John, my 17-year-old townie goyim boyfriend I picked up in a park." So I cried, and at the same time I rejoiced that I still had a heart to break. I never saw him again, but I still have a few of his awful poems. I still love Robert Frost.

*　　*　　*

My role models? None were local. Who else was there at the time? Liberace? Paul Lynde? Charles Nelson Reilly? They showed me nothing of what I was or wanted to be. I thought, even when I was in my late teens, that they represented straight America's wishful thinking: gay meant frivolous, silly, ornamental, expendable. What about the future? It was fine to have peers, but where were we going? I found people to look up to through the most unlikely avenue: my family. They were two old family friends from Boston, Harold and Charles, who happened to be gay. Charles grew up with my mother and had even dated my aunt during high school. They were a couple, roommates to us, and they were certainly not "out." They were not "in" either. They were thresholders. I had profound hopes, disguised as suspicions. They would be obvious to me today, but then I had not yet learned to recognize subtle cues. I watched them with outward contempt but with an inward longing I find difficult to recount. They were not in any way physically or verbally affectionate with each other. (No wonder, being surrounded by the enemy.) Here were two men who lived together; they joined us for dinner and I watched their every move. They were both academics; they were both funny and very kind. I asked as many questions as I could without attracting undue attention. Mom? "How did they meet?" "Where did they live?"

In my "research," I became obsessed with learning whether they slept together. Above all, I wished to see their bed. My hypothesis was, one bed meant a conjugal relationship. One couple meant the hope of a dignified and mature love. The diplomatic maneuvering it took to get an invitation from these two suspected fags and then to have my cagey Catholic parents accept I will leave to your imagination. In the end I was able to do it.

My folks nervously approached the Back Bay apartment. We had already attended Mass at Boston's Paulist Chapel to protect us from the sodomy of the evening. I was entirely single-minded. I hardly noticed the book-lined apartment warmed by a blazing fireplace. I tried to offer to take my family's coats, but Charles was a deft host. I remember sitting by the coffee table trying to guess which of the doors in sight was *the* door. I excused myself to go to the bathroom as the adults and my brother talked nervously chatted with the "roomies." "Second on the right," Harold dryly informed me. I walked down the hall; all the doors were firmly closed. I tried the first door, locked. The next door was open! The cellar gaped. I went into the bathroom close to distraction. I had to find out!

Out into the hall again, I tried the next door. Upon opening it I was greeted by a perfectly arranged linen closet, the Burberry blankets mocking my error. If I knew then what I know now... Harold came around the corner. "What is going on?" his voice was clipped. Obviously he was the Mistress of the Robes. I had an inspired lie on the tip of my tongue, "Er, I forgot something in my coat." He walked straight to the unopened door, and I followed him, holding my breath. Sitting in the middle of the room was *the* queen-size (I am not joking) bed. The love bed, the bed where they slept together. In my reverie I heard a voice: "Well, what did you want?" Harold was looking at the coats on the bed. "Oh, um, my wallet? Yeah, my wallet, thanks." "Wallet?" he repeated, staring straight ahead. I was too high to even hear him. I don't know what was singing in my head, but when I returned from the honest bedroom, beaming, to the hypocritical living room, I knew I was beginning one of the happiest evenings of my life.

To those who taught and failed to teach me about sex and love: Only through extraordinary efforts and great luck did I survive the lies, bigotry, and self-hatred you fed me.

I now speak to my younger self and those given a similar sex education: Those who taught you are perverts or bigots; liars teach you we are predators, lawless, shameful, and sex-obsessed; monsters profess that love and death are fused in you and that you would be better off dead; cowards are those who are silent when they know better. You must be very fierce to save your heart for the people worthy of your love.

Half-Breed

by Kevin Jennings

– 1974 –   *– 1998 –*

Cher taught me the limits of acceptance I would face as a gay person.

Well, maybe that's stretching it a bit, and maybe it's more my sister Carol with whom I should start.

I grew up in Lewisville, N.C., a small town outside the city of Winston-Salem, during the '70s. I wouldn't say the atmosphere there was stifling for a young gay boy. I would say it was completely airless, more like a vacuum, a veritable black hole into which all hopes and dreams were sucked like light rays from a dying star. With a fundamentalist preacher for a dad, "fabulousness" was hardly a concern for me. Survival was more the order of the day.

I wasn't ready to use the word *gay* to describe myself as a lad, but I'd known I was different from early childhood. I remember just loving my brother's muscle magazines in grade school, and I'd fairly prance around when his football-playing buddies would come over after practice, so excited was I. This occasioned a few awkward glances ("Hey, Jennings, your brother is *weird*"), but my enthusiasm was chalked up to a desire to emulate them, even though I was already realizing that what I really wanted to do with them was *copulate,* not emulate. I knew they weren't role models. They were future playmates, or so I hoped, in my most forbidden fantasies.

My sister Carol was my real role model. Seventeen years older than I, she lived in the mysterious North with her husband, an enlisted man in the Navy (now, that's an erotic fantasy for another story). She was outrageous by our small-town Southern standards. She had a McGovern bumper sticker on her Vega, sometimes didn't wear a bra, and (shhh!) *slept in the nude.* She was even friends with black people. *Quel scandale!*

I adored Carol. Far from trying to slough me off like some kind of itchy eczema (as my three older brothers did), Carol delighted in me, buying me gifts, telling me tales of life in oh-so-cosmopolitan Groton, Conn. (hey, I did live in North Carolina, OK?), and encouraging me to think about college. Although she had only a high school diploma herself, Carol had some serious intellectual pretensions, and she became my comrade-in-arms against the philistinism we both deplored in our family. She made me feel special, and helped me see that there was a life beyond the tobacco fields and strip malls of my hometown. She was my lifeline during grade school and junior high. She gave me hope I wouldn't be stuck in North Carolina forever. For this, I adored her.

I emulated her down to a tee. If Carol liked a singer or a show, I slavishly followed it. Her tastes were, for my family, unconventional. She loved soul music, so I became a big Gladys Knight and the Pips fan, as she was. This didn't earn me more acceptance from rest of my family: I remember my brother Paul saying to me once, after I had returned from a visit to Connecticut, "All you want to listen to after you've seen

Carol is nigger music." But, if Carol liked it, it was OK by me.

Of course, I was growing up in the '70s, so it was television that I used as my biggest escape. Here, Carol's nascent feminism led her to like shows with strong female characters, and I followed her lead. I was probably the only boy in Lewisville who made sure to take in *Phyllis, Maude,* and *Rhoda* each week. I identified with all of these women, who were sassy and strong and pushing the boundaries of what was acceptable. I watched every episode of *Wonder Woman,* longing for my own magic bracelets (perhaps to word off the taunts of my peers), as well as the *Bionic Woman,* who seemed so much more accessible as a role model than the *Six Million Dollar Man* (perhaps because I secretly longed to be romanced by Lee Majors, as the Bionic Woman was). I aligned myself with Farrah, Kate, and Jacqueline as my three angels triumphed over an assortment of masculine oafs. I lived vicariously through my TV heroines. They did what I wished I could do.

Especially Cher.

No, not the fabulous modern Cher, complete with her Academy Award, her Junior Vasquez remixes, and her frequent flyer program at the local plastic surgeon. I worshiped the tacky, early-'70s Cher, complete with her big nose, her Bob Mackie bell-bottoms, and her not-yet-out toddler Chastity, whom she would hold in her arms while crooning "I Got You Babe" to her not-yet-troglodyte–Republican–Congressman–ex-husband Sonny at the end of each episode of *The Sonny and Cher Comedy Hour.* She flaunted the rules: she swore, she showed her belly button, she wore outrageous clothes. She was my biggest hero in middle school. So, of course, during Spirit Week of my sixth grade year, when we each had to dress up as our favorite TV character, I chose Cher.

Now, I did not make my first attempt at cross-dressing without trepidation. I was regularly bullied as the smart boy (the "faggot") in our school, so I knew I was taking a risk. But, hey, I was also respected for my brains—hadn't the other kids elected me student body president that year? (Correction: I was elected white student body copresident—because of racial tensions, we had "separate but equal" races in North

Carolina in 1975.) Lots of people liked Cher anyway, I thought—I remembered how much everybody had loved my playing "Half-Breed" in fourth grade during show-and-tell, so proud was I of my first self-purchased 45. It was a risk, but I figured it was pretty safe. I was basically trying to find out what the limits were in my hometown.

I knew enough to wait until Mom had left for work to get dressed. I was an embarrassingly inadequate proto–drag queen. I tore one of my shirts into what I thought was a semblance of one of Cher's daring fashion statements, stole one of my sister's pairs of stretch pants, put on some makeup, and tied one of my mother's scarves around my neck, before heading out to the bus stop. The bus stop and ride were smooth enough. People avoided me like I had leprosy, but nobody said anything. So I was feeling pretty good when I sauntered off the bus and into reading class.

Here things started to go badly.

To this day I can't remember my reading teacher's name—Mr. Carter, I think it was, but I can't be entirely sure. But I will never forget his penetrating glare as I entered the room and settled into my seat. He began class with a silent reading assignment. After we got our books out, he slowly ambled to my desk and towered over me. I tried not to look up, and I pretended I didn't feel his eyes boring a hole though the top of my skull. I started to sweat, and the other kids started to giggle. The seemingly endless silence wore on, with Mr. Carter remaining in place, not uttering a word. I remained focused on my book, clinging to it as my life preserver with all the desperation of a drowning man. Finally Mr. Carter harrumphed. "Well, boys shore ain't what they used to be," he said in a loud, clear voice. The other students erupted in hilarity, and Mr. Carter snorted as he went back to his desk.

I could have died.

A part of me actually did.

That was the part that thought it was OK for a boy to have someone like Cher as a role model. You see, I didn't want to be Cher: I simply wanted to have Cher's pizzazz, her chutzpah, and—most of all—her freedom to be who she wanted to be. The roles boys were ascribed didn't offer me that, so I had turned to her. Mr. Carter and my class-mates—who harassed me in the halls that day and the rest of the year (hadn't Mr. Carter given them tacit permission to do so?)—told me I wouldn't be having that freedom in Lewisville, N.C., in 1975. I slunk home that day, stripped off my costume and makeup, and never wore drag again. I never told anyone in my family about the incident or the harassment that ensued. Not even Carol.

My story doesn't get prettier after that. The next year I received one vote when I ran for reelection as student body president—my own. I ate all of my lunches alone in junior high and early high school (as no one wanted to sit with the school fag), and finally I attempted suicide at age 16. I learned quite well the lesson that I couldn't be who I was (I was always a straight-A student, after all), and that lesson almost killed me.

Without even knowing she was doing so, my sister Carol once again came to my rescue. After my sophomore year she suggested that my Mom and I come to live with her and her husband at their new post-ing, at Pearl Harbor Naval Base in Honolulu, Hawaii. Here I indeed learned that North Carolina was not the limit of my horizons. Perhaps because of its multicultural population and lack of a fundamentalist es-tablishment, Hawaii offered a tolerance for diversity that stunned me, and I began to make friends for the first time since grade school. I lost the 40 pounds I'd gained in high school (a sort of self-protective armor and the result of years of having Doritos as my only friends) and rein-vented myself. I was even elected Student Council treasurer my senior year, reclaiming the leadership position my cross-dressing had cost me. I still suffered the costs of the closet—the shame, the isolation—but I began to realize that there were other rooms in the house and made plans to move. I used the *Barron's Profiles of American Colleges* that Carol had given me as my 17th birthday gift to choose Harvard as the college I wanted to attend and, wonder of wonders, I was accepted and went there. I escaped and ended up getting to be who I wanted to be after all. Those straight A's turned out to be my salvation.

My story doesn't have an entirely happy ending. While I was in high school, Carol began a long, slow descent into drug addiction and mental illness, a descent in which she hurt many of us and tried to take as many of us down with her as she could. (I guess she learned her own lessons about breaking the rules society lays down for women.) We haven't spoken for 15 years as a result of my decision to refuse to enable her in her illness. As an adult I would learn that the gay community has its own rules and regulations one must comply with to be accepted, ones sometimes no less daunting than those I faced in sixth grade, and I learned that acceptance in any community has its price. But at least now I know there are many horizons, not just one, and I am happy with myself as a hybrid, someone who probably won't ever "fit in" anywhere. A half-breed, as Cher might have put it.

Coons and Corpses:
A Lesson Unlearned

by Ed Brock

- 1984 -   *- 1997 -*

I can't believe I just impulsively spent close to 30 bucks on books. Fag books. Thirty bucks on fag stories. Thirty bucks!!!

Not that reading gay fiction is a sin—at least not in my book. And not that it isn't OK to treat myself every now and then to a book that I can read simply for pleasure (and they *were* for pleasure). I bought *Captain Swing* by Larry Duplechan and *Going To Meet The Man* and *Just Above My Head*—the *original* black gay novel, thank you very much— by James Baldwin. I guess I'm on one of my *let-me-rediscover-the-black-gay-brilliance-of-Brother-James* kicks again, because yesterday I also bought a copy of *Another Country,* in addition to buying the *Men on Men 6* collection of contemporary (white) gay fiction, edited by David Bergman.

No, reading gay fiction ain't a sin. But my consumption of gay literature seems to come in binges. Like the bulimic who gorges on bonbons in a moment of weakness, I splurge on books—gay books—when my self-esteem needs a boost. Just like I waste money and time enduring gay dance clubs and cruising guys on the A train when I need that boost. Or just like I get catty and trifling with other desperate-for-attention queens on Christopher Street, spend hours surfing the Net for anything gay-related, and desperately make my rounds at bourgie gay support groups, looking for that boost. All of this because at 23—after going to college and coming out and being a fierce black queer activist and scholar and graduating from college and getting a job and getting my own apartment in New York City and hearing people tell me that I'm *making it*—I'm still hopelessly and aimlessly looking for affirmation. I'm still looking for my damn fucking reflection.

❋   ❋   ❋

Lesson #1: *I remember when they beat me up in fifth grade. It was during recess, right after an intense soccer game between the kids from my homeroom teacher's class and the kids from Ms. Clark's homeroom class. I forget the exact reason why they beat me up. But I do remember that for several weeks prior, this white kid named Christian had insisted on repeatedly sharing his discovery of the word "nigger" with our classmates. I remember being jumped toward the far end of the soccer field by Christian and two or three other white boys as they called me "nigger" and beat me like I was one. I remember other kids—most of them white—passively watching, some of them confused, some of them entertained. I remember eventually breaking away and running inside, where Ms. Clark noticed my shaken demeanor, my grass-stained shirt, and my unrelenting tears. And I remember not telling Ms. Clark the reason why I was upset, for even back then I seemed to know that I wasn't supposed to speak up when white people used their power to hurt me. This marked the first time I could remember being aware, being overwhelmed, by the fact that I was different. And this marked the first time I could remember ever getting a lesson in how to be silent.*

*   *   *

Why the hell am I writing in fragments? Why can't I just script a cute and quick essay on how it felt to a be a closeted queer in junior and senior high school? High School?! Shit, do I even remember what it was like to be a closeted black queer in high school? As soon as I graduated, I ran away, far away, and never looked back. I went to college, I came out, and I conquered the world, or at least the fucking campus. Protected by the PC liberalism of an early '90s college campus, I erased the traumatic episodes of my high school career from my memory. Nobody wants to remember life in the closet after coming out. So now there are gaps in my memory and gaps in my story. My story resists being neatly compressed into a fluid, *Stand-By-Me*-style, coming-of-age narrative. While all of the excerpts in this piece are related to one another, fitting them into a narrative is impossible. Using them to formulate a fluid narrative would allow me to understand my story, and more dangerously, to control it. Clearly, the forces-that-be do not intend for me to control my narrative. They are too afraid of what I would learn if I could put all of the pieces neatly together. And quite honestly, I think that I, too, am afraid of what my narrative, in order and intact, would reveal.

*   *   *

Lesson#2: *Fifth grade was an important year for me. I discovered some crucial facts of life. One discovery came right before Christmas, when I played Ebenezer Scrooge in the fifth-grade production of* A Christmas Carol. *There I was, this cute little black boy in a predominantly middle-class white suburban public school, with the lead role in the school play. How the hell did this little Negro get the lead part? is what my father expected the white folks in the audience to say, or at least to think. Over weeks of memorizing lines, getting fitted for fab! costumes, and keeping my patience through long and tiring rehearsals, I feared that the audience wouldn't like me. I was worried, frightened. But you know what? When the curtains opened, Ms. Thing stepped on stage and turned that role out. I sang, I screamed, I pranced up and down that stage like an overanxious diva on Broadway. Basically, I worked (SNAP!). And the crowd loved me. They loved me. The well-dressed, well-paid white parents loved me. They smiled at me and praised me. My teachers showered me with adulation. Even my peers congratulated me (and, much to the heart's content of this diva-in-the-making, envied me). I enjoyed the applause, and I learned a valuable lesson. I learned that I could win people's affection when I pretended to be someone, or something, else. I learned that people enjoyed me when I was on stage; I learned that people approved of me when I pretended to be someone, or something, that I was not. When I pretended to be someone, or something, that they wanted to see. Of all the things that I was taught in grade school, this was one of the few lessons that I truly understood—that I truly learned.*

* * *

There weren't many images of black gay men circulating through popular media when I was in high school in the late '80s. Well, at least I didn't have access to many images. In fact, only two images come to mind: the flaming snap queens Antoine and Blaine on the TV show *In Living Color*, and the pictures of the men who were killed and devoured by Jeffrey Dahmer. As I struggled to construct a sense of self as a closeted black gay teenager, the only images I saw of other black gay men were the buffoonish derisions of Negro faggotry offered by homophobic black male comics and the hazy snapshots of the victims of a cannibalistic white gay psychopath. I remember the condescending laughter directed at those limp-wristed parodies of black sissies; I remember aunts and old black church ladies looking at newspaper pictures of Dahmer's victims, quoting verses from Leviticus and Romans, and declaring smugly, "That's what happens when you live *that* life of sin."

These were the contexts in which I received images of black gay men when I was in high school. During those ever so formative years, with no other resources at my disposal, I searched for my reflection in coons and corpses. When watching *In Living Color*, I scavenged for redeeming qualities in being oversexed and misogynist. I derived pleasure from saying "Hated it" every time Blaine and Antoine reviewed a movie starring women; I misconstrued their exaggerated appetite for male chests, cocks, and ass as an act of black gay sexual liberation. And while looking at the pictures of Dahmer's victims, I explored their eyes, their lips, and their smiles. I searched for indications of buffed black bodies, and I imagined them as my lovers, engaged in my embrace. I did all of this because coons and corpses were the only images of black gay men that I saw, and I mistook them for my reflection. Even though Bayard Rustin actually graduated from my high school, no one ever taught me about Bayard. No one ever taught me what I desperately needed to know about Bayard, Langston Hughes, James Baldwin, Joseph Beam, Marlon Riggs, and Essex Hemphill. Not at my high school.

*　　*　　*

Lesson#3: *I know there is a God because it was God who prevented me from stabbing Damon, Chris, Shane, and Jay in the tenth grade. This was the clique of macho-acting boys who played on the football team, bragged about the sex and the drugs that they really hadn't had, and asserted their fragile masculinity by harassing me, the class sissy, on a daily basis throughout the tenth grade. They mocked my effeminate manner and taunted me with epithets. They wrote* ED IS A FAG *on the walls of the boys' bathrooms. In gym class they ridiculed my lack of athletic prowess. In health class they brought attention to the fact that I surrounded myself with platonic female friends with whom I gossiped and even went shopping; they accused me of being one of the girls. And often they did these things in front of girls, as a way to advertise their virility to potential female lovers.*

I realize that I was lucky—they never hit me. They never hit me, however, because I never talked back. I always took these verbal beatings silent-

ly, afraid of the physical beatings that would occur if I were to speak up. My silence bred terror. I was terrified every time I had to endure their barrage of accusations. I died every time they brought my unannounced, but widely suspected, faggotry to everyone's attention. I felt powerless as they stripped my sexual identity on the auction block for public inspection. This sense of powerlessness in the company of my peers became the lens through which I learned to despise and hate myself—a lesson which Damon, Chris, Shane, and Jay taught me on a daily basis. I didn't speak up, not only because I was afraid of physical retaliation, but also because I didn't believe that I was worth speaking up for. They knew, our other classmates knew, and tragically, I knew that black faggots were pathetic, sick, worthless. I had no place, no right, to challenge such a commonly accepted truth.

Yet at the same time that I felt terrified, powerless, and worthless, I was also consumed with rage. Every time Damon, Chris, Shane, and Jay harassed me, a bloodthirsty rage threatened to occlude my air flow, cut off my circulation, trouble my bowels. At night, in the privacy of my own room, while still awake, I would fantasize about violent episodes in health class where I would wield ice picks, trash cans, metal pipes, and daggers to mutilate my four foes. Some nights in my room, after a particularly rough day at school, I would even act out these scenes after my parents had gone to bed. I would swing my arms through the air as if I were pounding Chris's head with a slab of wood; I would position my hands as if they were strangling the last breaths of air out of Shane's 15-year-old body. Then one morning, having been pushed to the edge with rage, I took my mother's 9-inch butcher's knife from the kitchen, placed it in my duffel bag, and got on the school bus. I had come to a decision: If they fuck with me today, I'll stab them. Never mind the fact that I would have gone to jail, that my life would have been ruined—another young black brother lost. No, they had pushed me to the edge, and their time to pay had come.

But as I said, I know that there's a God because God prevented me from stabbing Damon, Chris, Shane, and Jay that day in the tenth grade. Instead of going to health class, I was called to the guidance office to see my counselor—for what I cannot remember. All I know is that missing health class that day gave me an opportunity to catch my cool. It gave me an op-

portunity to rediscover my terror, my fear, and my disgust for myself. It gave me an opportunity to remember that I had no place, no right, to challenge Damon, Chris, Shane, and Jay. I've heard many stories of queer youth inflicting violence on themselves or on others as a response to the homophobic bullshit they experience on a daily basis. But I rediscovered my hatred for myself before I got the chance to carry out such violence. I guess I was lucky.

✳   ✳   ✳

"We teach who we are." Those were the words that accosted me on a late August afternoon at the George School, a private boarding school in eastern Pennsylvania. Just about two weeks before beginning my second year as a history teacher at an elite private school in New York City, I attended a series of workshops held at the George School for young teachers of color. One of the facilitators wrote this sentence on a piece of newsprint and proceeded to recognize how our demeanor, ideals, and character as teachers are the lessons that our students remember the most. In our students' eyes, names and dates of historical figures and events pale in comparison to how our own beliefs inform the ways in which we run our classrooms and interact with students. I immediately thought of my fourth grade teacher, Mrs. Sinters; the only thing I remember about my experience in her class is how she ignored and disempowered me and the handful of other black students in the class on a regular basis. She didn't care too much for black children, and she definitely taught who she was.

I sat in horror as my memory shifted from Mrs. Sinters's class to my own experiences as a first-year teacher. After being *very* out and *very* political in college, I had decided to revisit the closet during my first year as a teacher. With New York being one of the 40 states in which gay men and lesbians can be fired from their jobs because of their gayness, with the absence of "sexual orientation" from my school's antidiscrimination policy, and with the hysteria that erupts around the inclusion of gay issues in secondary education, I opted for closeted silence and a paycheck as a first-year teacher over job insecurity and political drama.

Sure, the kids knew—I didn't fool anybody. Kids can put two and two together rather easily. But since I evaded their inquiries into my sexuality, they accepted me. They knew I was gay, and they knew I was going to be silent, so they accepted me.

And so I sat in horror that afternoon at the George School as I considered what I had taught my students during my first year of teaching. I thought that I had taught them about medieval European guilds, Spanish conquistadors, and the American Revolution. But what I had really taught them was that I was beat up by white boys in the fifth grade and learned how to be silent. What I had really taught them was that I was harassed on a daily basis in the tenth grade and learned how to hate myself. What I had really taught them was that as a black gay teenager in a predominantly middle-class white suburban high school, I learned, as Paul Lawrence Dunbar once wrote, to "wear the masks." I learned to wear the masks of docility, assimilation, fear, and silence.

These are the lessons that my students took with them, and these are the lessons that make growing up so difficult for gay and lesbian teenagers, especially gay and lesbian teens of color. For while all teenagers suffer whenever they are taught to be silent, gay and lesbian kids of color face a particular dilemma. It incenses me when I hear people of color express their homophobia by proclaiming that homophobia and racism are not alike, that racism is clearly the more horrific of the two, and that gay people have no right to make such a comparison. It incenses me because I can recall from my own experience that while being a black child in a racially conservative community was difficult, I at least had resources that I could turn to. I could go to my parents, black teachers (the few that there were), or other black adults in the community for guidance. I could sit down at the "black kids' table" in the cafeteria during lunch, or I could attend a meeting of my school's Black Student Union when I needed to vent. I could call upon local black churches and the local chapter of the NAACP when I needed community assistance. When I got beat up by white boys in the fifth grade; when my ninth-grade history teacher defended "the white man's burden" in class one day as a worthwhile doctrine; when skinheads appeared in my high school during my junior year; or when the Ku Klux Klan held a march in my hometown two days before Martin Luther King Jr.'s birthday during my senior year of high school, there was a community of black people to whom I could turn for support. This community protected me, nurtured me, and provided me with the tools that I needed to face a racist world.

No equivalent support systems were available to me as a gay student. There weren't any openly gay students in whom I could confide. There weren't any openly gay teachers or other adults who could counsel and guide me. I didn't have access to any larger gay community that could shelter me, nurture me, and teach me the skills that I needed to confront a homophobic world. While I gradually gained confidence in and love for my blackness, and as I gradually learned to celebrate and embrace it despite racism, my gayness remained suppressed and despised. So homophobic people of color do have a point: homophobia and racism are, in fact, different. For gay kids of color, however, the former is not necessarily the lesser of the two evils.

Regardless of how racism and homophobia are different, one important similarity remains: both teach silence and self-hatred. These were lessons that racism and homophobia taught me all too well, and these were lessons that I taught my students as a first-year teacher. Which is why, during my second year of teaching, I decided to draw up a new lesson plan. Below is an excerpt from a statement that I posted on my school's "Speak-Out Board", a bulletin board where members of the school community can post their opinions on issues of concern:

I'm writing this because I've been in a terrible mood all week. I've been in a terrible mood because I've been silent. Over the past year, and especially over the past week—with the appearance of this speak-out board, as members of the upper school community have made their homophobia and heterosexism known— I've been silent. And silence is an active exercise, and an exhausting one, too. It takes a lot of energy and intense concentration to make sure that you walk, talk, and behave in a way that allows you to remain silent. I've been in a terrible mood because although I have so many things that I want to say, Riverdale forces me and many others, students and faculty alike, to remain silent. Tirelessly, we've served our duty well. And so I write this statement, not to force "my business" or some politically correct agenda on anyone, but simply because as a gay member of this school community, I just don't have the strength and energy any more to be silent…

Overall, coming out as a gay teacher was a positive event. Sure, there were those kids whose religious/moral beliefs, or whose immaturity and personal insecurities around sexuality, led them to make snide comments behind my back. But to my amazement, many students overwhelmed me in the halls with adulation and praise. Straight kids, closeted kids, white kids, kids of color—they all respected and appreciated what I wrote. Why? Because all kids want to learn how to speak up, speak out, and affirm who they are. This was definitely what I longed for as a closeted, petrified, self-loathing black gay teenager; some things just haven't changed.

But after the initial rounds of adulation and praise, my glorious moment of self-affirmation was tempered by the cool realization that coming out never solves all of one's problems. After all, we live in the same homophobic and heterosexist society *after* coming out as we did beforehand. Quickly I noticed which students and teachers did *not* offer me encouragement and support; I became paranoid about how our relationships would change for the worse. Quickly (and I do mean *quickly*) I became annoyed by and suspicious of fellow faculty members who wanted to tell me stories about gay cousins and lesbian aunts, proving how "cool" they were with "the issue." I revisited my anxiety over the parental disdain, administrative panic, and job insecurity that might result from my actions. Gradually—just like that day in tenth grade when my stabbing expedition got detoured by a call to the guidance office—I took a step back and surrendered my confidence to self-doubt, angst, and most of all, fear.

Ironically, in my attempt to unlearn the lessons of self-hatred and fear that I had internalized as a youth, I realized that these lessons, at least for me, will never be completely unlearned. Silence and self-doubt, for me, are like biting my fingernails and filing my income-tax at the last minute: habits I will constantly struggle to overcome. But I must say, for the time being, I'm comforted by the fact that after sorting through this messy warehouse of adolescent memories, for the first time in my life I finally realize what the struggle actually is. And with this knowledge, I can actually begin to fight.

From Batman and Robin to Same-Sex Marriage: A Tale of Two Generations

as told to the class of '97 by Loraine Hutchins, class of '66

– 1964 –   *– 1997 –*

NOTE: This piece is about censorship and gay bashing which took place at my high school in 1966. I was moved to tell the story to current students at the school after hearing about a new event of censorship at the same school 30 years later. In 1996 students at my alma mater produced a video show on same-sex marriage for the school's station, WBNC-TV/Channel 60. The video was part of a series called Shades of Grey, *which has already debated controversial topics like female genital mutilation, gun control, and euthanasia. The show on same-sex marriage, however, was barred from running, at the last minute, by the county's superintendent. I sent a slightly different version of this story, below, to the school newspaper,* Silver Chips, *which published it in February 1997. The students have charged censorship and infringement of First Amendment rights and have asked the county school board to overturn the superintendent's decision.*

*   *   *

In 1965 I started my senior year at Montgomery Blair High School in suburban Silver Spring, Md., right outside of Washington, D.C. I was excited because I'd been chosen editor in chief of *Silver Chips*, the school newspaper. I'd worked my whole high school career to win this position, and I was dreaming of becoming a professional writer someday.

I was avidly interested in current events and politics as well as real-life human interest stories, so the editorship of the school paper seemed a perfect assignment for me. The Vietnam War was already raging over-seas, and some of our classmates would be sent there soon after gradu-ation, never to come home. We never dreamed that years later the refugees from this war would move here into these same neighbor-hoods, go to Blair, and end up selling us spring rolls on Fenton Street.

At that point in my life I also never dreamed I was anything other than heterosexual. I knew I was attracted to boys, but no one told me you could be attracted to both boys and girls, and it took the women's movement a few years later to inspire me to act on my feelings for my sisters. I did already identify with homosexuals, however, because I as-sociated them with art and poetry and civil rights. The summer before I entered high school in 1963 my mother, who was a Washington, D.C., schoolteacher herself, took me downtown with her to march down Pennsylvania Avenue in the famous March on Washington for Civil Rights. This was something of a family tradition, my grand-mother having marched as a high school student with her class and teacher to petition for women's suffrage during President Woodrow Wilson's era.

My mom and I stood under big shade trees that day, on the grass on the Mall, near the Lincoln Memorial, with thousands of black and white folk gathered singing and swaying, listening to Martin Luther King tell us his dreams. Although I didn't know it then, that famous march had been organized by Bayard Rustin, a gay African-American.

As a budding writer, I read all the modern poets, essayists, and novelists I could find. Allan Ginsberg and James Baldwin were gay literary figures who especially inspired me. My friends and I all wore buttons that said HOMOSEXUAL RIGHTS along with our FIGHT RACISM and END THE WAR IN VIETNAM buttons, even though none of us were admittedly homosexual yet. After going downtown many times to the beatnik coffeehouses near Dupont Circle and eagerly soaking up the free verse poetry, smoky jazz, and social commentary, we even decided to organize a coffeehouse of our own, which we started in a local church basement. We called it The Real Dirt, after a passage in one of Jack London's books.

We hung old white bedsheets on the church basement walls for graffiti writing and scrounged card tables and chairs and lots of empty wine bottles for candle stubs, some cups and silverware for our own teenage coffeehouse, which we dedicated to raising money for SNCC.

When we weren't haunting the beatnik coffeehouses or going to demonstrations, we would all pile into Richard's car, one of those old boat-shaped Pontiacs, and catch the midnight movies downtown. That year, they were reviving the old Batman and Robin movies from the 1930s. We thought it was funny that they made all the villains look Japanese, until we realized it was serious war propaganda and racism we were laughing at. Still, since so many of us loved their corniness and their high sense of drama, my friend Jo decided to write a feature piece on these old Batman flicks for *Silver Chips.* She talked about how the revival of interest in them was a strange craze, so absurd one had to call it camp. We asked her to define "camp," so she added a sentence about how "camp" was a term from "the homosexual subculture." It means, "so extreme as to amuse or to have a perversely sophisticated appeal," she said.

That's all she said. Nothing more. Nothing about gay rights, gay love, or same-sex marriages. And for this, we got the copies of the school paper locked up in the vice-principal's safe! This is history. Your history, students of Blair today, as well as ours. You should all know this.

I marched down to the principal's office and discussed the situation with him, all the while knowing that we had held back a substantial stash of copies he knew nothing about. My staff was distributing these contraband copies in the halls even as he and I spoke. Eventually he realized he looked silly, and no more was said, that was that. But it intimidated us. We weren't sure anymore whether we really had freedom to write about what we wanted to or not.

I realized after that what censorship meant, what it could potentially do to stifle education and debate. Ironically, his action made us all the more curious about homosexuality and homosexual rights, exactly what he hadn't wanted to do. (He had told me that homosexuality "wasn't something that should be discussed in high school.")

Yeah. And neither was the Vietnam War, which our government was sending my classmates to die in that year, either. They could send the guys over but we couldn't talk about it in many classes or organize teach-ins about it on school grounds. Until later, that is, after many more deaths…

I did not know then that I was bisexual, nor that Jo, who wrote the Batman article, would seven years later become my lover. I didn't know that her boyfriend would later move to San Francisco and declare himself gay. I didn't know that one of my *Silver Chips* sports reporters would die years later of AIDS, nor that he would be so ashamed of it that he would not allow its mention at his funeral. I did not know then (because he was too ashamed to tell us) that my best friend was being beaten up every day in gym class, for being, or acting, or appearing, gay, that he was repeatedly humiliated, hit and shoved in his locker, that the coach was aware of it and considered it normal, did nothing about it, even after my friend asked for help. My friend, now a social worker who works with the elderly and with the families of people with AIDS, told me recently that he even went to the school principal back then, over the coach's head. The principal said there was nothing he could do. This friend can't face going back to the school even to this day, even when he needs to go for professional reasons related to his social work caseload. He has to beg off. Entering those halls still makes him physically ill.

I learned from that experience that none of us are free until all of us are free, and that free expression is the essence of democracy for people of all ages. I support and salute you, students of Montgomery Blair High School in the 1990s, in debating today's hot issues and reclaiming the lost history of yesterday's hot issues too!

Sarah W.

by Jaron Kanegson

Seventh grade
we sat on the gold carpet of my bedroom floor,
listening to Sting on my boom box
    the Murder By Numbers song.
We played it over and over,
listing all the boys we hated.
Picking three so we could do it like the song,
    murder by numbers, one-two-three,
we made up things to do to them
(we thought we were original).
We'd tie them to chairs,

and hack off their penises with kitchen knives
slice by slice,
and make them all watch.
We'd cook their flesh in a frying pan,
then feed them the crispy pieces.

Meanwhile she was pretty,
with dark hair and dark eyes,
pale skin and red lips, like Snow White.
She never wore her glasses, so she squinted a lot
making her cheeks look dented and beautiful.
Later she cut her hair extra short.
     Then I really wanted her,
especially once when she came after me
with the six-inch leg of a stuffed toy lamb.
Except she lied a lot.
One night, when I was coming to sleep over,
she covered the toilet seat with Vaseline.
I had to wipe and wipe my butt to get it off.
She said it was for her brother,
but I didn't believe her, because really,
how often do boys sit down?

Still, we were horror movie friends, watching three in a night.
One was about a woman killed by a monster.
She turned into a corpse with long bloody hair,
and came back to life.
She wandered around, covered with graveyard dirt
moaning and shrieking in the memory of someone,
"You could still love me, you could still love me."
After that movie she'd say it to me, "You could still love me."
     But she never tried to kiss me,
not even when I lay next to her all night in a broken-zippered sleeping bag
on her scratchy living room carpet.

She never kissed me, not even when she told me
that in first grade, after I said to her
    I could be a boy
    and no one would know,
she was afraid to go to the bathroom with me—
    she decided I was one.

Fifteen my parents got divorced.
Sarah and I met some guys.
She liked Adam, who everybody knew
had a valise full of different types of condoms.
I liked Zeke because he had long hair
and told me in a dark movie theater that he liked me.
But then he never talked to me again,
and Sarah said Adam came over to watch TV
on a night she was home alone—all alone.
    I couldn't decide if she was lying.
One Friday we hung out with two other guys, in a basement.
The blond one took Sarah into the boiler room,
while the skinny one kept trying to kiss me.
I lay facedown on the concrete floor,
shouting "No!" and breathing dust and mildew
'til he called me a bitch and went away.

I didn't see Sarah as much anymore.
My Mom said Sarah told her Mom not to jingle the change in her pocket
'cuz it sounded too masculine.
Sarah grew her hair out and got blue contact lenses,
so her eyes seemed cloudy and she always looked high.
She took lots of drugs, and her face got all puffy,
and she didn't go to class anymore.
She just hung out in the quad smoking Marlboro Lights,
and never said "Hi" in the hallway.
    I sat in Advanced Placement Math with three other girls

and 18 boys who thought they were brilliant,
arguing about parabolas, logarithms
and points of intersection.
    I'd just sit there not listening,
drawing boxes and knives, boxes and knives,
crying in the bathroom
when guys asked me out.

Preacher Man

by Michael Kozuch

– 1980 –   *– 1997 –*

"You're gonna be a preacher some day," they used to tell me. Boy, how I loved that. Here I was this four-year-old little sissy boy, sitting in the pastor's office while church people walked by saying how cute and sweet I was. I loved it. The irony of it today makes me love it even more. Today, I am sort of a preacher, but not the kind my mom and dad would have liked me to grow up to be. I am employed by the Massachusetts Department of Education to help set up programs in schools for gay and lesbian students. A couple of days a week I am leading workshops on how to end homophobia in schools.

At four years old, of course, I didn't know a thing about homosexuals or my fundamentalist church, nor the inherent conflict they posed to each other. In the 20 years following, the full meaning of growing up fundamentalist and gay is only now revealing itself to me. In my church, being gay was equated with the worst sins. It was evil and of the devil. Knowing my own homosexuality at an early age and being so much a part of my church, I felt oftentimes that I had the devil inside me. I felt that I should confess my sin and God would take it away. I confessed time and time again and prayed that God would change me, but it never worked. I looked homosexuality up in the Bible and found everything I could about what God said about it. The Bible I read and book they gave me to help interpret it, a concordance, didn't give me any hope. I was left to an internal fight between my feelings and how evil I felt those feelings were.

My fundamentalist church was more my extended family than my Czech and Polish relatives were. It weaned me on its dogma and its false sense of acceptance. It gave me positive feedback on my good deeds, even though I felt dirty on the inside. People in the church would come over our house and stay the whole day. We would have food and sing-alongs. They would play with me, teach me guitar, and make me feel important because I had such religious fervor at such a young age. "What a good little boy." "Such a follower of the Lord." "And at such a young age," someone would chime in. "Yep, that boy's going to grow up to be a preacher." They would say these things all the time, and it continued until I was in early adolescence. At four years old, it felt great. I just did what I was told and smiled like the best little boy I could be. At 13 it felt like an Oscar-nominated performance. Homosexual on the inside, preacher man on the outside.

One particular evening I studied homosexuality intensely. I was supposed to be preparing for my first sermon that I was to give to the youth group at my church. I must have been 13. It was the night before I had to give the sermon (typical teenage procrastinator). I felt honored, but also under pressure to perform my greatest act of piety yet. I prepared like I heard other preachers prepared—locking myself in my room and trying to pray. I knelt on my bedroom floor, which was covered with papers, my Bible, and the concordance, asking God for divine guidance, but I couldn't concentrate on anything but homosexuality. I tried to get it out of my mind, going through everything I could to draw my attention away, but I found myself looking up homosexuality in the concordance. I kept finding the traditional passages in Leviticus and Romans, which didn't really spell out what they meant, but the concordance, which gave the fundamentalist interpretation of the Bible, helped me out. It of course said how sinful homosexuality was. I also found Jesus' teachings about love and acceptance, which were very clear and didn't need any interpretation. It was torturous, praying, sitting, pacing back and forth, crying out to God to help me. I think I failed to see what God was trying to show me, that the Bible wasn't really that clear, that Jesus' teachings about love and acceptance were much more important.

I think I first realized I was a "sweet boy" when I was five. This is what my oldest brother, David, used to call me. In his 14-year-old mind, it was probably because I cried a lot, sucked my thumb, and ran to Mommy whenever he, his friends, or my two older sisters picked on me. Maybe he actually knew something that I didn't know until I turned 14. Whatever it was, it was obvious to him, but only a curious thing to me. I did know that "sweet boy" meant I wasn't as much a "man" as I should be, but it was with the same fogginess that I understood there really wasn't a Santa Claus or a stork.

I did think it was in some way connected to me playing doctor with Scotty Potty from across the street. We didn't call it doctor because that is what little girls and boys played. We didn't have a name for it. I just knew it must have been connected to my sweet-boy identity. It was pretty innocent stuff, things that people laugh about now. We hid behind big evergreen bushes in the front of his house and showed each other our wee-wees. He instigated most of it and it was always at his house, so he was the one to get caught with his pants down. A few times we even watched each other pee, but that stopped when we got caught by his mom. I was sent home worried that his mom would tell my mom what we were doing. I have no idea if she ever did, but it left an indelible impression on me that little boys shouldn't watch each other pee.

My first day of kindergarten brought excitement and trepidation. Scotty went to a different school because, although he lived across the street from me, I lived in Palmyra and he in Cinnaminson. These were different towns in southern New Jersey, with Cinnaminson being slightly more middle-class. My excitement came from my chance to reinvent myself without the label of sweet boy. Without Scotty around no one could find out my sissy tendencies. My trepidation was that I would not do a good enough job of casting off my sweet-boy label. Luckily my brother and his friends were already in junior high, so I had a chance.

It worked out OK. I played sweetest boy to the teacher and tougher boy with the kids. My mother also helped. She bought me a shirt with an anchor on it for my first day of school. It was perfectly masculine: dark maroon and white horizontal stripes with a yellow stitched anchor. I matched it with dark maroon pants and brown shoes. With my blond hair and blue eyes, I felt like the sailors I saw in *National Geographic.* I felt important and in charge. When we had playtime, I had the idea to build a ship out of the huge wooden blocks that they had for us to play with. I got to be captain. Orders were given—batten down the hatches, watch out for pirates, and no girls on the ship. Everyone loved it. They loved my shirt and loved me. Clothes did make the man, or at least they made this sissy boy a man.

Overall kindergarten was pretty fun. I learned what worked and what didn't, and I fell right into place. Masculine worked, feminine didn't. Captain worked, Scotty Potty didn't. Maroon worked, pink didn't. Good grades, but not too good. Impressing the teacher was important, but it was to be done mostly in private. Not in front of everyone else, or everyone would find out how sweet I actually was.

After kindergarten we moved to Cinnaminson. The new neighborhood was an upward climb into the middle class, but my family life was a strong descent into a black hole. My mother accidentally got pregnant with my soon-to-be little brother and had to stop working as a substitute teacher to deal with the pregnancy. My father was working for Whitman Air Conditioning and Heating, where he had pulled down a steady income and decent salary. But when my father lost his job soon after my brother Matthew was born, even our Czech and Polish frugality, as my mother called it, couldn't keep us from the stress and strain of poverty. I became acutely aware of tension and anger that I had never felt before.

The next few years are a blur of fighting between my parents and the kids. Anger and yelling reigned supreme in my house. When I would try to go to sleep at night, I would hear yelling coming from my parents' room next door. We were all affected by the poverty that we suddenly found ourselves in. We were all embarrassed by having to wear hand-me-down clothes and the constant struggle to put food on the table. Everything that could be watered down was. The orange juice, the apple juice; even the milk was part powdered, part "real."

The only thing that didn't get watered down was my mother's religious fervor. A new pastor came into the church and really shook things up. Women were encouraged to wear veils, and church services started on Sunday mornings and felt like they did not end until the next Saturday. There were Sunday night services, and Tuesday and Wednesday night prayer meetings. Thursday nights were spent at the "coffeehouse" that the church bought to do missionary work in the town. Friday nights were youth group nights and Saturday nights were spent on the street corner handing out tracts, singing, and trying to save souls. Soon we were being dragged to church what felt like 24 hours a day.

The congregation was convinced the Lord was coming soon. All throughout the church, people were talking about the Apocalypse and how the sign of the beast, 666, would soon be shown. It scared the hell out of me. I got saved as fast and as many times as I could. They showed us the film *The Late, Great Planet Earth* (based on Hal Lindsey's 1977 book) during a youth group meeting, a film about the impending second coming of Christ foretold in the book of Revelation. In the movie the believers are "raptured" up to heaven, and the heathens are left to endure the destruction of the world and the rise of Satan. After seeing the movie, every time I came home from school and no one was home, I thought I got left behind because I was such a sinner. The terror of my preadolescent mind was more than any horror movie could instill.

I'm not surprised that this book became so popular with fundamentalists. Jimmy Carter was president, and many people felt like the country was falling apart. The gas shortage was at its height, and inflation was out of control. The popularity of disco probably didn't put the church people any more at ease.

In my own family my father was moving from job to job, sometimes a heating and air conditioning technician, sometimes a used-car salesman. The used-car salesman part I loved, because he was always bringing home a different car. Big ones—Buicks with power windows, cruise control, and plush seats. It gave me and everyone else the illusion that we had more money than we did. Unfortunately, big American Buicks weren't selling well at the height of the oil embargo.

School wasn't much of a comfort either. It started off every year from first grade to sixth with me being called down to the main office to go get my free and sometimes reduced-cost lunch tickets. This humiliated me every time. I was called over the loudspeaker with the rest of the poor. I felt like I wasn't supposed to be with them. When I stood up in my homeroom to go down to the office, I silently pleaded with everyone that I really wasn't this poor. The humiliation continued because every day I had to hand my lunch ticket to the cashier in the cafeteria. I tried to conceal this as best I could. I tried not to stand too close to anyone in the lunch line. I sometimes let my friends to go ahead so they wouldn't see me give my ticket to the lunch lady or tried to get first in line before anyone had a chance to see. I had successfully shed off the sweet-boy label and hid it from everyone else, but my poverty was paraded in front of me and everyone else every time I bought lunch. My isolation grew because I stayed away from the other poor students so as not to draw attention to me or them, for their poverty amplified my poverty.

Luckily I found my escape in Luke Skywalker and Han Solo. Between *Star Wars, The Empire Strikes Back,* and *Return of the Jedi,* George Lucas gave me enough science fiction to occupy my preadolescent mind. My friend Justin also had the best collection of *Star Wars* figures on the block. He had all the toys, the Millennium Falcon, the Landspeeder, even the Death Star. I was fascinated by these things, but I think what really got me going was my crush on Luke Skywalker. I used to have fantasies of Luke Skywalker in all forms of undress and positions with Han Solo. Because I had the blond hair, I got to be Luke, and Justin with his brown hair was Han. I remember these play sessions as the most erotic experiences of my elementary school years. We made Han Solo and Luke Skywalker hug each other and go skinny-dipping together, and eventually we made them hump each other. We would laugh it off, just as I would later in my life as mere "horsing around," but this felt different for me. It was what I did with Scotty Potty years earlier. It was what I thought sex was. It was all I needed at this point in my life. It made it all the more erotic that I thought Justin was cute too. In the end my satisfaction was limited with Luke and Han. I never got to act out these fantasies with Justin.

Somehow my family and I made it to the 1980s intact and with another addition, my sister Christine. My father finally got a good, stable job with the U.S. government, working at the Walson Army Hospital at Fort Dix, N.J. We moved to a substantially bigger house in Mount Laurel, N.J. And I moved onto junior high. Mount Laurel isn't known for much. It doesn't even have a town center. But for a working-class family, it was a significant move into the middle class and the middle of the road. Mount Laurel did make a name for itself through a Supreme Court decision on equal housing. The town wanted to keep low-income housing from being built and consistently blocked any such developments, fearing they would bring property values down. They thought low-income housing would bring in all kinds of undesirables, especially from Willingboro or, as everyone would say, Wiwimbowo, trying to imitate the blacks who lived there. Housing advocates sued, and Mount Laurel lost.

Of course our neighborhood didn't have any blacks. The only people of color were the "Pakis" across the street. That was the name I heard my Canadian relatives give them. When I was confronted with

Pakistanians across the street from me, I used the same terms that I heard my relatives use. I made fun of the way they talked, looked, and smelled. My father and brother in particular didn't discourage me. In fact, I felt like I was finally being the real man they wanted me to be by putting someone else down. Any time I made fun of others' difference, I felt like I got a "that-a-boy" from the males in my family. Even though it felt bad to say these things, I thought it was another way I could prove I wasn't a fag.

The only thing that broke through my family's prejudices against the Pakistani family was money. If they could afford the neighborhood, they could be there. My little brother was even allowed to develop a friendship with their boy. However, every time he came home, choruses would ring out about how he smelled too.

I found how hard this must have been for my brother when, my junior year of high school, I made friends with the new black kid who moved into our neighborhood. I justified my friendship the same way my brother had with his Pakistani friend. Since the African-American family had more money than we did—which always silenced my family—he was an acceptable friend. I was constantly on guard, however, wondering what comment my family or others would make about him. My guess is that Darren was dealing with similar issues. He constantly tried to impress me with his money and frequently lied about status issues to make himself look better. Racism undermined our ability to be good friends, even as we tried to use class status as the an equalizer and justification of our friendship. Because we couldn't name the racism that permeated from outside our friendship, we couldn't begin to deal with how it affected us. When we ignored oppression's effects on our relationship and acted like they did not exist, we ignored a fundamental challenge to being friends with each other. If I could have articulated this as a child, maybe we could have talked about it and broken through barriers in both our lives. But this would have required me to acknowledge my own racism, which at that time in my life would have been very difficult. Instead I tried to be "color-blind" in a racist society, an impossible task.

I now feel guilty and embarrassed about the things I said when I was a kid. But I also feel like my family and the school system failed me in challenging my racism and, in the end, my own homophobia. My family must have been quite surprised when they found out in 1996 that I had moved in with a Pakistani lesbian and described her as one of the best roommates I have ever had.

But this was years later, and I had to still get out of Mount Laurel. When we moved to Mount Laurel, it meant that I finally got my own room. My oldest brother, David, had moved out and joined the Air Force. This was a good thing, because that was when my hormones started feeling a little more free too. My fantasies with Luke Skywalker and Han Solo turned into full-fledged erections with Chris, Mike, Jamie, and Todd. Soon everything around me seemed to be oozing with sexual energy. I could barely think of anything else. School became a place where everyone started talking about sex. I was in seventh grade when some girl had her period in school and everyone knew about it. I was so glad I wasn't a girl, at least I could keep my growing teenage body fairly private. Brazen sexual talk began to occur between friends during lunchtime, in gym class, and on the bus. The school looked the other way concerning this burgeoning sexuality, half hoping that no one would get too turned on, including the teachers. No adults wanted to acknowledge our sexual energy and the tension it created. I felt left out and confused.

Not surprisingly, no one mentioned homosexuality in a positive light. There was no context for me to deal with my feelings, so I shut them down. It became easy for me to separate what I was supposed to do, from what I needed or felt like I should do. My existence in high school became filled with what I should do—trying to play straight, get good grades, and make my friends, parents, and teachers like me—instead of what I wanted to do.

Instead, I did the things that I thought would convince myself and others that I was the straight person I professed to be. I joined the football team my freshman year and dated women. The dating was short-lived, but long enough (I hoped) to establish my heterosexual credentials. I was always timing my dating life. How long it had been since the last girlfriend? Did enough people hear that I had had a girlfriend? Every once in a while I thought I might have real feelings for the girl I was dating. Then, of course, sex would get in the way. I liked the women I dated, I just didn't want to do anything more with them than hang out. It was a constant juggling act to make sure I didn't get too close but didn't stay so distant as to let them think I might be gay. Try a little something, but cut it off before too much would be revealed. Endless and tiring.

My managing even spilled over to harassing the "art fag" along with everyone else. Words like *cocksucker, fudge packer,* and *homo* were the words boys used to hurt each other. These words enforced their distance from homosexuality and set up a challenge to find out who the real homosexuals were. I constantly felt like I was going to be discovered. I tried to learn the signs of a gay person and keep myself clear from anything that might give me away. I stayed away from art, drama, and Boy George. But I also knew that if people thought I was too afraid of these things, they would think I was gay. So I tried to develop a balance between hating gay things and gay people and not hating them too much.

On the outside people probably thought I was navigating high school pretty well. I was a pretty good student and had a fairly large group of friends. I was active in extracurriculars. I got an after-school job. I was always going from school to seeing friends to work. What they didn't know was that these were coping mechanisms as well. I always had an excuse if I needed one—"I'm so busy."

Seeing friends was always a little tricky because I wound up in love with many of my boy friends. When we were alone, it was incredible. I never wanted anyone else around.

One evening that remains in my consciousness was with my best friend Todd. He was in my gym class junior year. I spotted him from a mile away and knew I had to become friends with him. In the locker room when he changed, I noticed he had colored briefs, which I thought was a clue to homosexuality. That they were Playboy briefs didn't deter me. I tried to ignore any signs that he might be straight and instead felt like I got increasing signs that he was gay too. We spent more and more time together. His parents left for the weekend a lot so we often spent the weekend together. We cooked dinner together, just hung out watching TV, even took naps on his bed together. Of course these naps had to maintain some sense of heterosexuality, so on his small bed we would put our heads at different ends of the bed. Not what I wanted, but close enough. I was falling in love.

The culmination was when both his parents and his sister were away for the weekend and we had the whole place to ourselves. We had planned the weekend way in advance, and I couldn't wait until that Friday after school. I took the bus home with him, having packed my clothes the day before. It felt so romantic.

We planned to go out to dinner at the Vincentown Diner. Not the Four Seasons, but it was close to his house and what we could afford. I had chicken parmesan. I know this because after we rented a movie and came home, I started getting violently ill. By 10 o'clock that evening, I was throwing up every half hour. We thought it was food poisoning. Todd suggested that we go to bed in his parents' room, since there was a bathroom connected to it and I could get to the toilet much easier. I didn't know if he really meant that we would sleep in the same bed. I questioned him, not trying to sound too excited or too upset about the idea. When he said of course, I was thrilled. We got into bed together in only our underwear. I wished I could just stop throwing up. Every so often I would have to get up to puke in the toilet. He kept getting closer and closer to my side of the bed as the night wore on, until I couldn't get into bed without lying so close to him I could feel the heat of his body. I was so excited I could hardly contain myself.

Then my stomach would wake me from this fantasy, because it couldn't contain itself. That was the closest I ever came to actually making love for a long time. Todd and I slowly spent less and less time together. He got a girlfriend and I turned inward again. Not until I turned 21, five years later, was I able to have an evening that even remotely resembled that one, an evening that truly left me happy afterward.

Not until I escaped to Northeastern University and the relatively liberal environs of Boston did I get a chance to express myself. I finally fully gave up on trying to hide. It just became too much, too unbearable. I also found people who were open about their homosexuality, and one person in particular, someone my age, who was cute and whom I looked up to, introduced me to all kinds of gay people and took me to my first gay bar, Campus, in Cambridge, Mass. I found people "like me" (whatever that meant). I soon was making the journey that changed my life forever—one that brought me from self-hatred, loneliness, and despair to self-acceptance and love.

While religion and family played a major part in my struggle to accept myself, my schools also played a consistent and ongoing role. I give them an F. Throughout, my schools had no ability to deal with my homosexuality. When I needed it most, in high school, they reinforced stereotypes and hatred. I knew I was gay but found no ways to access what it meant for me. The silence and indifference around homosexuality on the part of adults kept me away from any meaningful experience. The violence and hatred of my peers made sure that anything regarding homosexuality would stay underground. The lack of information or civil conversation kept me in the dark for years.

I can't go back and change what happened to me or any of my gay brothers and sisters. I can do something now to stop the violence and the indifference. I can give straight kids a chance to understand their family members, friends, and teachers. I can give gay kids a chance to find their feelings. As a consultant with the Massachusetts Department of Education's Safe Schools Program for Gay and Lesbian Students, I have participated in over 350 antihomophobia workshops for faculty, staff, and students in schools across Massachusetts and assisted in the formation of over 95 gay/straight alliances. Hopefully, the work I'm doing is helping kids keep from feeling so tired they give up. Instead, they might even find the ability to give themselves and others love. After all, it is what we all want anyway.

Sissies and Tomboys

Singin' the High School Sissy Blues

by Larry Duplechan

– 1974 –

FACT: High school is no place for a small, effeminate, black gay boy with a high IQ, a high-pitched voice, and a penchant for phrases like "I daresay" and "heavens, no."

This I know from experience.

Not that it actually took me or anyone around me 14 years to realize that I was (as Michael Jackson once expressed it, albeit in quite a different situation) not like other boys. Heavens, no. I daresay, as early as kindergarten, my preference for the company of girls and for traditionally girlish activities (I mean, why roll a Tonka dump truck around the floor when somewhere there is a Chatty Cathy doll with no bouffant?) raised the eyebrows of parents, teachers, and schoolmates alike.

By the fifth grade my teacher, the minidressed, fishnet-stockinged, pale-pink–lipsticked Mrs. Byrne (her real name—I've no desire whatsoever to protect her) took it upon herself to bring to my mother's attention, at parent-teacher night, her concern that I was spending an inordinate amount of time in the company of girls, and with one girl in particular—Jacqueline Honor. At an age when other boys were feeling their first twinges of sexual identity, in the form of a strong (and usually quite vocal) aversion to girls, Jacqueline Honor was my best friend. We sat together in class, did our homework together (she was a whiz at long division, while my sentence diagrams were unsurpassed), drew pictures of fairies and dragons together, and spent our respective allowances at the local movie theater several times to watch and rewatch *The Sound of Music* together. At Easter time we coauthored a one-act play in less-than-imperfect iambic pentameter regarding the origin of the Easter Bunny. As I recall, my mother came home from parent-teacher night and immediately notified me that Mrs. Byrne thought Jacqueline and I were spending too much time together, but I don't remember her ordering me to spend less time with Jacqueline or even suggesting it. I do, however, recall the distinct feeling that Mrs. Byrne, Cimarron Avenue School, the Los Angeles Unified School District, indeed the state of California itself, had just poked its collective freckled, turned-up nose into something that was none of its collective beeswax.

By that time my lifelong aversion to any game whose name ends in "ball" was firmly in place. I was neither physically frail nor grossly uncoordinated. I simply didn't care who had the ball (whatever ball) or whether or not it got from here to over yonder.

True, I couldn't throw. Fact is, I could run, jump, pull-up, and sit-up well enough that I would have made the President's All-America Team (and you simply have to be a certain age to have the first clue what that was) but I just couldn't throw the damned softball. I was told then, as I'd been told before and would be told often and loudly thereafter, that I threw like a girl. I imagine I still do. However, since high school graduation, I have steadfastly refused to throw anything to anybody. Don't even ask me.

In the seventh grade, all around me, boys were discovering girls. In the eighth grade I discovered boys. I was a late bloomer. I still remember the night I awoke abruptly, lying on top of an aching boner, fresh from a dream in which I lay beneath a large, shady tree, my head cradled in the blue-jeaned lap of Ted Vrakas, a brown-eyed handsome boy from drama class. I also recall spending an inordinate amount of time spent gazing at Steve Duros, a short, muscular blond who played last-chair trumpet in the Winston Churchill Intermediate School orchestra, in which I played first-chair flute (yeah, I know, too phallic to mention). It was also in the eighth grade that Julianne Ponta—a seventh grader and a girl, for heaven's sake, said to me, "Larry, you are such a femme!" Unfortunately, I don't recall coming up with a dry, stinging, Dorothy Parkeresque retort for that one. And given what Julianne Ponta felt free to say to my face, I chose not to even consider what kids must have been saying about me behind my back.

And then came high school—everything I had come to despise about the public school experience multiplied exponentially and served up with a healthy side order of sexual confusion. I began high school smaller and considerably less developed physically than most of my classmates (I was described as "scrawny" by someone who purported to like me). I'd skipped a grade early on (the third grade, as I recall), and as I've mentioned, I was a late bloomer. Coupled with my (by now) well-known aversion to and utter lack of aptitude for team sports, this made physical education a fresh hell each and every day. I learned the true power of prayer through my daily entreaties to the Deity that a locker room full of sweat-stinky, body-hair sprouting, genital-swinging butt-ass-naked teenage boys not cause me to achieve full, throbbing penile erection. I'd actually seen one unfortunate boy pop a spontaneous boner in the locker room and, as I now recall, he was teased, mocked, and generally razzed on such a relentless and school-wide basis that he finally transferred out of the district.

The unspeakable horror that was, for me, boys' PE class can, I think, best be expressed with this little anecdote:

Having shown myself to be as utterly inept at volleyball as I was at every other team sport I'd so far been forced to attempt, one Bob Bruce, an unhappy teammate, endeavored to explain and demonstrate to me the proper finger position for tapping a volleyball up into the air, to be spiked down the collective throats of the opposing team. I feel at this point that a brief description of Bob Bruce is in order. Bob Bruce was possessed of full-lipped, long-haired '70's white-boy good looks (sort of Peter Frampton with a perpetual sneer), and through some extracurricular weight lifting, he'd built himself a set of bulky upper arms and a chest reminiscent of Gordon Scott (star of *Tarzan the Magnificent*). Bob Bruce considered me beneath contempt. Naturally, I was attracted to him. Anyway, Bob bounced the volleyball again and again off the tips of his fingers, which were outstretched in a stiff, conelike formation.

"See?" he said after bouncing the ball at me, hitting me in the forehead with it. He made the cone shape with his fingers again. "It's like you're grabbin' a chick's tits." And with a trademark smirk he added, "Or haven't you ever done that?" And of course, I had at that point in my life done absolutely no grabbin' of chicks' tits, and, from the smug look on Bob Bruce's face, he knew it. Thus, in PE, my complete lack of athletic skills and my painfully ambivalent sexuality could be rolled into a ball and bounced against my head in front of a contemptuous group of my peers. This was in my junior year. Which means, among other things, that I've gotten way ahead of myself. Meanwhile, back at my freshman year. I discovered that the attraction I felt for boys had not diminished, but in fact had increased considerably between the eighth grade and the ninth. I also discovered this infinitely more surprising

FACT: There are some heterosexual females who are actually attracted to small, effeminate, black gay boys with high IQs, high-pitched voices, and a penchant for phrases like "I daresay" and "heavens, no."

This I know from experience.

Linda Waples played the clarinet in the marching band (in which I, of course, played flute). She was a pretty, snub-nosed white girl, and she surprised me one evening during a football game when, sometime after the halftime show (I seem to recall the band playing the *Hawaii Five-O* theme while forming a portrait of Jack Lord), Linda said something like,

"Ooh, my hands are so cold," then scooted up close to me on the bleacher and proceeded to warm her hands in my jacket pocket (a pocket then nearly full of my own hand). I was amazed—didn't this girl see me for the sissy I obviously was? Didn't it matter to her? Unfortunately for both Linda and myself, I wasn't the least interested in her little cold hands or any other portion of her anatomy. I was at the time harboring a huge crush on Ulrich, the West German foreign exchange student who played oboe in concert band (reduced to schlepping a sousaphone in marching band); a tall, broad-shouldered thing with early Michael York good looks and an unruly mane of blond hair. I had an recurring fantasy of sitting in the bleachers, tucked in close to Ulrich, his arm around my shoulders. Which was about as far as I even dared fantasize at that point.

Never happened, of course.

By the tenth grade, I had moved on to Gil Cineceros, an achingly handsome Mexican-American boy from my American lit class. It was while grinding against the sheets one night, my mind full of visions of me kissing Gil Cineceros, that I accidentally discovered masturbation. The unprecedented physical pleasure of my first orgasm was immediately followed by the (of course, unfounded) fear that I had somehow injured myself and had spurted blood all over my bed. Which was, naturally, immediately followed by the desire to do whatever it was I'd just done, again.

And, of course, I did. Again and again and again—that night and (as I recall) each and every day thereafter for the next several years.

The tenth grade was, in fact, fairly jam-packed with big events. It was the year Dave Reynolds (a boy so blond, tanned, and effortlessly handsome that he looked like the personification of some Beach Boys hit) called from across a hall crowded with classmates, "Hey, Larry—are you a fag?"

Like any 15-year-old boy who habitually masturbated himself to sleep while thinking about other boys, I yelled, "Hell, no," and ran in the opposite direction.

That same semester Leroy Johnson—a homely, overweight black boy with a spot on the back of his head (site of a childhood injury) where no hair grew—in the course of a verbal disagreement of some sort, treated me to the following tongue-lashing:

"They must have cut too deep when they circumcised you—that's why you act like such a goddamned girl!"

Later that same school year, another boy (damned if I can remember his name), a good-looking, light-skinned black boy with a well-maintained little Afro and a missing earlobe, took it upon himself to instruct me in the fine art of behaving like a man. I remember he referred to himself and me (straight-faced and without a trace of irony) as men. As in, "There's certain ways you're supposed to behave, because you're a man." The 16-year-old "man" proceeded to demonstrate the proper way to walk (seems my own walk entailed entirely too much hip movement), to cross my legs (ankle over knee, of course, never knee over knee, the way a woman crosses her legs), to carry my schoolbooks (not, repeat not, propped against my hip). Very John Kerr and Darryl Hickman in *Tea and Sympathy*. As I recall, I thanked this boy for the (quite unsolicited) advice. I mean, he really seemed to be doing this out of a sort of brotherly concern, and it wasn't as if we were close friends or something—we just had a couple of classes together. But, needless to say, his efforts failed to change my lifelong behavior in any significant manner.

It was also in the tenth grade that another male classmate, Pat something, for reasons I have yet to fathom, began sneaking up behind me and whispering things like: "Larry, I want your body," and "Larry, I need you." Whether Pat did this as tease or torment or some sincere, if clumsy, teenage seduction, I didn't know and still don't. But between my heart-pounding fear and my equally heart-pounding (if desperately hidden) desire, the boy very nearly destroyed me. Pat was not one of the boys I fantasized about. And he was nothing special: lanky build, unkempt dirty-blond hair, a smattering of acne, just sort of a boy boy. And yet, when Pat approached me as I bent at the water fountain or looked up a book in the library's card catalog, the faint tickle of his breath against the nape of my neck, the slightly acrid, boy-sweaty scent of him, the heat of his body so close to me, all but drove me mad. In time (Was it weeks? Months? I really don't remember), Pat stopped doing whatever it was he was doing to me. And I suppose I was relieved. And I very likely missed it, just a little.

The summer before my junior year, my family moved from Los Angeles to Lancaster, Calif., some 85 miles northeast of L.A. in the high desert area known as the Antelope Valley. In 1973 Lancaster was a sleepy bedroom town built around nearby Edwards Air Force Base and Lockheed Aircraft, where my father worked. There, in Lancaster, I endured my last two years of public school at Antelope Valley High.

A.V. High was everything I had come to despise about high school, and less. In L.A., at Westchester High, the performing arts were well respected and well funded. The school took nearly as much pride in its theater arts and music departments as in the football team. Its twice-a-year musical shows were practically Broadway quality. At Antelope Valley, only sports, particularly football, seemed to matter. The school had no theater, not even a proper auditorium. The shoestring budgets allowed for the twice-a-year drama department productions were augmented by bake sales, candy sales and the allowances of the drama students, and the plays were produced in the minuscule theater at the local junior college.

The word *miserable* doesn't begin to describe my junior and senior years.

By this time I knew I was gay. I hadn't told anyone yet, but I'd definitely looked myself in the eye and said, "You're gay." I had by then managed to find and read enough about homosexuality to know there were others like me, somewhere. And this being the early 1970s, the materials I'd found on the subject were almost entirely negative, describing homosexuality as a mental illness at best. I distinctly remember huddling in a corner of the public library, reading the chapter on homosexuality in *Everything You've Always Wanted To Know About Sex But Were Afraid To Ask,* which alone should have warped me for life. I'd also read *The Boys In The Band* and had somehow completely missed how miserable all these gentlemen were—I was so completely taken by the play's bitchy wit and, I suppose, by the glorious fact of holding an actual piece of gay culture in my own two teenage hands, that it actually never occurred to me to fear growing up to be a miserable, drunken, self-hating homosexual. Such, obviously, was my need to see my gay self reflected.

By the middle of my junior year, my gay self was very much in love. Oh, I'd had countless crushes on boys by now, but this was love. I knew it was love, because it hurt.

ALL TOO OBVIOUS FACT: For a small, effeminate, black gay boy with a high IQ, a high-pitched voice, and a penchant for phrases like "I daresay" and "heavens, no," to fall in love with a straight boy is a very, very stupid move.

This I know from experience.

Frank Pryor was about a year younger than I (and two grades behind me). His photograph in my 1974 Antelope Valley High School yearbook (named the *Yucca* after a tree indigenous to the area, a tree sufficiently ugly to properly represent the Antelope Valley) shows a boy who wasn't quite handsome—a bit lantern-jawed, a tad nose-heavy, entirely too much wavy brown hair (it looks rather like a large piece of someone's birthday cake). Among the things the photo doesn't show are Frank's hands, long-fingered, well-padded, simultaneously masculine and graceful. Frank played guitar rather well and sang ("Duncan" by Paul Simon, Elton John's "Madman Across the Water," and a couple of Cat Stevens numbers) quite badly. I remember watching his beautiful hands as he played, ignoring his singing voice as best I could. Neither did Frank's 1974 yearbook picture include his well-defined, round-assed teenage body, which I carefully avoided glancing at in the locker room, but on which I feasted my eyes poolside at Frank's house. I couldn't swim—still can't—and I wasn't much to look at in swim trunks. Still, I'd have sprawled in an old inner tube on the Lake of Fire for the opportunity to see Frank in a Speedo, and, besides, he was the first male to invite me to spend time at his house since Martin Kirkwood in the fourth grade. I'd never had many male friends, and (as if to prove the existence of God and the distinct possibility that she might possess a rather bitchy sense of humor) Frank Pryor was my friend. So rather than admiring him from afar, I longed for him, up close.

Frank was in the Drama Club, as was I, and we appeared in three plays together. Drama class, after-school rehearsals, performances, and cast parties afforded me more than ample opportunity to spend time with Frank—all too often, unfortunately for me, in the company of whatever girl Frank might be dating, or hoping to date, or just simply longing for, up close. I distinctly recall Debbie Lindsay, a pretty, honey-blond, impressively breasted aspiring actress for whom Frank had a (quite understandable) letch. I remember the pain of watching Frank and Debbie holding hands backstage at some play or other, whispering and giggling, as one might remember the pain of a third-degree burn. I also recall the desire to introduce a small explosive device to Debbie Lindsay's panty hose. I thought of Frank nearly incessantly, wrote bad love poetry he never saw and the occasional unsent love letter, and spent one memorably sleepless night just banging my head with my fist and weeping. Love hurts. Roy Orbison said so.

Finally, I did something only a 17-year-old boy in love could ever be blindly stupid enough to do. I told Frank Pryor I was gay. Now, as I rapidly approach middle age (all right, so I've actually slammed smack into it), I find that (as Lily Tomlin used to say) my mind is more and more like Teflon—nothing sticks to it. Consequently, I must admit that I don't actually remember when and how I told Frank I was gay. Only that, to his eternal credit, Frank neither kicked my little black ass from here into next week, nor told everyone he knew and a few total strangers, rendering the remainder of my high school experience even more ghastly than it had been to date.

Fortunately, Frank does remember. On a recent whim I made contact with Frank after over 20 years, via the Internet, no less (Let's hear it for technology!). I'd told the story over and over since high school about how I'd been lucky enough to fall in unrequited love with the most emotionally mature, level headed 16-year-old straight boy on the planet, and as my 40th birthday approached, I found myself wondering how that boy had turned out, where he'd ended up. Fortunately, Frank was as happy to be found by me as I was to have found him—a professional photographer, living in San Francisco, never married, childless, and (believe it or not) still straight. I mean, what are the odds? Artsy, living in San Francisco, and not gay. What a world.

Anyway, while Frank did not remember Debbie Lindsay's name ("You broke my heart with this girl," I ranted via E-mail, "and you can't remember her name?" "I never forgot yours," he said), he did recall my coming out to him. It was during a break in rehearsal, and Frank was telling a succession of fag jokes. I asked him after each one to please stop, they weren't funny, but he obviously didn't take me seriously enough to stop the laughfest. Finally I took Frank to the side and said something to the effect of, "I'm afraid I don't appreciate this sort of humor, Frank. You see, I'm gay." Frank said something like, "Oh. I'm sorry." And probably switched to Polack jokes or dead baby jokes or something. And, as I recall, it was pretty much business as usual between Frank and me. True, I hadn't followed up with the big punch line: "Oh, and by the way, I love you." Never did. Which was undoubtedly one of my smarter moves.

As I really like a happy ending, I'm happy to be able to supply one for the story of my high school years.

It happened because of the annual choir concert my senior year. Between the two main sections of the concert, right before intermission, came something the choir director, Mr. Summers (a singularly unattractive, bald-headed, hook-nosed white gentleman bearing an uncomfortable resemblance to Erich Von Stroheim) called the "Interlude Numbers." These consisted of solos, duets, and the like by various members of the choir, chosen by the performers. That night, Jack and Jill Schramm (a brother-sister act of some local renown) performed a Peter, Paul and Mary number. A barbershop quartet in which I sang first tenor offered "My Blue Heaven" (complete with incredibly corny choreography and props—a light bulb for "a little white light," that sort of thing). And I sang a solo: "And I Love You So," which had been a hit for Perry Como, but which I knew from the *I Am Woman* album by Helen Reddy. Initially Mr. Summers had rejected my choice of material, telling me it was both "awfully adult" and "kind of a downer".

Fortunately, my fellow choir members, having heard my audition, banded together to convince him to include my song. In a nice little ironic twist, Frank Pryor accompanied me on the guitar as I sang, "and yes, I know how lonely life can be," eyes closed, hands clasping the mike stand, resplendent in my rented white, flare-pants, huge-lapels tuxedo.

After Frank strummed the final chord, there was a moment of total silence, followed by a veritable tidal wave of applause, filling the multipurpose room. Frank retreated, leaving me alone in the spotlight, awash in waves of love from a school, from a town, I largely detested, and which I generally felt detested me in return. It was the first of those wonderful, all-too-rare events in my life that I like to call "movie musical moments."

The following week I found my status at school had shifted. Kids who had never looked in my direction before hot-footed across the senior lawn to tell me how much they'd enjoyed my performance and to ask if I planned to sing professionally after graduation. Tit-grabbing, volleyball-playing Bob Bruce himself stopped me in the hall with a beefy hand against my shoulder (briefly frightening me—I mean, was this guy going to give me my senior ass-whippin', or what?). He smiled (something I don't believe I'd ever seen before), tossed his hair back in a Framptonesque motion and said, "Great voice, dude." After four solid years of nearly nonstop misery, for the final week of high school I was popular. Something I'd never been. Oh, I always had friends, of course. But I'd never been popular. And anybody who's been to high school knows there's a difference.

High school was very nearly over—and, as far as I was concerned, not a moment too soon. I'd never have to take PE again as long as I lived. And I'd already been accepted to my first-choice college, the University of California, Los Angeles—UCLA. Far enough from home that it smelled like freedom; close enough to home that Mom and Dad allowed me to go. And, most important, I'd heard —and, funny thing, I can't for the life of me remember where I'd heard, but I'd heard— that UCLA had a gay students union. Lord, have mercy! A gay students union.

And I'll never forget, that glorious last week of school, as we were passing yearbooks around, stupidly inscribing only first names ("Good luck in college, wasn't algebra a bitch, I'll always consider you a great friend, Bob"), as if no one would ever forget anyone else, I mentioned to some guy or other that I was going to UCLA, and this boy said, "Oh yeah? I hear that school's full of fags."

I just smiled and said, "So I've heard!"

Something Brief

by Ken Rus Schmoll

– *1985* –   – *1997* –

The following piece was written and performed on April 26, 1996, at a Watkinson School coffeehouse sponsored by the student group S.A.F.E. (Sexual Awareness for Everyone).

I had wanted to write something to read tonight.
An odd reflection.
A charming anecdote from my life.
Something brief but memorable
    like the time I was in Sweden and I went swimming with some
    friends in the Kattegat Strait on a moonless pitch-black night. So

dark we had to feel our way down the steep path to the dock as if blind, tentatively sticking out each leg until it sensed a solid foothold. To know where everyone was, we would call out and respond, not unlike Marco Polo.

But I'm a playwright
And not too comfortable with the personal essay genre
And my scribblings never really took form.
   I decided to just come and have nice cup of coffee.

Last night, however, I learned something that rocked my pen into action.
I'm not going to moralize.
Rather I am trying to put into perspective for myself
   —and maybe for you—
The ramifications of what occurred.
And here I am, nervous, yet resolute.

Frankly, when I sat down to write, I was seething with anger.

   A few weeks ago, an upperclassman in the Watkinson community decided to have a little fun. The object of the fun was a lowerclassman, in whom exists the ambiguity of sexual orientation. It seems the upperclassman, in front of a handful of his friends, picked up the lowerclassman, spun him around, and asked, in an affected voice, if he were gay. It seems too that everyone had a good laugh—including the lowerclassman, who needed to convey that, yes, the joke was got, the fun was had. The upperclassman
WENT AWAY
   gratified and feeling mighty clever and somewhat proud. And I don't know if these two are friends. And I don't know the sexual orientation of either one. And the incident recalled even now sounds harmless. But I don't know how the lowerclassman
WENT AWAY.

Something brief but memorable.

Growing up I spent year after year in school listening to the jeering remark:
    "Are you a boy or a girl?"
This became the essential question of the my life.
Am I a boy or a girl?
And though anatomically answerable, this question led me one day to
pack nothing
    and go. Out of the house, on foot, as far as I could walk. I took
    refuge in an alley and sat grinding my forehead into the brick wall and
    tried to convince myself that pavement indeed made a comfortable bed. I
    remember police cruisers gliding by on the street.

Am I a boy or a girl?
Today I am tickled by that androgyny.
Today I may even encourage it.
Luckily I had parents who said:
    "Your being gay does not preclude being the best son we could ask
    for."
Unluckily my parents' attitudes are rare.

    All of a sudden, I feel like now I should trot out the statistics of
    suicide among gay teens, or launch into the politics of "outing." But
    I'm thinking of my friend Mike, who was a student with me at Drew
    University in the mid '80s. One day, a friend of Mike's—who is
    himself gay—wrote in black Magic Marker the word
    FAGGOT
    on Mike's door. As a joke. And that night in the showers, Mike cut his
    wrists. The right way. Moving up the wrist. Not across it.

OK.
I wanted to be brief.
    And memorable.

In fact I feel better.

Which, to be sure, was not my goal.

(A pleasant aftereffect.)

And, no, I haven't told you that swarming in the water that night was a certain

type of phosphorescent plankton. Each microscopic organism emitting a tiny pin-prick of light. And looking down into the water was like looking down into the universe of stars. After we swam, we clamored blindly back onto the dock, dripping wet. And for a brief moment, we saw each other. We stood on the dock, in total darkness, covered in plankton. We saw human forms comprised of tiny lights.

Each one of us a universe.

And so.

We danced.

Barbie Doll Dropout

by Donna Arzt

– 1965 –

– 1997 –

I was a Barbie doll dropout at age six, the neighborhood tomboy at age nine, and leading batter for the local team at age 12. Ah, those blissful summer evenings at shortstop for the Levittown Swingers, in the girls' Class C softball league! Those double plays I assisted! Those death-defying leaps at line drives! Those ice-cream cones the coach bought us after the games we won!

I was a self-made athlete, I'm proud to say. With but a younger sister and no brothers, I had to pick it all up by myself, watching the boys at recess, eventually drawing up enough nerve to ask them to let me play. My greatest thrill came when my father offered to "have a catch" with me after dinner, though I sensed even then that he felt uneasy in the role.

My young athleticism wasn't without its lonely and unsettling moments. At Summerdale Day Camp I climbed trees while the other girls in the bunk played jacks. I did it more out of embarrassed frustration with those damn metal pieces than out of defiance or dissent.

I remember one Sunday, when I was about ten years old, that my great-aunt and uncle came for a visit. They hadn't seen me for at least two years and had brought a special present for me, a doll. It was a nice doll, daintily clothed, with delicate features, but not quite my idea of the perfect present. Imagine their surprise when they stepped out of the car and saw me playing football on the front lawn with the neighbor boy! I'm not sure who was more disappointed: me, in their gift (I really wanted a kicking tee), or them, in what they must have seen as their maladjusted niece. As they were hesitantly handing me the doll, I was calculating how to drop-kick it onto the roof.

My parents tried to direct me toward tennis, which they seemed to think was a more "social" sport. After all, the tennis court is the ideal place to meet young men. It's a graceful game—no sliding into base, anyway. And it's not too hard to find one or three others for a spontaneously arranged game on an open court. But how often do you happen upon a softball diamond, bats, balls, gloves, and 19 other players? And so at age 12 I took tennis lessons and made lots of new friends: all the other girls from the area whose parents had had the same idea. It was their idea of "finishing school."

I continued with softball, volleyball, basketball, and track through junior high, enjoying the surprised looks on my competitors' faces when this five-foot midget broke school records in the standing broad jump (7 feet, 4 inches) and softball throw (142 feet). It didn't bother me that I occasionally broke some minor bones (a finger here, a nose there). They were my trophies.

Then the worst happened. Or maybe the best. I developed breasts, asthma, weak ankles, and astigmatism, all in the course of six months. Donna the Tomboy became Donna the Hypochondriac. My throwing arm was soon replaced by thick glasses, my sneakers with orthopedic shoes. So I began to redirect my energies toward more intellectual pursuits. Although I played softball and basketball on the girls' high school varsity teams, I felt an increasing sense of intellectual superiority over my teammates, who were "mere jocks," while I also edited the school paper, chaired the Student Council's constitution committee, and presided over the World Affairs Council chapter. The baby butch was quickly becoming the future lawyer.

I had felt natural in the act of playing sports. The physical agility and use of concentration and strength combined in a very natural way. It would take me years to feel as comfortable in the act of scholarship. But as I see now, in the social aspect of athletics, I really was never quite at ease. When I played with the boys during elementary school recess, I knew I didn't really belong. True, my greatest childhood memories are of the summer girls' softball team. But even that ended when we moved away to a wealthier neighborhood.

Even now, I feel suspicious of women, as if they were expecting me to compete with them in a contest I didn't even want to enter, for the attention of men. Maybe it's because my first friends were the boys I played ball with, not the girls who played hopscotch or gossiped and flirted during recess. My later adjustment from tomboy to feminist would be a difficult one. It would take much effort before I could come to identify with the women's movement, with the cause of women as a whole. After all, I had always taken pride in the fact that I threw a baseball like a boy, not "like a girl."

Though it should mean less now, the sense of disappointing the adults still lingers. I've always suspected that my father had really wanted a son. Perhaps my tomboyism was my way of pleasing him, of meeting his expectations. I was sort of a compromise, not always a daughter, but not quite a son. When I finally *did* become a daughter, after puberty, I think my father felt aggrieved. Perhaps that's why we have so much trouble getting along today. If only we could still go outside "for a catch."

Esto Vir

by Matt Rottnek

$- 1987 -$ $- 1997 -$

I n the fall of 1980, I switched schools for the seventh grade—from a
parochial school, St. Justin the Martyr, to a Catholic boys' school, Chaminade College Preparatory, which my superstar older brother, Fred, had
been attending for two years of high school. The school had a reputation for
serious academics and less serious athletics. I was excited to attend a much
larger school with college-like facilities, where students wore ties, and that
was a 20-minute commute from home. I felt like I was growing up. I also
clearly remember hoping for this: a chance to start over, a chance to watch
my behavior more closely —so I wouldn't be hated, wouldn't be pegged the
faggot, pansy, homo, loser, wouldn't be the last pick of the team, wouldn't
be spit at, laughed at, joked about—a chance to try harder.

115

— Matt Rottnek —

November 1979

read the sign halfway up the front drive. From noon until 4 o'clock, the priests and brothers who ran the school were hosting an open house for all prospective middle school students and their parents.

Dad drove us slowly around the school and parked the car near a grove of trees that separated Chaminade from Our Lady of the Pillar parish next door. The lot was filled with BMWs, Mercedes, Cadillacs, Town and Country station wagons, and a few white Carriage vans. Chaminade fathers, I knew from Fred's descriptions of his friends, were executives. Or they were doctors, lawyers, accountants. Not only did Dad not have a professional degree, he hadn't even gone to college. And that was the first year he drove a Buick instead of a Cadillac. Already I was self-conscious.

Mom sat for a minute in the front seat to reapply her lipstick, blot her lips with a tissue from her purse, pinch her cheeks for color, and check her hair. She snapped the vanity mirror back up and Dad opened her door. I crawled out from the backseat and checked my clip-on tie. Still in place.

We entered the athletictron onto a platform between sets of stairs. Mercury-vapor lights buzzed over the sounds of a basketball team practicing in the abutting gym. In front of us, wing tips and Top-Siders skidded over polished terrazzo floors as upperclassmen distributed punch and cookies. At the top of the stairs, under a banner reading WELCOME, were three registration tables marked A-K, L-R, S-Z, where volunteering Chaminade mothers—all wearing red rose and baby's breath corsages—sat to welcome prospective families. We got in line behind a family of five: the mother in a pleated plaid skirt, white cotton blouse, and cardigan; Dad in khakis, loafers, and a blue- and white-striped oxford; two girls with matching blond bobs and plaid jumpers; a son with a green sports coat that matched Dad's.

"I don't see why we had to come at all. Jenny and I aren't changing schools. Besides, I have a tennis lesson this afternoon. I better not be late," one of the daughters was saying loud enough for me to hear.

"And I'm meeting Rachel at 3 to go shopping!"

We approached the R table and were each handed a red folder and a name tag. My name tag had a blue border, since I was the prospective student. Mom's and Dad's, as the parents', were red. Each name was written in calligraphy against a gray imprint of the school logo. I put mine on my sweater. Dad put his on the lapel of his sports coat and Mom carried hers in her hand for a few steps, then folded it in half and put it in her purse.

On the outside of the orientation folder, CHAMINADE COLLEGE PREPARATORY SCHOOL, ST. LOUIS, MO., flanked a larger, raised impression of the school logo, and in script at the bottom was printed: *PREPARING MEN OF TODAY FOR THE WORLD OF TOMORROW*. I opened it eagerly and read the inside flap, a key to the school's logo:

THE ANCHOR INDICATES THE FAITH THAT IS THE FOUNDATION
OF ALL WE DO; A SUPERIMPOSED "M" STANDS FOR FR. CHAMINADE'S
DEVOTION TO MARY AND HIS MISSION TO BRING ALL PEOPLE
TO CHRIST THROUGH HER;
THE MOTTO, ESTO VIR: BE A MAN.

This is what I needed, I thought. *If I worked hard and took the school seriously, I would come out a man.*

Mom was pulling at a stray thread on Dad's shoulder.

"Hold still."

"Marie. Don't pull it. I have a knife…"

We moved into the commons area. A man about 55, with slicked-back, yellow-gray hair, pockmarked skin, and glasses greeted us just past the registration table.

"Welcome to Chaminade. I'm Brother P., the school principal."

Like the rest of the brothers, he wore black pants, white shirt, and black tie. But Brother P. was distinct in size—he was by far the biggest. The back of his pants rode up the crotch, the waist stretched tight over a protruding belly, and the buttons of his shirt strained to stay closed behind his tie. His back was damp with sweat, and he seemed to strain for breath. I took his ill-fitting clothes to be a sign of his vow of poverty. *He* had substance, and I shouldn't have noticed the flaws.

Brother P. shook my hand. His palm was clammy. I returned with the firm grip Dad demanded. "A handshake says a lot…Chances are it's a limp man behind a limp wrist. No one likes to be handed a dead fish…"

"Hello, Brother," Mom and Dad both said.

"Quite a crowd today," Mom said.

"Yes. It is," Brother P. responded and then, in one continuous movement, he grabbed the left lens of his eyeglasses with three fingers, pushed them up on his nose, screwed up his face to a degree disproportionate to the gesture, and sniffed. "So you're going to be joining us next year," he said as he released the tension in his face and turned toward me.

I bit my lip to keep from laughing. I recognized the gesture from Fred and his friends imitating it.

"If he gets in," Dad answered for me.

"*He'll get in,*" Mom countered.

"Your brother has made quite an impression on us. We have high expectations for you," Brother P. added.

I smiled, and Mom tousled my hair.

"*Mom.* Don't!" I jerked my head away and checked my hair. Minimal damage.

Fred had told me earlier that fall that they almost *had* to let me in—since he was a student there already and Mom and Dad had given enough money to the school. "They'd be stupid not to," he said.

When enough registrants gathered around, Brother P. addressed the crowd: "Chaminade College Preparatory was founded in 1910 by the Society of Mary, or, popularly, Marianists, an order of priests and brothers dedicated to the mission of Mary: bringing souls to Christ, her Son. Hence, our motto in Latin, *Per Matrem Ad Filiam.*"

I looked at Mom. She nodded and gestured for me to pay attention and took a tissue out of her purse. She understood, since she went to Catholic high school before Vatican II, when the Mass was still said in Latin and Latin classes were mandatory.

"Through the mother to the Son," Brother P. translated and continued. "The school is named after Father William Joseph Chaminade, who founded the order in Bordeaux, France in 1817."

I knew Mom was pleased with the Marian emphasis of the school; she belonged to a Sodality of Mary and occasionally said the rosary on weekday mornings with a group of women at church. And I always thought I had a better chance with prayers said to Mary than to God the Father.

"Mom. I'm going to go over there to look around," I whispered.

"OK, honey."

I looked closer at the bulletin boards set up in the back of the commons—photographs of boys playing basketball, football, baseball, tennis, golf, and water polo, and swimming. Swimming. In *Speedos*. I sized myself up against the boys in the photos. Breeder's hips—just like a woman, Fred always said. No chest. And my dick... I began to feel numb. What if we *had* to swim in Speedos? I'd think of some excuse— to wear shorts. Or, I could get Mom to say that I couldn't swim since I had surgery on my ear when I was younger. (I'd used that one occasionally to get out of recess.)

I moved to a bulletin board that listed the school's clubs and extracurricular activities. Radio club; yearbook; the school newspaper; speech and debate; the chemistry club. Maybe I could get out of gym class all together if I joined enough of them.

After a few minutes, Mom and Dad walked over and stood behind me. Mom's lips were pursed and her jaw set. Neither one said anything. That was fast, I thought. Another fight. Over *what?* The principles of the Marianist order?

Next to the bulletin boards, a tall, thin priest was talking about spiritual life on campus. He spoke in drawn-out phrases and hissed on any *s* that ended a word.

So *that's* Father N., I thought. Fred and his friends were always talking about him. They called him *Sequoia*—since he was so tall—and they imitated his voice. Like Liberace, they said. Queer as a $3 bill.

"Studentsss participate in all-school Massesss on Holy Daysss—the middle school in the Immaculate Conception Chapel, and the high school at Our Lady of the Pillar Parish, next door. There are other opportunitiesss for studentsss to join in the spiritual life on campusss. Campusss Ministry, for example, aimsss to instill in studentsss, a social consciousness grounded in the Catholic tradition. Campusss Ministry sponsorsss a food and bundle drive every winter and takesss regular collectionsss for the Catholic charitiesss of St. Louisss."

"Chaminade is a Catholic school," Father N. continued, "offering a Catholic education. Any studentsss not from Catholic familiesss are still expected to participate fully in the Chaminade life."

We went back to the registration table to wait for a tour of the campus. All the teachers were men, I realized. I had only once before had a male teacher—for fifth grade math at St. Justin's. And I believed he hated me. Fred had told me that aside from the typing teacher and art teacher, the only women at the school were in food service or administration…

Starting at the north end of campus, we walked past practice fields, past the outdoor pool that was used now only for summer camp, though the football field, and paused at the horse stables. Up the hill, the brothers' house connected via breezeways to the concrete A-frame Immaculate Conception Chapel to the South. Next to the chapel was the dormitory. We stopped again at the front of Chaminade Hall.

"You realize what it would cost today to build a building like this?" Dad said. "All that granite…and a slate roof! You couldn't do it."

I wasn't sure whether he was talking to Mom or me, but I looked up anyway. The building did look quite solid, invincible really. And each gable was capped with a cross.

"Chaminade sits on a 55-acre tract of land—once Montezuma Farm—that now joins the borders of four St. Louis suburbs. The school opened on September 12, 1910, and graduated its first student, Felix Keaney, in 1912. This statue of Father Chaminade was dedicated on June 9, 1918." He gestured to the statue next to the front steps.

Mom stood silently listening with her arms crossed over her chest. Dad raised his hand for a question.

"How long did Father Chaminade have to pose for that statue?"

General laughter. I grimaced.

"Unfortunately, Father Chaminade died long before the school was built," the student answered.

We moved on and ended the tour at the old gymnasium. We walked through heavy old oak doors, through a mint-green cement-block foyer, and past a soda machine and vending machine, and stood inside the gym.

"Since 1970, when the athletictron was completed, Juergens Hall has been used for the middle school gym classes and basketball games…"

The boys in the group eyed the space over. "Cool. This space is just for us? The high school doesn't use it?" One boy asked.

"Yes. This is where your gym classes are held when the weather's bad. The only time you'll use the high school locker room is when you go swimming." The guide answered.

I rehearsed my question about Speedos, thought about whether we would have to change clothes in the high school locker room, wondered about showers, but said nothing.

He continued: "To the right is the middle school locker room. We can walk through there back to the athletictron. I don't think there'll be any urchins in there today."

A few mothers laughed. *Urchin* was the plebeian name for a Chaminade middle-schooler. My mouth went dry as we walked toward the door.

The room was an open space surrounded by cage-type lockers. Everything—walls, concrete floor, ceiling, and lockers—was painted primary red. A long bench extended in front of each wall of lockers, so that the whole configuration was an open circle. At one end of the room was a bank of open showers. No place to hide.

For two years I had seen Fred carrying a rolled-up pair of gym shorts and a T-shirt home for Mom to wash and, every once in the while, a swimming suit and jock strap. I'd never really processed the possibility

—no, necessity—that I would have to change my clothes and shower in front of other boys. I tried to imagine myself—in another world—having the courage to strut into the shower and snap my towel at a few asses on the way. I tried to imagine myself as a normal kid who wasn't cripplingly self-conscious about the size of his penis, the width of his hips, the fleshiness of his thighs, for whom undressing in front of other boys didn't feel so revealing, like impending humiliation, and, somehow, metaphysically significant. No success. And I had less than a year to blossom into a real boy.

January 1980

It was a slushy Saturday. Mom dropped me off at Chaminade at 7:30 for the school's entrance exam.

"I'm going to get my hair done and do some shopping. I'll pick you up at one. Just wait in the front of the school if I'm a little late. Then I'll take you out for lunch."

"OK."

"Here's some money for a snack, in case you're hungry before then."

"Thanks…"

"Good-bye, honey. You'll do fine."

At 11:30 we gathered in the school cafeteria. We had a 20-minute break in between the English and math sections of the exam. The room was full of sixth grade boys. I was relieved to see I recognized no one. All it would take was one boy from my old school to get the rest to hate me.

I sat alone at a table drinking an orangeade, rolling my two no. 2 pencils back and forth across the table, and worrying about the math section of the exam. The tips of my pencils were perfectly sharp, as I had had Dad sharpen them with an electric sharpener at his office. I was convinced this would help my performance. At the table next to me, three guys were eating chips and arguing about the football Cardinals' season so far that year.

"Hey, where's the vending machine?" I walked over and asked.

One guy looked up. "Upstairs," he said and turned back to the group. "What a fag," he said as I walked away.

February 1980

Mom was serving leftover chicken casserole for supper. She nodded at me to say the blessing.

"...name-a the Father, an'-a the Son, an-a the Holy Spirit," we each made the sign of the cross. "Bless us O Lord an' these Thy gifts which we are about to receive from Thy bounty through Christ-our-Lord. Amen." I slurred the prayer and made an abbreviated sign of the cross—in a circle instead of four points. Lazy for a Catholic, but standard for some Protestants.

Mom served each of us, starting with Dad. "So, we have some news for you," she said, looking at me.

"Marie!" Dad snapped.

"*Oh,* I'm sorry," Mom said, recoiling. She served herself last, taking only a small spoonful of casserole.

Fred grabbed the French dressing. "Don't use it all," I said.

"You can use one of the others."

"I want *that* one."

Dad was pouring a pool of Thousand Island onto the top of his salad. "Looks like you're gonna be an *urchin,*" he said.

Fred passed me the bottle of French. Three drops came out on a leaf of lettuce.

"Go put some water in it and swirl it around," Dad said.

"*What?...Gross!*"

"*I'll* take care of it *later,*" Mom said. "This means no more TV after dinner. You're gonna have a lot of homework to do."

"I know. Is there any more French?" I asked Mom.

"I think *what's on the table* is adequate," Dad answered for her.

March 1980

I dressed after dinner to go with Dad for the Chaminade acceptance interview. I felt like I needed to make a good impression, to seem mature—so I wore navy slacks, a new white Izod, and a new pair of black dress shoes (my first without laces).

We drove in silence the 25 minutes up Lindbergh in Dad's new yellow Cadillac Eldorado. The tufted leather still smelled new. I inventoried the myriad new controls: power windows; power locks; moon roof; electronic climate control; four-way adjustable seats (both driver's and passengers'); power side-view mirrors; lighted vanity mirror calibrated for evening, day, and office.

Dad was the only parent to park in the front lot (reserved for faculty). I didn't know if he was ignoring the sign or just didn't see it. We climbed the granite stairs past the statue of Father Chaminade into the austere lobby of the main building. Two high school students sat inside the door checking names off of a list, and just like at the open house in November, they handed out name tags. This time mine was red. I was in. Each father and son pair were then matched with a brother for individual interviews.

The Alumni Room was at the center of the first floor of Chaminade Hall amid award plaques and trophy cases. An index card was taped to the door: *Brother B.* We waited outside while the father and son pair inside finished their interview. It felt like waiting for confession, so to distract myself I scanned the award lists for Fred's name and found it, with only three other students, listed under Special Honors. Just then the door opened and Brother B. emerged patting a blond, freckled kid on the back and then squeezing his shoulder. "We'll see you in the fall."

Dad and I followed Brother B. into the room. I walked fast so Brother B. wouldn't have a chance to touch me. Dad took off his hat, and we sat down at a big oak conference table surrounded by Bank of England chairs. The room smelled musty. The walls were covered with an antiqued green and brown paneling. They looked like they were painted over so many times the wood grain no longer showed through, so now the grain was painted on, Victorian style. On each of the side walls, a series of swinging frames held photographs of each graduating class. Windows flanked a bust of Father Chaminade.

Another statue. I hoped Dad would keep his mouth shut.

"This is an interview in the original French sense—*inter-vue...*" Brother B. started out. "You're well above average for the incoming class in all these categories except mathematics." He pointed to a series of bar graphs on a computer printout.

I wondered how he had gotten my test scores.

"That's something you'll have to work on," he added.

I nodded. I'd gotten used to hearing that.

"I always tell incoming students, 'Don't be like a river,' " he continued. "Do you know what that means?"

"No."

"A river goes like this." Smiling, he gesticulated in a curving motion with his left hand. "It just flows and goes the easiest way possible." His fingers were remarkably long—delicate—and white, tapered like candles.

"Ya hear that?" Dad said.

"Yeah."

"*Yes...*" Dad corrected me.

"Yes," I repeated.

We stood up, and Brother B. reached out to shake my hand. "*Esto vir,*" he said.

I smiled.

"Thank you, Brother," Dad said, and we left.

August 1980

Mom woke us at 5:45 A.M. the first day of classes.

"OK. I'm up. Fred's going in the bathroom first anyway," I said.

"Don't make me come in here again," Mom said and turned on the overhead light on her way out.

"Mom!"

"You heard what I said."

I lay in bed with the pillow over my head, still hearing the water running, the teeth being brushed, a nose being blown, the medicine cabinet shut.

After ten minutes I heard the bathroom door open. Fred walked a few steps to my room, stuck his head in the door, and said, "OK, *dear. Your* turn."

"Would you turn out the light?"

"No. Get up! I'm not waiting for you if you're late. You can take the bus."

He went back into his room, shut the door, and put on Barbra Streisand's *The Way We Were* album.

I began to doze off to "Being at War With Each Other."

At 6:05 Mom stormed back into my room and tore the sheet off the bed. "Matthew Joseph! Get outta that bed."

Luckily I was lying on my side so she didn't see my morning erection. "OK. OK...I'm up."

I sat up, pulled my T-shirt down over my boxers, and walked to the bathroom to "The Best Thing You've Ever Done."

I showered and dried off and then blow-dried my hair, feathering my bangs back from my face. When it was dry and wouldn't take any new shape, I sprayed it with Vitalis hair spray, speckled my pimples with Clearasil vanishing, and doused myself with Polo cologne.

I picked out my new yellow Izod, khakis, and orange socks. Slipped on my Top-Siders—new that summer, but by then well worn— grabbed my new Chaminade book bag full of books, and went downstairs.

I poured a mug of coffee and sat down at the table across from Fred, who was busy reading *Newsweek*. At 6:30, after a quick bowl of cereal, we left the house so that Fred could be at Chaminade by 7. He was helping the chemistry teacher set up her lab, as he'd been doing for the past week.

As we drove up Lindbergh, Fred was playing the sound track from *Funny Girl.* Through the town center of Kirkwood, past the Presbyterian church where Fred had his Sunday night Bible study meeting.

Omar Sharif began wooing Barbra Streisand as the resistant young Fanny Brice in "You Are Woman, I Am Man."

"The eager man; the resistant woman," I said and laughed. "What was that chick's name you took to the Homecoming dance last year?"

"Melody...Why?"

"Mom always called her 'that sweet young woman' from your Bible study group. God, what a *dog.*"

"*Shut up.*"

We rode in silence the rest of the way until Fred dropped me off at the door to the atrium, where students were to wait until the doors to the main building opened. "Have fun," he said and drove to the faculty lot, where he would park and from which he would enter directly into the main building.

I walked to the smoked-glass atrium doors and stopped. My hesitation wasn't new. In the first grade, I waited in the morning for the school building to open not with the rest of my class, but with Fred and his friends, then in the fifth grade. I waited with him, that is, until Sister. P., the principal, found out and made me wait with the rest of my class. And the first morning I had to wait with the rest of the first grade boys, I cried so forcefully and so long that my teacher sent me back to Sister P. I lied and told her I was hit by a football that two eighth graders were tossing in the parking lot. "I know you won't grow up to be like that," Sister P. told me and patted my back.

There were only 11 students in the building. I sat alone watching more and more boys enter the space, until it was full of 11- to 19-year-olds. The older ones tended to arrive later, since they had their own cars. Remarkably they carried the least books. They also had facial hair and deep voices and men's bodies.

I stood up to go to the bathroom. I pushed my wallet back down in my rear pocket and pulled my khakis down over my thighs, since they had ridden up while I was sitting. The khakis were pleated, so they had much more material in the crotch than I was used to and they bowed out below the waist. Which was expected, the tailor had said, since the waist was 34 inches taken in to 29. But what was the alternative, Mom had asked the tailor, since I needed the room across the buttocks and in the thigh?

The buttocks and thigh. My "breeder hips," as Fred called them, "just like a woman." And like a woman, I was well aware; the hips and thighs were the first place I gained and lost weight. A five-pound shift on the scale translated on my body into the difference between "breeder hips" and a body that could pass for male.

The more I put into my pockets the worse the pants looked. Keys, change, a handkerchief, a wallet—all made the fabric bow out even more. I chose a thin wallet, but there wasn't much I could do about the rest—I needed house keys, change for the bus, and the handkerchief Dad insisted on.

I felt lost in the pleats. My penis seemed to take up so little room; the space behind the fabric was a void of hot air. But the pleats were necessary; the straight-cut, unpleated khakis were far too tight in the thigh. And besides, I liked the look of the pleats.

I retucked my shirt as I walked across the field of brown, short-pile, industrial-grade carpeting, past stands of boys in conversation, south towards the men's room. Ugh, a bubble the carpet layers missed—that'll be trouble—much easier to correct when the glue's still wet. Now, it will have to be steamed and rolled out. The atrium was much less challenging empty. My boxers were caught in the crack of my butt. That was another problem—if the pants were too tight in the thigh and the underwear hung lose, it wasn't long before the friction between the two caused the underwear to become bunched up. The result: chronic wedgie. As soon as I pulled it out, it started to creep back in with every step.

I chose the urinal farthest to the back of the bathroom, in a shadow where the overhead fluorescents didn't reach. The urinals had no dividers between them, so I pivoted my body toward the back wall. I moved even closer into the porcelain cavity of the urinal when I heard someone coming into the bathroom. He spit into the urinal, and I slipped my penis back into my boxers. For another ten years.

— Esto Vir —

January 1997

I remember wondering, from third grade even, why I was so disliked. Was it just my sissiness—my inadequate masculinity, my explicit femininity? Or were unappealing defenses already in place by seventh grade—did I come across as abrasive, aloof, superior? Why, for example, in the eighth grade, while I sat with a bus full of Chaminade boys on the way home from school, did someone call out: "Rottnek. What's wrong with your lips? Fuck man, look at Rottnek's lips—he's wearing lipstick. The faggot."? Why did virtually the whole bus laugh? Did I bring this on in some way I don't remember?

I came to avoid expressiveness as much as I could—because I worried that any revealing of myself would be seen as effeminate/homosexual expressiveness. And yet, at the same time, I became a Little Lord Fauntleroy: while some guys, for example, wore the same tie every day and kept it crumpled up in their lockers only to put it on for homeroom, my tie was always tied perfectly, chosen from an expansive collection, and matched carefully to the rest of my outfit. My hair was always neat and changed styles regularly (especially when I had it permed), and my clothes alternated between periods of preppy and Eurotrash. I felt I couldn't afford to break the rules and be sloppy, *and* I wanted to distinguish myself as a fine young man. A young playboy. Sophisticated beyond my years—an imaginative indulgence to distract myself from my social environment. Because in my social environment I felt subhuman.

I managed to have about five friends in those six years. We were all pariahs of some sort—who found an unspoken refuge in the group. And we didn't treat one another very well. I wonder now if we're not *all* queer. (Sex—even, especially, masturbation—wasn't discussed.) But the tentative companionship of five similarly alienated boys wasn't enough to insulate me from the pain of a lonely six years. I spent most of my time by myself: I studied hard and watched a lot of television—particularly on the weekends when the other guys were gathering at lawn parties, drinking illicitly, living their adolescence. For me, an ideal

Friday night was a series of nighttime soaps and a Domino's pizza with extra cheese.

Homosexuality was always the bogey: always present somehow; always the antithesis to maleness; always used to invalidate one's worth. A suggested prom theme Fred's junior year: Homosexuality. Pink Friday, the senior class forum for weekend announcements, told us, in preparation for Easter weekend: "And when you're grandmother says to you, "My how you've changed," say, 'Yes, Grandma. I've become a homosexual.'" The school exploded in laughter, and Pink Friday was canceled.

Faculty and students alike, despite any redeeming traits, were regularly vilified for any gender atypical behavior or the slightest suggestion of homosexual affect. Unfortunately, among the faculty, these tended to be the most sensitive, emotionally accessible and dedicated teachers.

On some level we knew that most of the priests and brothers were homos, and we had disdain for their perversity. In retrospect, they were self-loathing; then, they were just creepy, and we took every occasion possible to make fun of them. We taunted my freshman year Latin teacher, Brother L., for example, because we found him effeminate. There were times he became so upset he threw over a desk and stormed out of the room. Both religious and lay teachers—with some exceptions—couldn't conform to the very ideology they were propagating. In religion class we were taught that there was a direct correlation between homosexuality and Satanism. And, as if to prepare us for normal, heterosexual adult life, Father N. told us (and this is a quote): "Boysss. You must never enter a woman dry."

I never, by the way, showered after gym class—the whole six years of my attendance. And I started wearing boxer shorts instead of briefs in the eighth grade because they were more modest—and fashionable.

Reading, Writing, and Ridicule

by *Kerry Lindemann-Schaefer*

– 1962 –

– 1997 –

I've gone through a wide range of sexual identities during my life, and what I consider myself at present doesn't fit neatly into any easily recognized category. However, during most of my adolescence I was what one could only call a "gentleman tomboy." In other words, while I wasn't the rough-and-tumble, sports-oriented, physically active stereotypical tomboy, from about sixth grade on, I consciously wanted to be a man. Not a boy, mind you, but a man. There's a big difference, especially considering that I came of age in the late '50s, amid beehive hairdos, black leather jackets, and the suburban housewife/working husband culture.

Being an intensely serious, scholarly type, I saw nothing worth emulating in the typical teenage boy. But a grown man—ah, now there was a proper role model! Strong, silent, competent, emotionally reserved. I could picture myself like that, except for the unfortunate fact of having been born female. This attitude made me a total misfit, especially when I reached high school, where I did my best to dress like my father. I wore tailored jackets, shirts, silk scarves knotted around my neck to look like ties, and oxfords; carried a brief case; and slicked my short hair back with—believe it or not!—Brylcreem. The only thing that ruined my pseudo-masculine image was the fact that I was forced to wear skirts to school and on other formal occasions. I hated wearing skirts with a passion, because they totally destroyed the possibility that I might be mistaken for a male, something that did happen now and then when I wore pants. However, these were the bad old days before the women's movement came along. It never occurred to anyone that wearing pants should be an option, except at home and in other such informal situations.

High school became the bane of my existence. Being both the class scholar and the strangely dressed freak did nothing to endear me to my peers. While I had a few friends, most others just stared, laughed at, or made fun of me. All this was before knives, handguns, and violence became routine in classrooms, so I was never physically assaulted. The worst anyone ever did was throw a firecracker at me. (It landed at my feet, where I ignored it with the proper disdain when it went off.)

Although I certainly never thought in terms of being homosexual—*gay* wasn't even in my vocabulary back then—I can recall a rather attractive girl who asked if I wanted to kiss her. Such a thought had never even crossed my innocent mind, but when I said yes, she presented her cheek, in full view of a classroom of students. So what could I do? I kissed her. It was nice, but no big thrill. To this day I wonder about her motives, since I barely knew her. Perhaps she was struggling with her own sexual identity, or perhaps she was simply attempting to embarrass me.

Mostly, however, it was the contempt and mockery of the other students that bothered me. I really didn't want to be a freak and an outcast, but I simply couldn't dress and act like the other girls without doing violence to my own self-image. I never got used to the stares, whispers, and laughter that greeted me wherever I went. It took many years before I could hear strangers laugh and not feel sure their laughter was directed at me, even after I had learned to dress like an ordinary woman.

And yes, I did finally realize I couldn't get by in adult society if I didn't change my appearance, but I waited until graduation day to do it. No scholarly caps and gowns for our class. The girls had to wear white dresses, much to my disgust. I changed my hairstyle that very day to something at least reasonably feminine, and I left high school determined to be a "normal" girl—a decision which got me into no end of trouble further down the line! Although I walked off with a majority of the academic awards during that graduation ceremony, the whole thing represented no triumph to me, for I had compromised my ideals and integrity by finally giving in to society's pressure.

Were my experiences in school major factors in forming my sexual identity? No, not really. If anything, it was the books, the movies, the TV shows that told me what it was to be a man or a woman. Men did all the interesting and daring things. Women took care of people, as wives and mothers, if they were lucky. If they weren't so lucky, they got into trouble and had to be rescued by a man. To my mind, this was a no-brainer—why would anyone choose to be female?

What I learned in school was only bitterness and hatred, not only for the popular culture into which I could not fit, but for myself as well.

Although it took many years for the bitterness to dissipate and the hatred to be set aside, I'm happy to say that I did make a sort of peace with myself, thanks largely to the changes brought about in society by feminism and the gay movement. I still don't fit in, but now I know that's all right. It would have been so much easier to have learned that lesson as a teenager.

Waiting for Spring

by *Marcelo F. Pinto*

– 1968 –   *– 1997 –*

I always enjoyed the early morning hours in the winter. As a small child I was always the first out of bed. I would sneak out the kitchen door into a large back yard. Winters in São Paulo, Brazil, were mild, but chilly and damp. It felt as though the morning fog and drizzle created a dome around my private backyard jungle, dominated by a single avocado tree. While I walked around exploring that space in solitude, I felt what today I call inner peace. I was five at the time and had no inkling that such a feeling wouldn't last forever.

In 1973, when I was 13, came the day I would remember best, one that I will always remember, one of such damp early winter mornings. The morning fog made the eucalyptus trees I passed on my way to gym

134

class look uncannily tall and powerful as they gave off their mentholated scent. Wisps of acrid-sweet smoke rose from piles of raked leaves still smoldering. It was a good uphill walk to the outdoor sports facility from the street where my mother dropped me off on her way to work. I dreaded each step of the way, each step toward a place I'd rather not be. "Basketball practice. Why do I have to practice basketball?" I grumbled. "I'm not good at it. I'll never be good at it." I don't think I minded the sport itself. I did dread what it meant to be a 13-year-old male. I dreaded the things that were expected of me.

When class started our gym teacher told us to pair off with someone and practice dribbling. None of the better players would want to play with me, which I found both relieving and humiliating. I was the youngest in the class and small even for my age group. The other kids were larger and stronger. And they were also…different. At the time I did not consciously know or understand why or how. They were just different. Other kids my age talked about growing older with excitement. They talked—rather, bragged—about changes in their bodies. I didn't really like the changes I felt in me. For the most part, I felt awkward about those changes, especially if they had anything to do with sexuality. I didn't quite understand what there was to brag about: first kisses, being with girls, erections over photos of nude girls. The things that were supposed to make a boy feel "cool" didn't seem to have much appeal to me. Sometimes I thought that my classmates were different just because they were older. But why did they sometimes call me *mariquinha* (Portuguese for sissy), *veado* (queer), *bicha* (faggot), *mulherzinha* (little woman)? True, any boy acting nonmacho, perhaps being "caught" playing with girls or acting effeminately, was called those names. But those words usually hurt like no others. Those words aroused a lot of anger and feelings of rejection.

Gym class was the one place I was most likely to be called those names. That morning I wasn't so lucky as to be ignored by the older boys. Somehow I ended up with a bully I never particularly liked. He was good at basketball, and he was definitely very different from me. He intimidated me, but I wasn't about to show any weakness. I had to do what I could to take the ball away from him. I tried hard. He was older, faster, and better at it than I was, and I'm sure he knew it. He laughed and sneered harder and harder at every failed attempt I made.

"C'mon, *veado*. Can't you get it? What a *mariquinha!*" he said provokingly. I felt increasingly angry. "You play like a *mulherzinha!*" I had to do something about that. As part of my culture, I knew that something very serious was at stake. My maleness was at stake. I just had to get that ball away from him. I tried. I tried again. What shame if I couldn't! He laughed with each twist and turn. He laughed when he got the ball right past me despite my clumsy attempts to be swift and supple. He laughed, and he called me those words out loud until he got other kids' attention. One by one my classmates joined in. "*Mariquinha! Mariquinha!*" What a spectacle it must have been for them. The harder I tried, the harder they laughed and called out names.

My playmate unexpectedly stopped and held the ball against his hip, laughing derisively. His sudden move confused me, and I froze. He started making effeminate gestures with the other arm and hand, wiggling the rest of his body, waddling girlishly. All the other kids started mimicking him. I soon found myself surrounded by my classmates' faggy frenzy. I stood there in bewildered embarrassment. I knew I didn't make those gestures, yet I felt humiliated. I didn't know how to make them stop. I fought back tears. My crying would have proved that I really was a *mulherzinha*. The saying "*homem que é homem não chora*" (real men don't cry) was well ingrained in my mind.

The gym teacher brought the commotion to an abrupt halt. He was very different, too. I liked him, even though I hated those early morning classes. We all looked up to him. He was once a player on the national Brazilian basketball team, which made him a hero to us all (and explained the emphasis on basketball practice). A slender, tall, strong man, he towered over us. I don't remember how we ended up sitting on the basketball court in a semicircle around the teacher. I do remember how I felt. I felt both bitterly humiliated and relieved for my rescue. I also feared I might get in trouble for causing all that commotion. After all, if only I had been a little rougher or a little faster. If only I had tried a little harder. I just knew I hadn't acted like the other guys, even though I had no clue what I could have done differently. What followed partly explained that to me, or so it seemed.

The teacher's voice thundered over our heads as he told us a story that, as much as I can remember, went somewhat like this:

"Everybody, quiet now and listen to what I have to say. I wasn't always this tall. I was a very small, skinny little guy. As I was growing up, I remember a time when my arms and legs grew faster than I could keep up with. My whole body was changing, and I was clumsy as can be. I couldn't get a glass out of a cupboard without dropping another. No matter how hard I tried, I couldn't seem to do things right. I was about your age. I had to work hard. I had to learn to toughen up and ignore the other kids making fun of me. Things changed, though. I grew strong and learned to coordinate my hands and my feet. Some of you are good at one thing, others are good at other things. You never know who will be ahead of you tomorrow. Some of those guys that used to give me a hard time turned out to be no-good losers today. So don't pick on each other, because we all have our talents and we all have our shortcomings."

He then matter-of-factly went on with the class. There were a few giggles here and there after his inspirational speech. For the most part, however, nobody really wanted to mess with him. I still felt humiliated, but I struggled to overcome the feeling. After all, I now had the answer! I just had to toughen up, learn to ignore the other kids, and wait until I was no longer different. That lesson wasn't much different from the advice I sometimes got at home. But this time it was different somehow. That morning had been the worst it ever got. Besides, even my gym teacher had backed me up and given me the assurance that I'd grow out of it—whatever "it" was.

In the following years I learned to play safe. I went on to high school in a different part of town. I had new classmates. They didn't know about that horrendous morning. I learned to stay out of trouble. I usually sat in the back of the class and spoke very little. I avoided social events. The few friends I made, I socialized with only at school. I got good grades. I dedicated myself mostly to the subjects for which I had a knack, English and biology. I had learned to concentrate mostly on things I was good at to avoid being ridiculed.

As I grew older, my interest in sex increased. I observed my classmates talking about going to a dance, flirting with a girl, kissing. I saw classmates smooching inconspicuously between classes. I was very interested in all of it. I envied my classmates because they seemed so "cool" about the whole courting game. The sheer thought of walking up to a girl put my stomach into knots. I thought, though, that I just needed to grow a little older. I dreamed about the day I'd grow out of all that shyness and insecurity and feel truly excited about my maturing sexuality.

During high school I had heard many stories about foreign exchange trips abroad, mainly to the United States. I was very attracted by the idea of spending a year abroad, living with a host family, and attending high school in the United States. I had learned to speak English fluently by the age of 16, so six months after I finished high school, I was boarding a plane in Rio de Janeiro, destination: Richmond, Va. I was 18, and I felt more confident than I had since adolescence had begun a few years earlier.

I was placed at a small, private all-boys school in conservative Richmond. I was different from the other kids. Different culture, different social class, different values. Feeling different was nothing new to me, but this time it was OK to be different. Being different was actually some kind of an asset. I was often the center of attention because I was "the foreign exchange student from Brazil." Being in an all-boys school, I had no choice but to socialize with the guys. (That wasn't much of a problem.)

Although I was a senior, I attended some classes with the juniors. For the first time, I was older than everybody else. I felt self-confident. Except, there were three major topics among the guys: sports, cars, and…girls.

My American classmates were very curious about Brazilian girls and about dating in Brazil. I learned to give them short, evasive answers, like "It's the same as in the U.S." or "I'll only know the difference when I've dated a few American girls to compare." There was a lot of male bravado going around, so I didn't feel I was being too dishonest. I usually found a way around the topic, though I felt awkward nonetheless.

Something else happened during my American senior year. I actually made friends with a few of the guys. It felt good to fit in, to have a sense that I belonged to a group. For the first time I felt that I was finally becoming a part of a peer group. One of the guys I befriended was Michael, one of those people I used to think was so different from me: athletic, popular, self-confident. Never before had anyone like him paid much attention to me unless they wanted to taunt me in some way. It felt good to have him as a friend. But for the first time, I realized almost consciously that I felt something different for him. I had had similar feelings for boys when I was younger, but I didn't know what they were. I thought they were just feelings of intense friendship. For the first time, I realized I felt attracted to another boy.

I learned as I grew up that it wasn't OK to be gay. I learned to associate being gay with being a sissy, with being a girl. Certainly, nobody wanted to be a *mulherzinha, bicha, veado*. I wasn't about to believe, now that my life was turning out to be so wonderful, that I was starting to be attracted to another guy. It just couldn't be. With deep denial and shame, I unconsciously believed that too would change. I learned to ignore the fleeting thoughts and shameful feelings that meant I was gay. That too would change. That too should change.

I had a handful of girlfriends. Dating was exciting. It was meant to be exciting, and I played my part. I talked to the guys about my dates. Sometimes I even bragged about them. But I never shared with them how awkward it often felt. I never shared with anyone how I would sometimes be thinking about sex and catch myself daydreaming about Michael. When I was around Michael, I sometimes feared I might be too obvious. I didn't want anyone to think I was a "faggot," a "pervert," a "homo," or a "queer" (my newly acquired vocabulary words in English). I did not want Michael to think I was gay...

I carried that secret within myself for another 14 years. I played the part I was taught to play. The discovery of my sexuality was marked by much shame and denial. When I finally came out at the age of 32, I had to contend with the loss of an eight-year marriage. I had never planned as part of parenthood for the day I'd tell my two young boys "Daddy is gay." I had to answer questions about my self-identity at age 32 in ways that made me feel awkwardly adolescent.

Despite the turmoil in coming out, I finally began to feel whole. I also came to realize that I was never really a clumsy, weak 13-year-old. Rather, something in the teenager was shining through: his homosexuality. Somehow others had learned to identify it and reject it, as I myself did. I was never really that different from my classmates until some of us went on to be heterosexual and a few of us gay. It was almost 20 years between that foggy winter morning and the time I realized that my gym teacher's lesson was disastrously wrong. The flourishing of a child's sexuality, gay or heterosexual, is to be cherished, not wished away. I don't feel angry at my gym teacher. He probably meant well. If only he had helped me with my rite of passage—the gay child's right of passage. He didn't know how.

Boys in the Band

by Jon Barrett

- 1981 -

- 1997 -

A gangly, stumble-prone boy inside me still cowers when I think about seventh grade. The insults still sting. And when I allow it, the name-calling picks at my memory just as I once did my pimple-pocked forehead. Mine is a familiar story, though: Gay boy caught in his fey ways before he knows what hit him.

Not that I didn't know I was different. In fact, when I learned that seventh grade PE included community showers, I spent all of sixth grade playing mind-over-body games. *If I think of naked boys when I shower now,* I thought, *maybe I won't get excited when the real thing happens.*

In that case it worked. But I couldn't keep everything down.

I confided my fears to no one, but my slight lisp whispered my secret. I avoided eye contact in the halls, but the three-ring binder clutched to my chest screamed, "Could there be any question?" The stereotypes fit almost as well as my Sperry Top-Siders, and it scared me.

I was never threatened physically, so I didn't fear for my safety. It was just that if people realized I was gay there was little hope that I could pull off a straight-boy charade. If I couldn't pretend to be straight, I'd never have a girlfriend, a wife, or a family. And knowing no other ingredients as important for a happy adulthood, I thought being gay equaled a lonely, dejected, hermitlike life. Nobody ever told me otherwise, and little was more frightening.

So when my classmates called me names, I pretended not to hear. When they scrawled things on my locker, I erased them. And when they suggested my best friend, Todd, was gay, I never talked to him again.

My memories of Todd as a friend are vague; our friendship didn't last more than a semester. The decision to write him out of my life wasn't difficult. It was impulsive, a defense mechanism. How could I hide my sexuality if I hung around somebody as effeminate as he was? It didn't matter that I knew, even then, that there was something special about our friendship.

We met in seventh grade band. As the only boy in the flute section, Todd was hard to miss. I noticed him from over my clarinet music as he positioned his lips in the "just ate a lemon" flutist pucker and peered through his owl-like glasses at his own music. The attraction wasn't sexual. But in the same way a flicker of sunlight catches my reflection when passing a pane-glass window, there was something familiar in the way Todd carried himself. In retrospect, maybe it was prepubescent gaydar that brought us together. I don't know if Todd is gay. We never talked about it. We never talked about girls or boys. We didn't have to. He was the first boy I was comfortable around, the first I could relax with. There was no posturing. And we spent our lunch hours, always an endless, lonely time for me before we met, wandering the halls and school yard together.

But he wasn't in the library with me that morning when a classmate named Sue said, "People are wondering if you and Todd are gay." He didn't feel my heart race with fear at the suggestion. And it kills me today to think how confused and hurt he must have been when I stopped talking to him, when his "Hello" in the hall was first met with my blank stare. How he must have grown to hate me over the next two years of junior high band, watching me every day in the clarinet section. I was little more than an instrument of the ignorance and hatred that kept me in the closet for the next 13 years.

I moved away after ninth grade, and don't know what became of Todd. I would like to think that he wasn't hurt by classmates' insults, that my cowardice was nothing more than a point of confusion for him. I hope he found other friends and loved ones. I hope he loves himself.

It's been three years since I came out of the closet. I wasn't able to do so until I met people who, through their own lives, discredited my misconception of the parallels between being gay and being lonely. I couldn't be myself until I found friends who contradicted my fears, fed by cloudy, one-dimensional images of gay men. And today, when I hug a friend, attend a gay chorus concert, kiss a man, or swell with pride in June, I sometimes think about my old friend Todd. For these are the true ingredients of happiness, and I hope he's relishing them as much as I am.

Some Vignettes in Awkwardness: The Puberty Years[1]

by Kathryn Hamm

– *1980* –   – *1996* –

"My name is Kathryn Elizabeth Hamm. Please call me Kathryn, or you can call me Kath. I like sports, books, movies, fried okra, Chinese and Italian foods, Dallas Cowboys, Nancy McKeon, and Kate Jackson. I hate homework. This year in school I plan to change my old image in some ways but keep it the same in others. Forget it! I'm me, and I'll always be me. Why change?"

That's how I responded to the fill-in-the-blank introduction of myself in my Judy Blume Diary in September of 1982. I was 13 years old and entering the eighth grade. I had already survived the worst year of my life, seventh grade, and was looking forward to a better year in school. I had big plans for myself. In my diary I vowed that I would "be myself no matter what happens;" I decided I wanted to be a professional golfer; and, as a strictly pants kind of gal, I even considered wearing a dress on the first day of school.

OK. So maybe it wasn't going to be easy to be myself. I had had trouble fitting in in the seventh grade when recess was no longer a part of our schedule at school. Recess had been my world. Every day, twice a day, up through the sixth grade, I would play football with the boys. As the only girl that they welcomed into their game on a regular basis, I was always picked last to join a team, and it was a big day if someone actually threw a pass to me. I loved every minute of it. I felt I had to work hard to remain worthy of this privilege. I learned a lot about competition, camaraderie, and fair play in those days, and still, to this day, I miss those times.

For all that I gained during recess, I realized quite abruptly on my first day in seventh grade that I did not have a clue about what the average 12-year-old girl in my class did in her free time. In my free time I played any sport I could find: football, golf, soccer. Anything. And, as long as I had recess, it didn't really matter if I could hang with the girls. Once recess was eliminated, however, I was left to my own unpracticed devices of standing around and talking with all the girls. It was agonizing. I was lost because all that the girls seemed to want to do was talk about the boys—a subject in which I had little interest.

I came to see myself as a misfit. I felt alone and different from everyone else. As a result I began to struggle between being myself and being the person that I thought everyone would like. Somewhere along the way, I decided that if I was skinny enough, nice enough, cute enough, funny enough, or smart enough, then I would finally be accepted and no longer feel so lonely.

"3/1/83—Diary, It's March 1. School just drags on and on. It's only Tuesday and it seems like Saturday was eons ago. I saw Judy today. She must have been in a bad mood. But we talked in the parking lot. She really seems to like me. Well, Junior Assembly is this week. I'm kind of excited about Andy and kind of not."

In eighth grade I began to write in my journal about the "crushes" I had on a few of the boys I knew. These mentions were usually limited to my exclamations that I thought they were cute; I said little else of substance. Following these mentions, I would (often in the same entry) talk about some of my female friends and mentors, usually with gushing enthusiasm.

"4/83—Dear Diary, Right now I'm going into a depression about being inexperienced (kissing) compared to anyone else. I had a dream and the guy was interested in me. It gets me sick. I would like to kiss someone, but at the same time it seems pretty stupid…. Softball is fun! I just love my coach Betty! She's so nice."

Because boys were not my priority, I found other pastimes to fill the void. I played sports, especially soccer, and watched a lot of TV. My favorite show was *The Facts of Life*. I watched it religiously and had created a small videotape library of episodes. I was enthralled with Nancy McKeon, the actor who played Jo on the series. One night a boy—a boy who seemed to have a crush on me, and the first boy to ever call me at home—called while I was watching *Facts*. I was flattered (and a bit panicked) by the call but did not hesitate to tell him that I would have to call him back at 8:30. Clearly, I thought he could wait, but Nancy McKeon could not!

Looking back, it all seems so obvious. Living it just felt awkward.

"5/17/86—Tonight is the prom. Again I get to hear about it second-hand. I don't like the thought that next year I may be scraping for a date. Almost everyone at school is out tonight, but I'm at home watching movies and walking the dog. I've been feeling so lonely these past few weeks. I talk to Kris, but it's hard to do things besides talking or the movies. I never realized that the things that I do by myself are my ways of beating this loneliness. We talked about it in Human Relations and I realized that riding my bike, watching TV, or going to the movies were my ways to avoid being lonesome. So now I notice it. It only makes me more aware that I'm lonely, and I hate it. Ralph (my younger brother) has a better social life than I do. I always think: This summer, things'll be different, but they never seem to be. I only hope…"

I think there are many reasons I was still capable of hope even though I felt so isolated in my middle and upper school years. Most of the credit goes to my parents, who raised me with an unconditional love and the message that I could be anything that I wanted to be. I also surrounded myself with other adults and mentors who believed in me and nurtured me. These surroundings were secure and reinforcing, and they gave me opportunity for stubborn optimism amid the tough knocks. Though I had so many doors opening in front of me, I still felt like I kept walking into the wrong room. There was something missing.

"6/27/91—Rereading the past entry (dated 11/30/84) makes me wonder whose life I was living. Well! I do know it was mine, but so much has changed. Every bit of who I am is different…including what I want, how I feel, and how I act. I guess I realize that sports were the only thing that kept me going through high school. It was my community because I was uncomfortable everywhere else."

At 21 I finally realized just what had been missing. I hadn't known that falling in love with a woman was an option for me. Of course, I had gay teachers and gay friends; my parents had gay friends. But any mention of their sexual orientation was usually suffocated in silence. On some level we all knew they were gay, but no one uttered a word about it.

Down deep, throughout my adolescence, I was always afraid that someone might think I was gay. As I look back, I realize that I endured loneliness because the truth—the truth that I am lesbian—was far too scary to confront until I was in college. And so during "the puberty years," I hoped for a boyfriend so that I might put my fears to rest. While I swallowed my fears, I gritted my teeth and assumed the attitude that "growing up hurts like hell, but you've got to start some-where" (1/26/86).

As I look back I can remember what it feels like to be on the outside, and I am stronger for it. These days I use that strength every day, especially in my job as a school counselor. Not only do I strive to be a role model by valuing and advocating for all youth, regardless of sexual orientation, but I am also able to entertain TV aficionados and couch potatoes alike with my astounding ability to answer almost any *Facts of Life* trivia question I am asked.

After all these years I know who I am, and I am proud of who I am. I know that I can be whomever I want to be: a soccer player, a school counselor, a daughter, a lesbian, a girlfriend, a mother. I think that I said it best, only half convinced, back when I was 12. Without excuses, without apologies, without shame, I can now say proudly, "Forget it! I'm me, and I'll always be me. Why change?"

NOTES

[1]Some names have been changed.

Draining the Gender Status Quo

by Warren J. Blumenfeld

– 1959 –

As the clock drew nearer to 10, my fear became almost unbearable. I had long since stopped listening to my professor's lecture, even though the material he was covering would undoubtedly be included on the final exam. I sat in the classroom shaking and dripping with perspiration. Suddenly the bell rang and class was over.

On that September day back in 1970, I had to make the most important decision of my life. Was I going to keep my appointment with the unknown woman in the College Student Union building, or was I going to stand her up and retreat to the security of my apartment? I made up my mind to carry through with the appointment, and I walked to the Student Union trying to maintain an air of composure.

I took a deep breath and went inside. I looked for the woman dressed in a green blouse and blue jeans. This was the outfit she had told me she would wear when I talked to her over the phone four hours earlier.

Suddenly I saw her; she saw me at the same time and got out of her seat to greet me. She took my hand and brought me over to her table. "You must be Warren," she said. "My name is Lee."

She was not at all as I had envisioned her. She had a kind, friendly face and long sensitive fingers. She spoke with an air of understanding, which allowed me to relax in her presence. I wished, however, that we were alone somewhere instead of here in the cafeteria where an acquaintance might walk in and find out the nature of our meeting.

"Lee," I said, "I called you because…" At this point I became extremely tense and could no longer continue.

"I know why you called me," she replied after almost an entire minute of silence. "It would really help to say the words that are so disturbing to you."

"Lee, I called you because…because I think I…I think I am a ho…a homosexual." At that moment I placed my head in my hands and felt like fleeing as fast as I could. After a minute or so she took my hand, and as she did, I could see her own eyes welling over with tears. It seemed that she knew the torment and self-hatred that I was feeling because she had gone through the same feelings herself.

I suppose I have had "homosexual" feelings since I was six or seven years old, but until that time I was afraid to "admit" it to anyone, especially myself. My meeting with Lee, the coordinator of the student group (the Gay Liberation Front) on my college campus at San Jose State University in Northern California, was so threatening to me because, as in most other areas of society, school for me was not a very "gay" place to be. For me, the schools I attended were extremely oppressive, lonely, and alienating places.

I was born during the height of the Cold War, the so-called McCarthy era following World War II, a conservative time, a time when difference of any sort was suspect. On the floor of the U.S. Senate, a brash young Joseph McCarthy sternly warned the nation how the

Communists corrupt the minds, and how homosexuals corrupt the bodies, of "good upstanding Americans." Within this climate, in the schools, anyone who deviated from strictly defined gender roles was considered "a homosexual" and, therefore, a prime target for harassment and attack.

For me, it started the very first day I entered kindergarten in 1953 at my public school in Bronxville, N.Y. As my mother dropped me off and kissed me good-bye, I felt very alone and began to cry. The teacher walked up to me and said in a somewhat detached tone of voice, "Don't cry. Only sissies and little girls cry." Some of the other boys overheard the teacher, and began mocking me. "The little girl wants his mommy," one said. "What a sissy," said another. The teacher simply walked away. I went into the coat room and cried, huddling in a corner by myself, until she found me.

Even before I entered school, some of the older boys in my neighborhood called me names. Soon after my fifth birthday, my parents, not knowing what else to do, took me to a child psychotherapist for counseling. Although it severely strained the family budget, I attended therapy sessions twice a week for nearly eight years, until shortly before my 13th birthday.

There was a basic formula to each session. I walked in, took off my coat, and hung it on a hook behind the door. The therapist asked me if there was anything on my mind that I would like to talk about. I said "no." Since I did not understand why I was there in the first place, I surely did not trust him enough to talk to him. Then he took down a kit of a model boat or an airplane or a truck from the shelf, and we spent the remainder of the hour assembling the pieces with glue. No playing with dolls, no cooking; we simply did "boy" things. I later learned that he advised my parents to demand that I mow the lawn and take out the garbage, and not to have me wash or dry the dishes, which, until that time, I was expected to do on a rotating basis with my sister. Also, I would have to join a Little League baseball team.

Soon after I started seeing the therapist, I began to believe that there was indeed something wrong with me, or why else would my parents be sending me, for the therapist and my parents were trying to change me, my "mannerisms," my interests, my likes, my dislikes. "When you wave," my father sternly warned one afternoon on the front steps of our apartment building when I was eight years old, "you MUST move the whole hand at the same time. Don't just move the fingers up and down like you're doing." He grabbed my arm, and through my tears and shame, vigorously demonstrated the "proper" handshake for a man. Then, as if anticipating the scene in the films *La Cage Aux Folles* and the U.S. remake *The Birdcage,* my father took me into the back yard and coerced me into walking and running "like men are supposed to move," not the way I had been moving. "Of course the other children pick on you," he blamed. "You do act like a girl."

Years later, in 1970, after I came out to my parents, I asked my mother why she and my father had sent me to "the toy doctor," as they had once called him. She responded: "You wouldn't have understood at the time, but we sent you because we felt you were too effeminate and we thought you would grow up to be a homosexual. Your effeminacy," she continued, "was the reason why the other children couldn't accept you and why they hurt you. We sent you because their taunts hurt us too, and we couldn't think of anything else to do." She also confided another reason for sending me.

"As you know," she continued, "Dad was one of only three Jewish children at his high school in the 1930s in Los Angeles. Because of the anti-Semitism of the time, he was beaten up by the other boys nearly every day. He tried to make you fit in so that you wouldn't have to go through what he went though."

My parents sent me to therapy, at least in part, in an attempt to direct my eventual sexual orientation and to have me conform to my gender role. My school reinforced this every day for all students

Even back in kindergarten, children were channeled into gender-specific activities. Boys were encouraged to participate in sports, girls to hone housekeeping skills such as cooking and cleaning. This channeling seemed to grow more rigid each year of grade school.

Despite this I developed what would become a lifelong appreciation of music and art. In the fifth grade I auditioned for the school chorus and was accepted along with only a handful of boys and about 50 girls. The reason more boys were not included in the chorus was not that girls generally have better singing voices than boys of elementary school age. The determining factor was one of social pressure. I and the other four boys in the chorus were generally disliked by our peers. In fact, most of the other boys in our class despised and picked on us, and viciously labeled us "the chorus girls," "the fags," "the sissies," "the little girls," and "the fairies." The girls, on the other hand, who "made it" into the chorus were well respected and even envied by the other girls in the school.

Because of the constant verbal and physical abuse, I was involved in a great many fights. To avoid confrontation I planned each day to arrive at school as close as possible to the opening bell and leave as soon as the school day was over. Often, however, a few of the more aggressive boys waited for me outside and taunted me. I then wished I could become invisible. At night in my bed I lay weeping, wishing I were someone else, and wishing I were dead.

This all set the stage for the most oppressive three years of my life— the years of junior high school. I attended James Madison Junior High School in North Hollywood, Calif., from 1960 through 1962. During this period I began to develop physically and became more aware of my body. Though I had had sexual feelings for other boys since I was six or seven years old, now these feelings became much stronger. Once I had a strong sexual attraction for a boy in my math class. When I told him I wanted to hug him, he looked at me in the strangest way and called me a "faggot." I felt hurt and scared that he would tell other students what I had said to him. By that time in my life, I knew what the term "faggot" meant. I was told that "faggots" were homosexuals who were sick and who needed to go to a psychiatrist in order to be "normal."

In junior high "normal" was defined by the teachers of our sex education class—the physical education staff. During the course the teacher talked about homosexuality during the unit on "sexual deviates." The teacher showed us a film, which included a number of interviews with supposed deviates: so-called "pederasts" who had sexually molested young girls and boys, and a "homosexual" strategically seated, face obstructed by a potted palm to conceal his identity, talking about his unnatural desires for other men, which he attributed to his close relationship with his mother. These men were undergoing shock treatments to alter their desires. I saw myself seated behind this palm tree. I saw myself as sick, as perverted, as deviate. Being in such a desperate state, I even considered submitting myself to shock treatment. This film and the course in general taught me to keep my feelings well hidden. Whenever any of my peers told antigay jokes, I was always the one who laughed the loudest, so no one would discover my true feelings and desires.

Junior high school sufficiently prepared me for my high school, teaching me never to question the conditioning I was being given. At Ulysses S. Grant High School in Van Nuys, Calif., from 1962 through 1965, I did not question the military drills in tenth grade physical education class; in 11th grade I did not question the transfer of a fellow classmate to a "continuation school" for alleged "homosexual tendencies;" and I did not question the statement of my 12th grade English teacher that "even though André Gide was a homosexual, he was a good author in spite of it." I felt too threatened to speak out. I tried, instead, to play the games social pressure dictated. I "went steady" with a girl in my history class during my senior year because the few friends I had were going steady, and I felt isolated for not having a girlfriend myself.

My self-hatred was not because I knew I was gay but because I did not know how to handle it. There was no one to whom I could turn for help, so I shut down emotionally in order to simply get through each day. Though I did relatively well academically, I basically missed most of my adolescence and delayed it well into my 20s and 30s.

I graduated from high school in 1965 with the hope that college life would somehow be better. To a great extent, it was. During my undergraduate years (1965-1969) for the first time I joined with other people to demonstrate my opposition to the war in Vietnam; now I felt the joy of joining with my black and Latino/a sisters and brothers in our struggle against racism on campus; now I was able to voice my disgust at the state of the environment by helping to plan ecology workshops and "teach-ins." But something was still missing. There remained within me a great void from which I could not escape. I knew the time was drawing near for me to make a decision of either coming out with my homosexuality to myself and to others or else remaining stuck and depressed as I had been ever since I could remember. I began seeing a counselor in 1967, and after a while grudgingly and painfully came out to him.

During my first year of grad school in 1970, in the campus newspaper I saw the headline, in big bold letters, GAY LIBERATION FRONT DENIED CAMPUS RECOGNITION. The article stated that the chancellor of the California State University system had denied recognition of the campus chapter of the Gay Liberation Front on the premise that: 1. "…the effect of recognition by the college of Gay Liberation Front could conceivably be to endorse or to promote homosexual behavior, to attract homosexuals to the campus, and to expose minors to homosexual advocacy and practices, and 2. "…belief that the proposed Front created too great a risk for students a risk which might lead students to engage in illegal homosexual behavior."

After my initial disgust and outrage (and also an overwhelming fear) over such absurd reasoning, I came out of my closet even further. I joined a therapy group in the university counseling center and eventually gained the courage to call Lee, the student coordinator of the Gay Liberation Front.

A few months later, at dinner over the Thanksgiving turkey, I came out to my parents and sister. Apparently it was no real shock to them, for they had known. Though my parents were not particularly thankful over my news that Thanksgiving eve, they were, at least, greatly relieved that the truth of my life was open for discussion. Since then, my parents have also come a long way in their process of understanding and genuine support.

The Gay Liberation Front chapters on my campus and at Sacramento State University eventually won a lawsuit and were reinstated the year following my graduation. The court upheld the students' contention that "To justify suppression of free speech, there must be reasonable grounds to fear that serious evil will result if free speech is practiced. There must be reasonable ground to believe that the danger apprehended is imminent."

Using this precedent, other gay, lesbian, bisexual, and transgender groups, which had been denied official campus recognition, have won numerous court battles throughout the nation. Though this ruling came after I had graduated, I still felt somehow vindicated for all those years of isolation and harassment.

In my work as a diversity workshop facilitator, I am contacted by people interested in having me lead workshops in schools, businesses, and community and religious organizations. Recently a high school teacher called to invite me into her classroom to diffuse what she termed "a very uncomfortable situation." As it turns out, students were taunting a young man in one of her classes whom they perceived as gay. Though she had led discussions on the topic of prejudice, shown films, had students read novels with positive portrayals of gay and lesbian characters, and finally made it known to students that name-calling and other forms of harassment had no place at the school, she wanted me to come and talk to the students to personalize the issue.

I talked with her about possible ways to reduce prejudice at the school, and I thanked her for her sensitivity and willingness to confront the issue. I then set up a time to meet with her to design the workshop.

Immediately on saying good-bye and hanging up, I found myself staring into space. As I did a flood of memories washed over me. I visualized this student, this young man, harassed and isolated from peers, as myself in another time, though often I find it difficult to believe that those awful school years ended for me over 30 years ago.

As the saying goes, "The fish is the last to see the water because it is so pervasive." I did not realize at the time how gender-role tracking and stereotyping had saturated my school environment. When looking back through the window of time, however, the "flood" becomes apparent.

I do have hope, though, for I can see the water slowly receding. I have hope for the future, one in which all people will live freely, unencumbered by others' notions of "proper" gender behavior, one in which the "feminine" and "masculine" as well as all the qualities on the continuum in between can live in harmony and prosper in us all. A future where all school-age girls and boys, young men and young women, are supported for behaving, dressing, living authentically, where gender stereotypes are merely taught in history class as relics of a time long past.

The water, the flood, is slowly ebbing. Let's open wide the floodgates.

Youngsters

Bad Influences

by Carter Wilson

– *1950* –

– *1994* –

I was surprised and excited (flattered I would say now) when I figured out Ned Akers and I were going to be friends. Ned was the new kid who'd moved in down the street from us. He was small and quick, precise-looking with his neatly combed blond hair and his dark eyebrows. At eight I had already begun to be bigger and clumsier than most of the kids I played with and had come to admire the perfection of smaller people.

What Ned and I had in common, our initial bond, was that we were both bad.

I'd started out that fall in the back of a combined third and fourth grade at the old Fillmore School. But even before Halloween the

161

teacher, Mrs. McCreary, said to me, "It's going to block the view of the board, Carter, but since you refuse to be a good citizen I'm going to have to put you where I can keep my eye on you," and moved me up to the second row. When I was especially disruptive, McCreary would jerk my desk out into the middle of the aisle to keep me from what she called "pestering others." Then after Christmas Ned was introduced into the class. His father was in the Navy, as mine had been, and his family had been stationed overseas. One afternoon for show-and-tell Ned brought in all the fans and sashes and stuff his mother had collected in Okinawa. He was just explaining how the ladies in Japan always took these tiny tiny little steps when McCreary was called out into the hall. In a flash Ned was up on his desk and shouting "Like this, everybody!" and mincing across the room from desktop to desktop, fanning himself and batting his eyelashes. We all burst out laughing, which brought old McCreary charging back in. "Ned Akers, you get down from there!" After that Ned had to sit all by himself in the front by the door to the hall, and I wasn't the class's only big behavior problem.

* * *

We lived in a little Washington, D.C., neighborhood called Burleith, two-story single-family row houses on streets shaded by maple trees tucked in between fashionable old Georgetown on one side and the in-town estates along Foxhall Road on the other. Some of our fathers were lawyers and accountants and clerks in the government; others were streetcar drivers or maintenance men. Most of the mothers kept house; a few had secretarial jobs. Though the buses and trolleys had been integrated, Washington at the turn into the 1950s remained a profoundly segregated city. The only black kids we knew were maids' children who occasionally had to come along and sit all day in our kitchens when their mothers couldn't find anyone to watch after them at home.

A smoky wet February afternoon. It was spitting rain when school let out and Mr. James, the Fillmore janitor, was leaning out the second grade window gathering the flag to him with one hand and reaching to unsnap the hooks with the other.

"You can go to jail for that," Ned said. "I'm going to report him one of these days."

"You're *supposed* to bring the flag in when it rains," I said.

"Yeah, but you're supposed to fold it up too. My dad says. And Mr. James, he just stuffs it in an old paper bag. What you got left to eat?"

Ned knew I bought large amounts of penny candy on the way back to school every day after lunch and sneaked it into my mouth when old McCreary's back was turned. I fished in my pocket and came up with a couple of leftover Mary Janes in their yellow and black wrappers. But Ned made a face and shook his head. So I told him I was on the way down to the Clover Dairy, and if he wanted to come along maybe I'd buy him something.

We walked along the cobblestones by the apartments. The patrols on the corners were boys from the fifth and sixth grades, trained by a kindly white-haired D.C. policeman named Officer Arlos. We all knew Officer Arlos because he was usually stationed at the light in front of school to get us across 35th Street. Today the patrols all had on their yellow slickers with the three A's on the back.

"I got another beating."

"How come?"

"Oh—" Ned drew it out, "'cause my mom went to the PTA and old Spider Lady told her I was running out of control."

"Your dad did it?"

"No, my mom. My dad had to go back to Japan."

The Clover Dairy was a white stucco building right across the street from Western High School. Even with the wet weather, after 3 o'clock the pavement out front was crowded with teenagers. The boys clowned around, cupping cigarettes down by their sides in case a teacher should go by, talking to the girls in their long plaid skirts and white socks with their books and big three-ring binders held up to their chests. There were couples too, the girls leaning back against the wall of the store and letting their boyfriends make out with them right there in public.

We were about to go in the store when a guy called out to Ned. He was big and fleshy, wearing a baseball jacket with the collar up in back, his hair combed back on the sides and left a shiny tangle of curls on top. Ned talked to him, but I hung back a little.

Ned turned to me. "You got a *lot* of money on you, Carter?"

"Four dollars. Why?"

Ned and the older guy both laughed. The older guy said, "Then I wouldn't go in there if I were you. Those hoods see you got money, they'll take it—and then beat you up just to keep you from telling."

"Yeah," Ned said, "Don't you know *anything*?"

"I—"

I was about to pretend I wasn't afraid, but Ned started backing off and I decided I'd better go after him. Halfway up the block, without looking first, he jumped into the street and ran for the far side. A car coming down 35th Street skidded and pointed almost sideways before it could shudder to a stop. The driver was honking, and through it I could hear the patrol up at R Street yelling, "You, kid! What's your name? You kid, stop!" But Ned went skipping along the sidewalk bouncing higher and higher, as though he hadn't heard. Way up the block he waved and ducked into the alley between R Street and S Street.

The patrol said to me, "What's that kid's name?"

"I don't know."

"Oh come on, he's your friend."

"But I don't know his name," I said.

"You want to get a report too, kid?"

I lined the toes of my shoes up right at the edge of the curb. "No."

Finally there was a break in the traffic and the patrol said, "All right. Go on quick. But I'm going to remember you guys."

*   *   *

Outside of school, none of us put much stock in the categories imposed on us by the adults. Just because Ned Akers and I were in trouble with the teachers or their kid cops didn't mean other boys thought badly of us. Our friends admired our audacity and to a certain extent even commiserated with us when we were blamed for things we didn't actually do. Often the really bad kids —the bullies we all feared and the tattletales we despised— passed along under the eyes of the grown-ups with little halos over their heads.

I had known most of the boys in my neighborhood since before kindergarten. As "little kids"—when we were three, four, five—all of us had been relentless voyeurs and exhibitionists. Midmorning at nursery school we were formed up into two lines to use the toilets. My best friend and I would wait till the teacher's back was turned, then run up and throw open the wooden doors and expose the children doing their business to everyone else. On summer afternoons or when we were allowed out of the house again after supper, our idea of fun was to go into the woods at the end of my street and heat ourselves up by chanting aloud all the dirty words we knew (there weren't that many), and then —most exciting of all—to turn around, whip down our pants and underpants, bend over and spread our cheeks. This procedure was called "bare backsides" and it was the most dreadful, engrossing game we knew how to play. Doing it made us giddy with pleasure. When we got caught, as we did several times, it was because our parents had heard us from half a block away and came down into the woods to find out what was the cause of all the hooting.

By the time I became friends with Ned Akers, however, the boys I hung out with had finally knuckled under to the adults' edicts about the body's shamefulness. The period often called "latency" was for us an era of repression. At five we had gotten our pleasure (perversely enough) from mocking the grown-ups. Now our still-intense sexual curiosity had been forced underground, or at least into new channels.

Some kids appeared not to remember all we'd done together in the past. They acted as though our hot little games had never taken place. It could be very confusing. Now a "sissy" was not just a kid who wasn't brave enough climb over the Cyclone fence to get into the Western High stadium. Or you could razz on somebody by calling him a "fairy" or a "homo" or a "cocksucker," and if he didn't get so angry he tried to punch you in the mouth, you could reduce him to tears—which was supposed to be the proof he really was one.

But one what? None of us was at all clear about what the powerful new words really meant.

*　　*　　*

Ned and I stood on his back porch sharing a Coke. The Akers's backyard had been all plowed up and reseeded and then covered with straw. It was the only good way to get a whole new lawn, he said. We went out to look, and in a couple of places we found single yellowish little spikes working their way up through the damp underside of the matted straw. "Go and get our garbage can lid from there in the alley."

"What for?"

"Just do it. I got an idea. I'll be right back."

Ned ran into the house and came back with a box of wooden matches. He struck one and dropped it in the straw. It went out. Ned crouched against the wind and told me to get over beside him. The second match made smoke and it looked out too, but then a pale little flame burst up and slowly spread, leaving a black center behind as it traveled out. We took our hands from our jacket pockets and turned them over the fire. I couldn't feel any real warmth coming up.

"Now!"

"Now *what?*"

Ned took the garbage can lid away from me and pushed it hard down on the fire and held it. He let it up and there was a huff of smelly thin smoke and the fire was out, except at one edge. Ned put the lid back over that part.

"You should count to ten just to be safe. You want to try one?"

"Sure."

"Lighting or putting out?"

"Lighting."

My fire came up nicely on the first match. While I watched it burn, Ned took the box and began a second one of his own right beside mine.

"What is that you boys are doing?"

Next to the fence there was a wrinkled lady peering through the dead branches of some rosebushes.

I counted to ten and picked the lid off.

"Ned Akers, are you deaf?"

"I'm doing this for my mother, lady. Now go away and leave us alone."

"Is your mother at home, Ned? Does *she* know you're playing with matches?"

"Sure. And she gave me permission to burn your old cootie hair off anytime I like."

The neighbor woman's head disappeared. Maybe she was spying on us from farther down the path, but I couldn't see her anymore.

Then we both had fires going. I ran to get the garbage can lid, but Ned grabbed it away from me and used it to put his out. I stamped around the edges of mine. "Hey, Ned, hurry up. This one's running out of control!" Finally Ned brought the lid and dropped it down over my fire and we both stood on it.

"Hey Ned, your other one didn't go out!"

There was a little line of flames blowing along the back fence.

We ran into the kitchen and filled saucepans with water, which took a long time, then ran back outside and dumped them by the fence. But the fire there was mainly finished by now, a whole wide burned-out black patch. The flames were moving in another line down toward the porch.

"You better get out your hose if you got one," I said.

"It's in the basement."

I followed Ned into the house. He had left water running into a big pot in the sink, but it wasn't even half full yet. I could hear Ned crashing around downstairs. There was dirty smoke blowing in the back door. Ned came up and said, "Well, I don't have any idea where in hell my dad put it. I think we better just leave now for a while."

Out front the corridor of black, wet tree trunks and branches along S Street was quiet, very few cars going by, lights already on in some people's windows. We walked along quickly, hands in our pockets. At the corner I said, "Think maybe I'll go on home."

"Oh, no you don't," Ned said.

So we walked up toward T Street. As we passed the alley I took one quick look back down toward Ned's house. A woman pulling a raincoat on over her house dress was hurrying down in that direction.

The grownups were bound to figure out who had done it. If nothing else, that old woman Ned had called a cootie would tell. Then I *could* claim it was all Ned's idea, which was mostly true, and that *I* didn't know what the rules were at Ned's house and—

Ned stopped and listened. "Hear that?"

"What?"

But then I could hear it too, the clanging of a fire bell and, below it, the growl of a heavy siren, coming nearer, grinding down, stopping.

We walked along faster. At the end of T Street was a NO DUMPING sign and a steep clay embankment. I led the way up, first through blackberry brambles, then hanging on to bushes and roots from the big trees at the top, and sat by the barbed wire fence. Right away I could feel the ground wet through my pants seat. Ned shivered and wrapped his arms around himself.

"We used to slide down here," I said, "and ruin our clothes and when we got home we all got—"

Spanked. But I didn't say it. Not the right moment.

After a few minutes Ned wiped first his eyes and then his nose on his sleeve. His jacket was the blue, silky, padded kind airplane pilots wore, much too big for him. He said maybe we had better leave now.

I walked him most of the way home. Ned decided he should go in by his front door. I came around into the alley and stood on the edge of the crowd of mothers and kids watching the firemen folding up their hoses and feeding them back into one of the trucks. Mrs. Akers was tramping around in the black straw turning over clumps of it with the toe of her shoe. I heard her laughing and telling one of her neighbors well, now she was mainly just relieved it hadn't gotten the porch or the house. There were cops there too and then, on the far side by the hook and ladder I saw my aunt Frannie Lyon's head above the others, the

wing of her glasses, so I ducked out and went up to T Street and home
the longer way around.

✳   ✳   ✳

Although I spent days in fear, they never pinned any part of the
Akers's backyard fire on me. I don't think Ned was punished either, but
he and I stopped spending so much time together. Was he told I was a
bad influence and to steer clear of me? I don't know. More likely, the
cooling of our friendship was our own doing. Even bad boys have their
limits. The fire had frightened us.

We sometimes still walked home together. I remember particularly a
day Ned let a guy a year behind us in school come with us. Leonard. I
thought he was creepy—hunched shoulders, a long, narrow face and a
pointy chin, his hair plastered down flat with some smelly goo. After
Leonard peeled off up the little side street where he lived, I asked Ned
was Leonard really his friend.

"No, not really."

"Then why do you let him hang out with you?"

Ned didn't say anything. We walked on a way and then, as though it
was another subject entirely, he mentioned that Leonard was supposed
to *do things* with older kids. When I asked what kind of things, Ned
just shrugged. "How would I know? Ask him."

I bided my time, waiting for a moment when no one else would see
me talking to him. It came one day after a kickball game in the street.
The other kids had left, and Leonard was still there, just hanging
around as usual. (We wouldn't have let a second grader play with us
anyway.) I told Leonard straight out I'd been hearing things about him
and I wanted to know if they were true.

"What things?"

"Can't talk about it out here," I said.

He said, "You want to come to my house? My mother will still be
at work."

We walked there in silence. Leonard had a key. Inside his house smelled musty to me, unclean. There was no chitchat between us, no raid on his icebox for milk or juice, no cookies. We went right up the creaky stairs to the second floor and into Leonard's little room on the front of the house and lay side by side on his saggy narrow little bed, not touching.

"All right, what is it you do?"

Leonard said well, if you hung out in the men's room at the Calvert Theater Saturday afternoon, especially after the end of the matinee, older kids from Western and even grown men would come in, and if you offered to put it in your mouth, they'd let you. Some of them would give you money even. I asked how much. Leonard said sometimes $5, sometimes just a quarter or 50 cents. Whatever they wanted.

Then we just lay there. Before my heart had been thumping, but now that I had the information, I felt completely at ease. Leonard asked if I wanted him to blow me. I had to ask what he meant. He said that was what the older guys called it. I said no, I didn't think so, and pretty soon I got up to leave. Leonard begged me not to tell anybody. He was already in trouble with his mother because sometimes he had money and she couldn't figure out where he got it.

After that, sometimes when we were all at the Calvert on Saturday and I went in the bathroom to pee I would look for the men. But I was too scared to hang out in there for very long. My life was more structured than Leonard's. His mother cleaned rooms at one of the big hotels downtown, I think. Whatever it was, the situation gave Leonard a lot of time to himself I didn't have. No matter what trouble there was in our family, when the Saturday double feature ended my mother or Frannie Lyon or somebody was always double-parked out front waiting to pick me up. Or if we were allowed to go with somebody's older sister, *she* was expected to have us home by a certain time.

*   *   *

By late May, early June, the oncoming heat and the closeness of freedom left us barely containable. All day Fillmore's high-ceilinged old classrooms rocked with our noise, and when we were let loose at 3, we shouted and pushed our way along toward home. One afternoon halfway down S Street I came up on Ned and a boy from fifth grade named Robert talking with an older kid. He looked like the one Ned had spoken to that day outside the Clover Dairy, but I wasn't sure. It sounded like they were planning to go up into the woods by the Archibald Estate. The older kid leaned against a parked car and showed Ned and Robert the contents of his pocket. He let me get close enough to see: some change, a couple of streetcar tokens, a key chain with a tiny pearl-shank penknife with two blades hanging from it.

The older guy asked me did I know him. I said no. "That's good," he said, laughing. Then, surprisingly, he stuck out his hand to me and said, "Joel."

I wanted to hang around some more, but Ned started pushing me and telling me to butt on out, this wasn't any of my business. So I went on home.

My father had been in the first stages of making a rock garden out of the slanting hillside in our backyard before he got sick. I had it in my head to complete what he had started. Sometimes I got as far as taking a trowel and a sack over into the woods and digging up some wild plants or finding some rocks I liked to bring home. My version of the rock garden was going to have a waterfall, so today I took the hose up to the top of the steps and began experimenting with letting water run down in different paths. But I couldn't think about anything except whatever it was Ned and those guys were going to do. So, feeling completely confused and numb, I went and got my trowel and a paper bag and set out after them.

I told myself I was going looking for plants again, but I stayed out of the woods until I got to the top of 39th Street, then ducked in along the broad path toward the meadow. I found Ned and the two older boys right away. (I must have heard more of the talk about where they were going than I remember now.) They were in a little circle of trees and vines, half hidden from the path but not more than five or six paces off it.

No one seemed surprised to see me. Joel was lying back against a log with his white shirt open, having a cigarette. Ned squatted beside him, and Joel was letting him take a drag every once in a while. When I asked them what was going on, Joel said not a helluva lot.

Robert said, "Ned said he was going to blow him in exchange for the penknife. But now he doesn't want to."

I waited. Ned took Joel's cigarette, stuck it in the corner of his mouth and dragged on it with his eyes half shut against the smoke. He looked up sideways at me. "Changed my mind."

"What about you, kid?" Joel asked. He squeezed the front of his jeans. "You want to?"

I said to Ned, "Did you do any of it?"

"I did some," he said.

"Well somebody better do *something* quick, or I'm going home," Robert said.

Joel opened his hand and showed me the penknife again. "Don't you want it?" he said. "It's yours, kid. Easy—" He unbuttoned his pants. "Come on."

Suddenly there was movement. An older couple went strolling by, the man probing the ground ahead of him with a walking stick. My heart was pounding.

Robert followed the old people almost to the edge of the woods, then came back. He stood off the path well away from us and began to take a leak. Ned got up and went to watch him. Joel lit a new cigarette and undid his fly enough so he could push his pants down.

"Come on, guy," he said softly.

It was just the two of us. The others weren't watching, but I couldn't bring myself to do it another time. I got up and brushed the dirt off my knees.

"Is that it, kid?"

I said it was. Joel didn't seem too concerned. I asked was I going to get the penknife and he said no, I hadn't really done what I was supposed to. But I deserved something, I said. He nodded at that, reached in his pocket and held his change out to me.

"Leave me the tokens," he said. "I need those."

I picked out the coins. Sixty-three cents.

"I've got to go now," I said.

"OK, kid," said Joel. "See you around."

*   *   *

And there the story of me and Ned Akers stops cold. That summer I went to a day camp out in Maryland and didn't play much on our street. In August I was sent to visit an aunt and uncle in Chicago, and by September my mother was so unhappy and confused that the rest of the family decided I should stay and start school out there where life was at least orderly. When I finally returned to Washington, for sixth grade, many of my other old friends were still at Fillmore, but Ned was long gone.

What had happened? Was Ned like Leonard and having sex with older boys and grown men all along and just afraid to risk asking me directly if I was interested? If so, the story at least has symmetry: the matter of reputation, which had thrown us together in the first place, then put an end to our friendship.

For years the recollection of that afternoon in the woods continued to fill me with a sensation that was hot and pleasurable, yet close to dread in the way it lodged in my stomach and my chest. Almost immediately I realized I had been a dope not to do what Joel wanted. If I had, I would have been the proud owner of the highly desirable little pearl-handled knife. I never thought of myself as having been molested or forced or even cajoled into anything I didn't want to do. I was too aware of my own collusion for that. I had found out what a cocksucker really did, and the knowledge that I turned out to be one myself didn't really surprise me.

Though Ned had disappeared, in the year I was back at Fillmore for sixth grade, I did see the older guy, Joel, around the neighborhood a few times. In a convertible at a stoplight with a long-haired girl leaning up against him. Seventeen or 18 by then, a man. I gathered from other people that he had spent some time in reform school, but now he had shaped up ("reformed") and had a job. "Hey kid," he would call out, "how you doing?" And I would say back, "I'm fine. How are you?"

Miss Ellingson

by Susan Gorrell

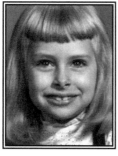

– 1950 –   *– 1997 –*

Miss Ellingson was my brilliant uncle's third grade teacher, so she began showing an interest in me from the time I was in kindergarten at Madison Elementary School. Once it was established between us that I probably had some of his intelligence and creativity, she was lavish with her attention and affection. I know now that what her interest sparked in me was a crush, my first. All I knew then was that someone was finally noticing me: smiling, looking right into my eyes, patting me with a warm hand. Up until then my relationships with adults had pretty much consisted of kissing dressed-up, nice-smelling parents good-bye and promising to mind the baby-sitter. So it's no wonder that an affection-starved little girl fell in love.

175

Miss Ellingson was regal, very tall. (Today I know that could mean anything over 5 foot 7.) She was thin in that bony, clotheshorse sort of way and had short, permed, steel-gray hair. She wore a steel-gray suit to match, with a sheer high-necked polka-dot blouse showing at the throat. Stern wire-rimmed glasses failed to harden the gentleness of her gaze.

With determination and craftiness, I found a reason to go down Miss Ellingson's hallway for a dose of kindness almost every school day; she always complied and hoped with me (or so she said) that when I reached third grade, I would be in her class.

The summer after second grade, right before school started, my parents received my class assignment: Miss Ellingson. Oh joy, oh rapture, oh love requited; I was beside myself and looking forward to school as never before.

The first day of school, I was new from hair bow to Mary Janes, smiling so hard you couldn't see my eyes. I took a seat as close to the front as I could get and sat silently with feet together on the floor and hands folded on the desktop, demonstrating perfect studenthood.

Miss Ellingson welcomed us to third grade, called the roll, and then re-called the names of seven students, mine among them, asking us to line up at the chalkboard. My stomach fluttered at the thought that I would so soon be asked to show what I knew. Would it be spelling? I hoped so. Or would it be addition? Please, God, not addition.

My agitation prevented me from concentrating on what she was saying, but I tuned in in time to hear: "So the seven of you will be in 3-B in Mrs. Reiter's class this year."

No, it can't be, I thought. I've heard this wrong. I whispered to the boy behind me: "What did she say?"

"We're moving," he replied.

It was true. She was sending me away. I had thought she liked me, had been sure she liked me, had counted on being liked by her this year, and suddenly it was all disintegrating. Third grade was turning from a fairy godmother story into a nightmare of the unknown right in front of me, and I was powerless to affect the outcome. Away we marched, and the door to my dreams closed behind me.

*   *   *

That's really the end of the story. It wasn't until months later that I understood that the part of her speech I had missed went something like this: "We're sorry to lose the brightest students in our class, but we're seriously overcrowded this year, so we're allowing these students to skip half a grade. They'll begin the second semester of third grade today."

It was an honor. Everyone said so.

Sixth Grade

by Peter Dell

– *1985* –   – *1997* –

When I was in sixth grade, I was in Ms. Chung's class. I remember her father died in that year and she was gone for a few days. "Alzheimer's disease," she said when she got back. "My father died of Alzheimer's disease."

When I was in sixth grade, we did a musical. It was Gilbert and Sullivan's operetta *H.M.S. Pinafore*. Nicole's parents said it was too advanced for us, but we did it anyway. It went very well. It wasn't too advanced. I was Sir Joseph Porter, K.C.B. I sang "Never Mind the Why and Wherefore" and "When I Was a Lad." My parents said I was the best part of the play, and I believed them.

When I was in sixth grade, some kids in my class decided to have a seance. They found out what a seance was because Shana had read about it in her book report. They went into the classroom at lunch with candles and a Ouija board. They pulled the shutters closed and called to spirits. They sat around the round project table, the one next to the chalkboard and the jack-o'-lantern on the bulletin board. Shana's aunt was the only ghost who came. Ms. Chung didn't mind, not at first. When the parents started to call, she said they had to stop because it was bad to call spirits in a public school.

When I was in sixth grade, Ms. Chung took me outside and told me I was a good student. "You're very smart, Peter," she said. "I'm going to give you some special work to do, if you like to, that is." I made up my own island nation and did a map and a report about it and called it Patarnia. Later I wrote a long report about ancient Greece. I used the encyclopedia entry for "Greece-Ancient" and rewrote the entry using my own words. I got an A on both projects. I liked Ms. Chung.

When I was in sixth grade, Jason tried to get me to go around with Shana. Shana and I were both fat, and it made sense to sixth graders like Jason that the two fat kids should stick together. That was fair. But I told Jason, no, I didn't want to go around with Shana. Then he said, "What about Julie?" and I said no again because Julie was almost like Shana except a little prettier. He said, "Why don't you want to go around with them?" and I said, "I don't know." But I was lying.

When I was in sixth grade, I started swimming at the YMCA pool. I swam three days a week like I was supposed to. When I swam I liked to look at the lifeguard. He was nice to look at. Kind of…pretty, but I guess you called pretty men handsome. But this was different than just handsome because when I looked at him, something inside me felt different, felt more alive, felt excited like right before I had gone onstage in *H.M.S. Pinafore*. Something jittery and nervous and wonderful. Is he sexy? Is that what that means?

When I was in sixth grade, I would sometimes sleep over at Robert's house on the weekends. "Sleep over"—that's what we still called it, not "spend the night." My dad would drop me off. I went to Robert's room right away because we played on his computer. His parents were always busy with his other brothers so we spent most of our time alone. What started a year earlier as looking at each other's penis became oral sex. We slept in each other's arms some nights and woke up before his mom.

Now that I am a sixth grade teacher, I live with my boyfriend. We share an apartment. When my students ask me, "Who do you share your room at home with?," I lie and tell them the only thing I can— "No one." They ask me if I have a girlfriend or a wife and I say, "No, no." Occasionally, a joker will ask me with a smile on his face—a smile that says "I dare you to say yes"—he'll ask me, "*Tienes un novio?*" ("Do you have a boyfriend?"), and I have to shake my head and laugh and pretend that his question is the joke he intended it to be.

Now that I am a sixth grade teacher, I think of Ms. Chung. She never said she was married, and she never had a wedding ring. I think how small Santa Barbara is, and I know it must have been smaller 12 years ago when I was in her class. I wonder now if she might have been a lesbian. Ms. Chung smiled like my godmother Bess, who was with Judy when I was in sixth grade.

Now that I am a sixth grade teacher, I look around my room and wonder which kids are experimenting with sex and which ones are masters at it already and which ones have yet to explore the wonders of the body. I count my roll book—31—and think of the three kids who watch me every day who are gay or bisexual. I think of how I wanted to talk to someone then, talk to anyone about the lifeguard and my sleepovers with Robert and not wanting to go around with Shana and Julie. But I can't say anything, not yet.

Now that I am a sixth grade teacher, I hear my students calling each other "gay" and "lesbian" with the impact of an insult. "You're gay." "No, I'm not; you're a lesbian." Last week a student wrote on the board, "Maria is gay. She likes girls." So I erased it from the board as quietly as I could, hoping no one would see, especially not Maria. No one has called anyone else "faggot" yet.

Now that I am a sixth grade teacher, I talk to Ben sometimes after school. I think he is gay. There is no evidence, no words spoken, no accusations. I just know in that way like I know sometimes that it's going to rain. He looks at me and I see so much of myself, so much of that feeling I knew so well then but that's hard for me to remember now, that feeling that I wanted more than anything else in the world to be older, to not be around these kids any more, to know—more than anything—that everything is going to be OK. Just OK. It's not too much to ask. I see Ben asking me urgently, with his eyes, "Is it going to be OK someday?" or at least, "Can it be OK?" And I smile down at him.

Now that I am a sixth grade teacher, I remember when I was in sixth grade. I would not like to go back.

Walking Past the Playing Fields:
My Sexual Landscape Before Puberty

by Randy Clark

– 1963 –   *– 1997 –*

When I was in elementary school, I used to make detours on my walks to and from home, so I could get a better view of the junior high or high school playing fields and watch the older boys at their sports.

Today, when I visit the neighborhood in San Diego where I was a schoolboy, I am impressed that the walk to school was a long one for a child. Our house was on the top of a hill in a suburban neighborhood that was and remains mainly lower-middle-class. To reach school I went to the end of our street, then down the hill, then on a flat stretch past the higher-level schools, then uphill again to where my grade school stood.

The playing fields were on either side of the flat stretch. On my left as I went to school in the morning was the all-purpose high school field. On my right was its football field, and adjacent to that, further along my walk, was the field for the junior high. All the fields were higher than the level of the sidewalk. They were hard to see unless I climbed a small retaining wall and then a bank that was covered with an ice plant. Once at the top I walked along a narrow ledge of earth between the ice plant and the chain-link fence that confined the fields. It was out of my way, and a third hill to climb at that, but I remember taking that route often. I don't remember the older boys on the other side of the fence ever taking notice of me. I was securely alone, and I was unaware that my looking might invite disapproval or hostility.

The football field had a lawn, but the rest of the playing fields, like the one I played on at my elementary school nearby, were barren gravel and sand. In retrospect they were nasty places, good for giving you scrapes and cuts. The older boys wore gym outfits that were all of simple gray sweat material: T-shirts and shorts. On warm days the T-shirts often came off. That was what I liked to see.

Two particular boys from the high school side remain in my memory. Both were tall and slender. One had a tan and brown hair hanging into his eyes, even though crew cuts were still the usual haircut for all but surfers. The other was blond and pale but he had a very dark trail of hair leading from his navel into his shorts.

Some boys besides the ones I saw on these walks remain in my memory. I was in Sunday school, five or six years old, when an older boy said he had burned his ankle on the exhaust pipe while riding his scooter. "Barefoot?" a girl asked. "No, bare-legged," he replied, and I got a thrill imagining him riding that way, in shorts.

In second grade our class was led, along with all the other classes in our school, out to the sidewalk to watch President Kennedy ride smiling and waving in his motorcade down the long commercial street that passes one side of the school. I remember being startled by his red hair. I had seen only black-and-white images of him; our television was a black-and-white set (color TVs were still a novelty), newspapers were entirely black-and-white, and even in *Life* magazine, which came to our house, color was still used almost solely for the ads.

Kennedy's visit to San Diego must have been in the spring of 1963. In November we were called into our classroom from the playground to be told he had just been shot. Then we were sent home. It seems that the next few days were spent almost exclusively in listening to the news, either on TV or on the radio in our car.

Even though I made a habit of walking by the playing fields, I also remember times the male body made me uncomfortable. I was especially uncomfortable, despite my enjoyment of the young athletes, with seeing the bodies of people I knew personally. One day I discovered I was not the only one who felt such discomfort. While at play with a neighbor who was a friend, I opened my shirt. He said, "Don't do that, it makes me nervous." With a sense of recognition I said, "Kind of makes you stare?" He nodded. I buttoned my shirt again.

As I grew I made a resolution not to fantasize about people I knew. The chain-link fence that separated me from the anonymous boys on the playing fields made a safe barrier. If I knew the person, the fence was down, and that was not safe.

Some people made me break my resolution. I especially remember a family friend, Matt, a schoolteacher who worked with my father and at whose house we used to swim. He was tan, dark-haired, and hairy. I'm sure I would still find him handsome. I think that in my attraction to him, I first realized I could be attracted to an individual, as opposed to sex in general. I tried to suppress that realization. It scared me.

No one ever told me in so many words that fantasies like mine were wrong. No adult ever mentioned such things. No classmate ever noticed me watching the older boys or harassed me for it. Nevertheless I knew I should keep such things secret. By the time I was seven I had created my own taboos. They were based on unspoken clues in the world around me. Maybe they were based on the adults' very silence. I had built a fence in my mind, my private counterpart to the fences around the playing fields I liked to walk past.

"Sissy" was one of our insults at school (I didn't hear "fag" until I was older), but among us it referred to personality and behavior. We didn't connect it with sex.

I was not a sissy. I was different in another way and knew I was. I had been told so. The year after I was born, the Soviet Union had launched Sputnik. The launch caused a panic in U.S. education and sparked a push for science education and a glorification of technology. I was tested—it seems all children were tested then—and found to be "gifted." That was the jargon of the times. It meant I should study science. My family and my teachers encouraged it. I got grief for this from some of my classmates. They found it peculiar. They told me I used "big words." They teased me. Not cruelly—most of the time I enjoyed school. But the sense of being singled out made me feel isolated. I lived in my head a lot of the time.

Today I don't remember much of the remoter realms of science such as physics or astronomy, but I do remember those close at hand: the form of the land where I grew up, its plants and birds, its other animals, its history.

My best friend, "Ross," also enjoyed natural history, hikes, and camping trips. He was a redheaded boy I knew from school. He lived at the bottom of the hill, past the high school. Our families became friendly. Often our camping trips included Ross and his father. Sometimes I went along with just the two of them. Besides the outdoors, we both liked science fiction and building improbable inventions in one of the large sheds in Ross's back yard. (A large part of childhood play seems now to have involved finding or building shelters: tents, "forts," caves, sheds, basement enclosures.) We would create potions—not very safely—with his chemical set. We liked to set off fireworks. We also talked about sex a lot—about straight sex. He told me a lot of things I hadn't known.

I don't recall ever wanting Ross physically. There was never any sex. The most physical moment I remember is that once he asked me to give his back a touch massage—something he must have learned from another friend. We were in his parents' bedroom watching TV at the time. I complied. Ross's mother came in and told us rather sharply to stop. I was embarrassed, but not as much as I would be now. I couldn't feel too guilty when it had been his idea in the first place. Hadn't he known she would disapprove?

If, from that point, Ross's mother suspected me of being queer, I wouldn't be surprised. But even afterward she never supervised us closely. I know Ross's mother did disapprove of my piano teacher, a young man named Roger who lived with another young man named Roger. My mother liked him and his teaching, but now and then she would make fun of his mannerisms, which today I would describe as "flaming." We laughed especially at his fondness for overly dramatic music. He liked to play Chopin's "Revolutionary Étude" and "Sunrise, Sunset," which he would sing loudly as he played. He taught me for a few years.

My mother's remarks about Roger and Roger, and not any comments from peers, are some of the first explicit mentions of homosexuality I can remember. When I was ten I overheard her and my father discussing which other schoolteachers in the district might be that way. One my father suspected, to my surprise, was my own fifth grade teacher: a small, unkempt, grumpy, and thoroughly unfeminine man. Another was a family friend and a favorite of mine: a slender, elegant man of Jamaican descent.

Both of my parents made disapproving remarks—that homosexuality was a mental disorder, that it was illegal—but at the same time they were accepting enough of some individuals to entertain them at our house and to let them socialize with me or teach me. I couldn't know how liberal that was for the time.

The remarks my parents made were clichés of the times. It was in those same years that Isherwood mocked the straight world's view of homosexuals: "Even when they are geniuses in spite of it, their masterpieces are invariably warped." I remember my mother making a similar comment, not using the word "warped" but saying such works were "emotionally sterile."

Did I relate myself to such remarks in any way? Not yet. The people they were describing seemed to have no relation to myself, and what they did together—of which I had only the vaguest idea—bore no apparent relation to the fantasies I summoned from my voyeurism. The fantasies frightened me, but I went on thinking of myself as normal except for the "gifted" label.

During those six years the landscape of my world—aside from the cherished excursions and camping trips—was mostly the streets of the hill between my school and my house, aligned along the walk that had its side paths where I could watch the older boys in their gray shorts, not knowing why I habitually did so, and with no premonition that those detours were indicative of desires that would have as much effect on my future life as any of my schooling or any of my family's hopes and plans for me.

I don't often think about my childhood. There was a time when I described it to friends as an unhappy one. But on a summer day not long ago, some friends and I were driving in a pickup along the ocean in Northern California. We were keeping an eye out for good-looking boys, especially ones with bare bodies—surfers or runners or skateboarders. We laughed at what we were doing, so much like straight boys except for the objects of our attention. Suddenly I remembered how I had used to walk by the playing fields as a boy.

That memory has brought back these others. Now that I've consciously recalled more details of my elementary school years, they seem neither happy nor unhappy but a mix of those extremes just as the rest of life has been.

Yet the big boys were on one side of the fence. I was on the other. The fence is part of the landscape, too.

Toughskins

by Michael Mitchell

$-$ *1977* $-$ $-$ *1997* $-$

Not only am I starving, but I'm beginning to get upset. David always meets me by my locker so we can go to my house for lunch. I live across the street from the Jefferson Middle School. I like it. Sometimes I watch my family coming and going from our house as I sit by an upper window in the tall, turn-of-the-century school. On the other hand, if I play sick, it's nearly impossible to escape the house without being seen by one of my friends or, worse yet, one of the teachers. And Mrs. Webb, the school secretary, lives right next door—treacherous when you're playing sick.

Preston, Ida., is the seat of Franklin County and lies nine miles north of the Utah border. It has five Mormon churches, two grocery stores, one stoplight and two dentists. David Mills is the oldest son of one of those dentists. He's my best friend. Between school and church, I'm guaranteed to see him six days a week. We've fallen into the habit of eating lunch at my house, a meal that usually consists of Lucky Charms, nachos and Hi-C. With Dad either in school or on patrol and Mom working, we're usually assured of having the entire house to ourselves. Unless, of course, my older brother Jeff comes home. I enjoy it when Jeff is there because he's more manic than usual when he has an audience; then again, he steals the attention away from me whenever he walks into the room. He is golden: mischievous eyes, hair turned flaxen by hours spent hauling hay with the Gregory boys, and a chin that has just finished shaping itself into a near-perfect square. He infects the room with a certain chaotic enthusiasm, a restless energy that quivers around him like mercury on a dish. Interactions with Jeff usually end in laughter or exasperation, depending on your tolerance level. Since being cast as Lancelot in the high school version of *Camelot* last week, he's been unbearable.

Even without Jeff, David and I spend most of our lunches laughing and generally being silly. One day last week I snapped a coat around my waist so it hung down past my knees and draped an old quilt over it and danced around the kitchen like I was Cinderella, singing and making lunch. I noticed at one point that David wasn't laughing as much as I was, that he looked a little nervous. I think he was having fun like I was because he's my best friend. David's part of the routine. That's why I'm upset I haven't seen him yet. Earlier I noticed him hanging out with some of the other guys from church; they were roughhousing at the other end of the hall. I don't think he saw me. I watched for a minute from where I stood, nervous that I might get pulled into the vortex of their horseplay, secretly aching that I would. They had disappeared around the corner, and I had continued into my English class. I figured I'd see David at lunch.

Now I'm hungry and getting pissed off. He's always here to meet me at my locker. My stomach growls. I take another look around the hall, decide to scope out the schoolyard, jaunt down the two flights of stairs and out the front door. Taking a sharp right around the corner of the building, I run smack into Casey Pratt, the unofficial head of the rowdy pack of boys I'd seen David with earlier in the day. It's an unseasonably warm late winter afternoon, and the school yard is full of shrieking kids without their coats. I feel conspicuous in mine. David tosses a ball back and forth with some other boys several yards past Casey; I can't catch his eye. Casey doesn't let me pass.

"Whatchya doin'?" he sneers innocently.

"I'm waiting for David so we can go to lunch."

Casey strips the flesh from a branch he has pulled from a nearby bush. I can see the green layer beneath the bark and the bone of the newly exposed wood underneath. In a few months it would have sprouted forsythia blossoms.

"Didn't you read the note?" Why does Casey make it sound like the final word should be capitalized?

"What note?" Something's not right; he obviously knows something I don't. I instantly think I've done something horribly wrong, and my heart begins to race. Maybe David told Casey about my dancing around like Cinderella. Or maybe Tad Benson opened his big mouth and told someone what he and I have been doing behind the garage after curfew. I feel more naked standing there on the playground than I do with my pants down in the dark with Tad. I shiver.

I notice David and the others have stopped tossing the ball and are looking at me. With a sickening feeling, I realize they all must know about this unseen note. The sense of panic that began to rise in me as soon as Casey said the word "note" is now accompanied by a cacophony of voices in my head that choruses "you don't belong here" and conjures up invisible slate walls sliding with the hiss of stone on stone into a circle around me with a silent, deafening thud. Riding on the shock wave of that thud come the whispers: "You're stupid. You're not good enough. You don't belong here."

Having finished stripping the branch, Casey now holds the wet, white switch in his hand, a few wispy tendrils of curled bark flesh tenaciously holding on. I can feel the sting of it on my cheeks without him moving a muscle. He looks at me. I taste hatred for him in the spit gathering in my mouth. He smirks.

"Didn't you look in your locker?" The whispered chorus chimes in: "You're stupid, you should have looked…"

The gaze of David and the other boys scrawls a deep sentence of defeat in the invisible slate walls around me. I have the sensation that I'm standing ankle-deep in a cold stream. The red Toughskins that my mom had ordered for me out of the Sears catalog gently flap several inches above the tops of my shoes, which suddenly look very soiled. The stitching is coming undone and the sole separates from the upper shoe. A previously unnoticed stain screams at me from my untucked shirt and points the way to the hem of the graying old T-shirt I've inherited from Jeff. I realize I'm standing on a bit of a rise that has eroded away from the rest of the pavement, grooves of dirt revealing the pebbles below.

You don't belong here.

Casey is walking away when I look up; to him I'm not worth the time spent gloating. He walks with his cowboy father's gait as David marks his approach. This is the drowning of the runt for Casey, nothing more. I turn and walk back around the corner and watch myself put my hand on the gouged red brick of the building. There's a hole in the elastic cuff of the my ski coat. My hand looks wiry and white, as if a layer of green bark has just been torn away.

With most of the kids taking advantage of the sunny day, the empty halls of the school echo woodenly as I climb the steep stairs to the floor where the seventh grade has its classes and the metal square that holds my locker sits incongruously by a huge window looking out to the school yard, my backyard across the street, the 100-year-old trees of the town and the mountains beyond. They look crisp and flat against the sky, like a stage set.

Shards of sunlight fan through the slits in my locker door and create an abstract design of the contents of my cluttered locker. There is no note. The sounds of the next round of hungry, anxious kids begins to flood the hall. Where is it? Didn't Casey say it was in my locker? I can't even remember anymore exactly what he said, it being so muddled in what I have already made it mean. I pull out the tattered English book I have spent the better part of the term decorating with graffiti. A folded piece of paper falls to the floor in slow motion. I try with hands that aren't mine to grab it, my legs attempting to help and, dropping the English book and all the papers it held in the process, scatter the whole mess onto the floor with a crash. Nevertheless, I recognize David's handwriting through the petals of the folded note. I grab most of the papers and the book in one hand crumpling the pages, and the note in the other. I shove the stuff in the locker and lean into it as I unfold and read the note.

Mike,

My mom says I can't come to lunch anymore because you don't eat healthy lunches.
I can't be your friend because you have a messy room.
Don't talk to me.

David

A sharp intake of air catches in my throat, invoking an uncontrollable sob from deep in my stomach. I choke it down—I won't cry here. The hole in my stomach now might as well be from a shotgun. I slam the locker door shut through the blur of my hurt and run down the hall and steps, hurtling out the front door toward home.

By the time I've crossed the street and the Webbs' lawn, cleared the hedge, and leaped up the stairs to our house, the tears are streaming down my cheeks and staccato sobs rack my chest. I slam the door behind me just as a good wail escapes my mouth. Katie, our dog, comes barking into the living room. Ignoring her, I blindly run into my room, though once there, I can't think to do anything but stand and look wildly around the clutter and cry.

"Mike, what's wrong?"

I barely recognize my brother's voice because I've never heard this tone before. Not only does everyone at school know I don't belong, but Jeff soon will as well. I'm pulled at once by the crushing thought of his knowing what happened and the uncontrollable urge to tell him everything. I'm feeling so hysterical and sorry for myself at this point that having Jeff hate me too seems fitting. I shove the note at him and in broken sobs say, "David…gave…me this…he says…he…doesn't want to…be my friend…anymore." Saying the words for the first time doesn't convey the weight of meaning they hold for me.

"Aww, Mike. Let me see it," he says as he unfolds it. In all my worship of my brother up to this point, I can't say I remember his once being this gentle with me. Not without his flashing an evil grin and snatching whatever toy he had wanted from me directly afterward. But I had learned the look of his eye when he did that; none of that plays behind them now. I try to breathe through the snot, tears and involuntary shaking of my chest.

He reads the note, folds it back up, and hands it to me. The gold chain around his neck jumps a little as he says, "Jeez, Mike. I'm sorry. He's such a dork."

All that comes out of my mouth is a slobbering, half yelped "yeah." I sit on my bed, put my head in my hands, and really begin to cry. Jeff stands there. After a few moments I feel the bed shift as he sits next to me and puts his arm around my shoulder. I turn into him and completely wet his shiny patterned shirt with everything issuing forth from my head. When I gasp for air, I smell his sweet cologne. After a few minutes, when I've begun to breathe normally, I notice that he's been gently patting my shoulder this whole time. It's this gentle repetitious motion that brings me back to the real world. The house is silent except for this sound.

"That's really low, man. You're better than he is."

The wet spot on his chest is the size of my fist. The medallion on his gold chain is practically embedded in my cheek, dangerously close to my eye. When I break away, wiping my face, I catch my reflection in the mirror and see the imprint it's left there.

Jeff rubs my knee.

"Have you eaten?"

I shake my head.

"Want a grilled cheese?"

"Yeah." A couple more pats and he's down the hall to the kitchen. By the time I've taken off my coat, thrown it on the bike in the corner of my room, and stared at my streaked face in the mirror for a minute, the smell of melting butter sizzles in my nose.

Jeff has already pulled out the chips and is eating them with one hand while shaking the frying pan with the other. I sit on one of the stools and watch him.

"You don't have to go back if you don't want to. I'll write you a note." I know for a fact that he's not the best at Mom's signature, but I also know that he could convince the Idaho school board of the rightness of it if we got busted. It's that noble Mitchell thing we do when we've been wronged.

Just then, in his shiny disco shirt, Elsha Cologne and Angel Flight pants straight from *American Bandstand,* I love my brother more than I've ever loved anyone in my life. Even Brigitte Bowles, whom I've loved since third grade. Even David Mills.

After we finish lunch and dump our dishes in the sink, Jeff watches me get up and go to my room for my coat. The bell at school has already rung and my squealing classmates have gone to class; I'm not only empty and aching after what's happened, but now I'll have another tardy. When I come out Jeff is bent over the counter, willing his hand to write like Mom's.

"You'll need a note so you don't get a tardy," he says, making a flourish with his pen. David's note sits within inches of his hand. He brushes it aside a little to make room for his forgery. I leave it there.

Jeff accompanies me to the corner and continues walking without a word when I cut off to go toward the steps of the Jefferson. He knows to act as if nothing has happened. I'm thankful for that. I turn and look through the glass doors as I open them and catch a glimpse of him, walking slowly with his head turned a little so I can see him. He's carrying it all for me. I can read it in his face. This is the prince they saw when they cast him as Lancelot.

I walk directly into the main office and hand Mrs. Webb the note.

*　　*　　*

I'm standing in the bathroom staring at myself in the mirror, as I have been for the last 45 minutes. It's not that big of a deal, I say to myself. Really, it's not. Dad's old Norelco sits on the sink unplugged. I pick it up and hold it in my hand, look in the mirror and try to discern what I'll look like clean-shaven. Not that different, I decide. Cleaner, maybe. But everyone is going to notice. All the kids at school will know I...I... shave. I'm uncomfortable having everyone know something that seems like such a personal thing. I hold the little machine to my face and feel the pads that hide the mini–lawn-mowing rotary dials against my skin. I imagine a jovial Santa as he hops on the back of it and rides over the contours of my face. Rubbing the light coating of fur under my nose, I put the shaver back in the medicine cabinet and leave the bathroom. Not yet. Santa's just gonna have to wait a bit.

The living and dining rooms in my house are separated by small French doors that my mother picked out and my father put up, but no one has ever bothered to paint or finish. Dad isn't around much because he's been working as a sheriff's deputy, going to school, and substitute teaching at the high school. I think Mom refuses to finish the doors herself in order to make a point about Dad's schedule. Not that I mind; the little doors allow light to flood into the hallway that leads into my bedroom, the family room, and the bathroom. When we moved into this house from the Old House around the corner, I was given the only bedroom on the main floor. Mom and Dad took the largest room upstairs for the master bedroom, and Jeff took a room in the farthest corner of the basement where he's currently listening to his music at full throttle. Jeff has had eclectic tastes in music: last summer, Kiss's *Destroyer* constantly rattled the family room directly above his bedroom. Now the Bee Gees rule his turntable.

The living room is the quietest room in the house, as much from its location as the aura Mom has created for the room. I flop down on the avocado and gold floral velvet brocade couch and look out the huge picture window that opens directly on to the church and the backs of the buildings that face Preston's Main Street beyond. While the builders took out several century-old trees when they built the gold-brick church a few years back, the church elders and town officials (probably one and the same) had the sense to leave the perimeter of huge maples, giving the new, sprawling edifice an air of permanence. Their branches trap the late afternoon sun, casting salmon light and dark purple shadows on the snow banks and street.

Slouched in the deep couch, I'm wondering (rather uncommitedly) if I brought my math home to finish. Today, in front of the entire class, Mr. Marshall rather unceremoniously suggested that I might want to consider coming prepared to class once in a while as he tapped my head from behind with his good hand. His other hand was deformed in some youthful industrial accident. Of course, Roger Sparks and I have decided it was probably something much more grisly and kinky. Mr. Marshall gives me the creeps.

My mind drifts to the dance taking place after the game Friday and, more precisely, what I'm going to wear. I'm beginning to hate the sweater vest and matching Toughskins combos my mother insists on my wearing all the time. Especially after that incident last year when some eighth graders hung me by my belt loop from one of the ancient hooks lining the halls of the middle school. Between the strength of the belt loop (in keeping with the Toughskin Promise) and my own aversion to making waves, I hung there silently until the teacher came out in the hall to make one final check for tardy kids and saw me dangling in a cloud of embarrassment and some amount of pain. And besides, every pair I own are high waters. Risking notice in stupid, berry-colored floods is bad enough on a normal school day; on the day of a basketball game and dance, it's social suicide.

"Stayin' ali…ah-i…ah-i…ah-ive." Jeff has the bass turned up so loud the crystals on the light fixture above my head are tinkling to the beat.

I move down to the sea of chocolate-brown shag carpet my mother has just installed and lie on my stomach with my head close to the heating vent. We have an old coal furnace with huge heat registers that measure almost a foot square. Lying with my ear close to the register and my head on my folded arms, I can hear the music distinctly. I also hear Jeff moving around the room, no doubt perfecting the moves he's becoming notorious for at the high school dances. Jeff and Colleen Lloyd have made it their mission to make disco's presence known at Preston High School. As I think of Colleen and Jeff slithering through their choreographed moves, I realize I've been unwittingly rubbing my furry upper lip. I kind of like the way it feels: more than fuzzy, but not quite hairy. I guess it's no big deal. I should just do it now…but my body just stays planted in the carpet. I'm also in need of a haircut, not so much because it's long, but because my hair is so thick. Right now it's just big. I'll need to ask Mom for money to get it cut when she comes home from work.

The music stops at the end of the song. Expecting the strains of the next song to begin playing, I'm vaguely disappointed. I wish I had my own copy of *Saturday Night Fever*. I wish I had a decent stereo to play it on. I could play it on the huge console in the living room, but it's not as cool as having a stereo in my room. I hear Jeff coming up the stairs. He calls my name as he walks down the hall.

I answer him.

He pokes his feathered-haired head through the French doors. "Do you want this?" "This" is a sky-blue shiny disco shirt, one of the first ones he had bought with his own money.

"Sure." He tosses it at me. The sweet, musky smell of Elsha and sweat hits me almost instantly as the shirt floats to the floor in front of me. "What am I going to wear it with?"

I'm not trying to be snotty or ungrateful. Or looking for something else for that matter. It's just that, as much as I've been wanting a shirt just like this one (Jeez! and to have the original!), I also know I'll look stupid wearing it with the worn-out, straight-leg pants that make up most of my wardrobe.

I know exactly what I want to wear it with: a pair of navy blue, bell-bottom corduroy pants with embroidered stars on the back pockets I saw at Block's. I'll be the only kid at Jefferson who owns a pair; I've been keeping a keen eye out for anyone else sporting them over the past several weeks. I've hinted at Mom that I want them, but she's ignoring me. I'm approaching the age that unless I find a way to pay for them myself, no new clothes are coming my way until the beginning of the school year. I have no job, and we're months away from a Sears "Back to School" catalog in our mailbox. I'm screwed.

"Well, I don't want you wearing a pair of mine and ruining them," Jeff says. Ruining them? What could I do to ruin them? Then I remember that the polyester that Jeff's pants are made of snags easily. I desperately want my own pair. Defeated, I put my head back down on my arms. "Besides, I don't think I have any that would fit you." The sound of my scratching my stomach where the brown shag carpet has been making it itch is louder than I expect and punctuates my mood. Jeff breaks the silence. "C'mon. Let's check."

Jeff has invited me to the Inner Sanctum of disco and Jeffness. I jump up and practically run into the wall dashing after him. I silently follow him down the stairs and long hallway to his room. First thing he does is flip the record over and put the needle on the Beethoven's Fifth redux. If we stay here long enough, we'll get to hear "Night on Bald Mountain," my favorite song on the album. I plop down on his fake fur bedspread as he starts to pull things out of his closet.

He chucks me a pair of black bell-bottoms. They shine even in the dim light of his bedroom, and they're just like the ones that John Travolta's wearing on in the poster on the wall, only black. The fabric feels luxurious. "Try those on first."

I have no idea how people can tell that Jeff and I are brothers. First of all, there's that hair, blow-dried into a perfect part down the middle like the Red Sea at the hands of Charlton Heston. I know I'm going to be tardy when I hear his 2500-watt dryer rev up before I stumble out of bed. Like there's any chance of sleeping when he turns the music up loud enough so he can dry his hair and shake his groove thing at the same time. Thank goodness the Kiss phase is over.

He is also much better looking than I can ever hope to be. A perfect nose that mine has already outgrown; twinkling eyes; that square jaw; and just the hint of a dimple when he smiles. I look manic whenever I smile.

Finally Jeff and I are not built alike at all. He's stockier than I am. And he's got a bit of a humped back for which he wore a brace for a while last year. Given the choice, I'd take the hump over my back, if someone could find my back. Right now, it's just pale skin pulled taut between my shoulder blades. I had gotten some color this last summer lying out on the roof and riding my old bike out to Lamont Reservoir, so at least I'm not scary-white as I'm prone to be in late winter. Jeff still holds his golden tan in perfect tones.

I turn away from him and take my pants off. At least I had talked Mom into getting me colored underwear this Christmas. To have taken my pants off and have Jeff see me in white briefs would have been too much. I'm not *that* uncool. I pull the pants on and, before I button them, shuck off my shirt and pull on the sky-blue wonder that's now mine. It feels cool and smooth against my skin. Untucked and with no chest to hinder its drape, it looks huge, but once I tuck it in and zip up the pants, it looks better. I absentmindedly look for the button below the collar to fasten. My hand keeps sliding down until I reach the first button directly in front of my lower sternum. I look in the mirror at my ribs and the constellation of moles littering my chest. I've never worn a shirt that showed this much skin.

The sleeves are a little long, but some intelligent designer put an extra set of buttons on the cuffs which, when fastened, hide the fact that my wrists are half the size of Jeff's. The extra length of fabric that would look funny in the hand-me-down cotton shirts I usually get from him almost fashionably blouses out on this shirt. I've never felt so dressed up in my life—and vaguely feminine at the same time. How come Jeff looks like such a man when he wears it and I look like such a girl?

The length of the pants is fine, but they sag at the waist, so much so that a belt would make them look worse. My heart sinks. I knew it was too good to be true.

"Nope," Jeff says jauntily and throws me another pair. These are kind of taupe-colored and have an exposed seam down the leg. I pull them on. Worse. I slide them off.

"Well, looks like we're going to have to buy you some," he says, hanging the two pairs back up. Buy me some?

"Mom's not going to be home for a while and Dad's on duty. Besides, I don't think they'd let me buy anything anyway."

"C'mon." Jeff grabs his ski coat and heads out the door, throwing me his I'm-the-big-brother-I-know-what-I'm-doing look, leaving the music on the stereo behind him. I'm caught for a minute, wondering if I should take the needle off or follow him. I hit the light as I run out the door.

Block's is the nicest clothing store in town, with other stores in Pocatello, Rexburg, and Idaho Falls. I love the way it smells of new carpet and hidden pins in shirts. The only time I've ever been able to buy anything here was to fill the gaps in my Boy Scout wardrobe I'd inherited from Jeff. Now I was thumbing through the racks looking for the star-butt jeans I'd been pining for.

Jeff pulls them out first. "What about these?"

"Yup," I answer, grabbing them and moving into the curtained dressing room. I take off my moon boots and pants and stand there in my tube socks, which look really sick in the fluorescent lights of the dressing room. I hear the young salesman asking through the curtain, "How do they fit?"

"Hold on. I'm still working on it," I answer, very aware of the fact that they can see my tube socks (and probably the huge hole in one of them I've just now noticed with horror) underneath the curtains. Jeff begins an affable conversation with the salesman, a guy a year older than him and cute, with blonde hair, high cheekbones, and smooth skin. He's one of the Rawlings boys. He caught me staring at him once at a football game, and I've been vaguely embarrassed every time I've seen him since. I think Jeff hauled hay on one of his cousin's farms. Jeff is in here all the time, so they carry on an easy banter.

"Rehearsals started yet?" *They started for Jeff the minute they announced* Camelot *as the play,* I think wryly. He's only gotten more full of himself as rehearsals have continued. I have to admit, I have enjoyed listening to his clear tenor voice as he shows off around the house.

Jeff is talking about the role of his lifetime when I walk out from behind the curtain. They both turn to look as I move in front of the three-way mirror. They fit me perfectly—a little long, but I think that's the way they're supposed to fit. And snug. So much so that you can see the seam of my underwear riding midway across my butt. The salesman crouches behind me and smacks some of the lint off the back of my upper legs. My face flushes as he does it.

"You like 'em?" Jeff seems genuinely pleased with himself.

"Yeah. They're nice. What do you think?" This is the first time I've ever had a pair of tight-fitting, bell-bottom pants on, and I want to make sure it's the expert who makes the decision.

"They look great. You can wear 'em with your church shoes." He's right. While they're not the platform ones I was hoping for to complete the outfit, they'll do. Besides, the pants are long enough to mostly cover them. "Wanna wear 'em home?" Nope, I shake my head; I wanna keep them nice. I'm going to look so cool for the dance! I return to the dressing room, change, and begin to walk towards the counter with the Rawlings boy. "What size is your waist?" Jeff inquires as he rifles through some boxes with his back to me. I think he's making a smart comment about my being skinny again when I realize he's in the underwear section.

"Twenty-seven," I say quietly. Jeff grabs a box with a picture of a hairy-chested man in red bikini briefs and a small sticker that says XS. I feel something like Cinderella. Jeff tosses them on the counter next to my pants and says, "Charge it."

Charge it? When did he get an account here? I shoot him a look.

The salesman smiles. "On Travis Mitchell's account?" Jeff nods and smiles. My stomach sinks. Mom's gonna kill us.

Jeff signs the slip and hands it back to him. In return, the salesman hands me the bag containing the pants and underwear; it feels heavy in my hand. As it's closing time, the Rawlings boy walks us to the door and locks it behind us, saying good-bye with a genuine grin. I kind of feel included, like one of the guys. It's just past 6 and already dark outside. The February wind catches the bag and turns it in my hands.

"Won't we get in trouble?" The magic of my shopping spree clicks down a notch as the lights in the front section of the store turn off behind us. I'm getting more nervous with every snow-crunching step closer to walking in the door with the bag past my mother, who's no doubt home by now.

"Don't worry about it. The store's closed now. The dance is Friday. By the time the bill comes, they're already used to the fact that you have them. It's cool." I wonder how much of Jeff's fabulous disco clothes have been procured this way. While I don't feel right about it, I desperately want these pants. No choice but to trust him.

When we walk in the door, rosy-cheeked and red-eared, I make a dash for my bedroom, throw the bag and my coat on the bed, and go directly into the bathroom. Without pausing, I open the medicine cabinet, take out the razor, plug it in, and, taking a deep breath and a quick, last look, lower it onto my fuzzy lip. *I hope they'll play some Bee Gees at the dance,* I think as I contort my face to get at it better. The vibration feels warm on my face. I run it over my chin and still-pink cheeks for good measure. For some reason, I thought it would hurt. This isn't so bad actually; in fact, it feels good. When I'm done I put the thing down and feel my freshly naked and slightly humming skin. And then rub my chin like they do in the commercials.

Entering the kitchen, I pass Mom, who reaches over and grabs my chin and says, "Let's take a look at it." My skin flushes. I realize I'm a good half foot taller than she is. She looks so small and pretty at the other end of her arm. Her face glows under her halo of dark hair.

"Nice. Very nice. You look like a nice clean boy again." I look over at Jeff, who's making a face at me. For the first time, I don't take offense and share in the joke. I pull my cheeks in and cross my eyes. Then smile a big, stupid, naked grin.

Down the Hall From my Mother's English Classroom

by Janet B. Stambolian

– 1969 –

– 1996 –

My mother worked in the same junior high school I attended from 1960 to 1962 in Madison, N.J. A very popular English teacher, she taught in a classroom down the hall from the bathroom I came to know and love in eighth grade.

Between classes the halls were the setting for many hysterically funny interactions involving me, my mother, and many of my friends who were taught ninth grade English by her. In fact, I loved having my mother in the same school; we were quite close and she often called out to me in a very pretend-stern tone, "Miss Stambolian, I will see you in my room right now, please," really loudly so that all my friends who heard her would tease me and we'd crack up laughing. Of course I complied with my mother's every command and went directly to her class-room whenever so instructed.

I particularly loved my mother's enthusiasm for her work, her students, for literature, and for learning. Often in the summer months, her former English students would come over to our house and sit on the porch reading Shakespeare plays together. When my sister and I were very young, we would sit on the stairs to our bedroom and listen to them all laughing, reading, and sharing what for each of them must have been a truly wonderful experience.

Even though she and I were buddies at school, she actually treated me and my sister very strictly at home, permitting us very few of the typical social interactions so many of our friends' parents regularly allowed. In fact, she permitted me to attend one, and only one, slumber party during all of junior high and high school. I think she had some vague notion that slumber parties were breeding grounds for all manner of inappropriate behavior. After attending my one slumber party of junior high in 1962, I figured she really knew what she was talking about.

It happened at Barbara Stern's house one Friday night when her parents were out for the evening. The girls at this slumber party were the fast girls—popular with the boys, cheerleader types, except for me. Definitely the only tomboy in the crowd, I had crushes on a lot of these ultimate WASP girls but kept it to myself.

I was in the living room watching *The Twilight Zone* episode in which that woman had had an accident and her face was totally bandaged. They shot the whole episode from the point of view of the doctors who were treating her as they peered at her in her pitiful condition, trying to figure out what to do. At the end of the episode, the bandages came off, and from her point of view we finally saw the "doctors" who were treating her. They all had these really ugly distorted pig faces, and she was completely gorgeous. All of us were horrified and screaming.

In the midst of all this, someone said, "Where are Barbara and Marcia?" Since the party was at Barbara's house, it was kind of strange that she had disappeared. Someone else chimed in: "They're down in the basement making out." I had never even heard the term before, but before I knew it, all the girls at the party had made a beeline for the basement. The song, "Devil or Angel" was playing on WABC out of New York, the DJ a guy named Cousin Brucie.

No sooner had everyone made it to the basement but they paired up and started slow-dancing to "Devil or Angel" and later another popular slow song, "Forever." I paired up with Ruth Elsis, and we danced and made out (my first French kiss) for the whole song. I couldn't believe this was happening to me. Then we'd change partners, and I got to dance and make out with almost everyone at the party. All those WASPS, so little time. I quickly learned what making out meant, changed forever by a healthy dose of adolescent hormonal power and my emerging and profound sexual attraction to girls.

On Monday, back in school, everyone went back to being popular with the boys, and I wanted so badly to talk to someone about what I was feeling, but of course did not, since it was 1962. Instead, I kept my secret inside, hoping that I would get another opportunity to build on what I learned at the slumber party.

My opportunity came later in the school year. I'm not exactly sure how it happened, but one day between classes my friend Lynn Telore and I locked ourselves in a stall in the bathroom down the hall from my mother's classroom. Girls kept banging on the stall door, yelling: "What are you two doing in there, anyway?" What we were doing amazes me to this day. She would unhook my bra and kiss my breasts. I am totally serious. Then we would make out and she would kiss them some more. I have absolutely no idea why we did this, since it's not like we were in a relationship or anything. Quite the contrary. She was one of the fastest girls in the whole school with boys, and in fact had kind of a reputation for being sort of loose (As my best friend, Cathy, says: "From The Book of Duh").

Obviously, I was open to it and invited her, but it remains such a puzzlement to me because I have no memory of how we actually ended up in this situation. We definitely did this on more than one occasion, but we never, ever talked about it. It was 1962, for chrissakes, and not fashionable to process feelings!

Mostly I kind of can't believe that I had the chutzpah to do this with my mother only footsteps away. I often replay the scene in my mind, and cannot explain how or why I had the nerve to so brazenly tempt the fates. The bottom line is that it helped me form my love of female sexuality. I loved the feelings that were ignited in me! The whole experience fit me very well, since I only went steady with boys because that was what you were supposed to do, not because it felt right. For the rest of junior high, high school, and college, I got crushes on girls, but dutifully dated and went steady with boys, trying so hard to prove that I was just like everyone else. I would say things like: "I'm going to be a virgin when I'm married," and stuff like that—all the time hoping against all hope that I wouldn't really ever have to do IT with a guy.

By the time I did do IT with a man, I was in my junior year of college. The student revolution against the Vietnam War had erupted on our Boston University campus in 1968–69, and I was getting a little bit desperate to prove that I really was just like everyone else. Since everyone else had embraced the sexual revolution, I figured it was time I did, too. The only problem was that it was a heterosexual revolution, and I was not heterosexual, so the experience left me wondering what all the hubbub was about.

In the spring of '69, I found my opportunity with a Rhodes scholar in one of the men's dorms on campus on a very tumultuous night when students were marching in the street to call off classes or take over the administration building (again). There I was, having sex with a man with whom I had been politically involved, organizing the student strikes. We were not particularly close, but we did do the sexual dance with each other, until he called my bluff. I figured, "What the hell," and decided to go for it.

I found sex with him kind of unpleasant, actually, but since I had not really had sex with women yet, I had scant data for comparison. I just knew that it did not feel right, as they say. Still, I ran back to my dorm and called my sister, who was in college in D.C., to announce the news!

In 1974, when I finally came out to my mother, she said something like "I have been trying to ward this off for years." Do all parents read the same What-To-Do-When-Your-Kid-Comes-Out-To-You book? Her problem with my sexual orientation had more to do with not wanting me to experience difficulties in life because of ignorance and discrimination, and I certainly appreciated her point of view. (She also wanted more grandchildren, a point that did not make much of an impact on me, since I knew I would be much more drawn to the role of Aunt Extraordinaire to my sister's children). Still, she never pressured me to alter or modify my own truth in any way because she really loved me—always did, always will. Just knowing that I had her love and respect played a major role in the development of a healthy self-concept.

The most important point is that all those early experiences shaped me because they spoke to the core truth that I knew was the real me. I did not have a voice for it, however. I simply knew that I had tapped into the part that was really me, and I did not wish to not ignore or explain it away. To the contrary, I waited until it was safe(r) to come out, and for that I thank feminism and the enlightened openness of women in the late '60s and the '70s.

To Generation Xers (also known to some as Thirteeners) who might read this: Be of good cheer, really know your brothers and sisters, and treat each other with dignity, honesty, and respect. I hope that our work lightened your load just a bit, brightened the way for you ever so much more. Trust that you are connected to something much larger than yourselves, and that we are collectively living through the greatest transformation the planet has ever known.

To my Baby Boomer sisters and brothers who might read this: Be of good cheer, and know that the threads that join us are much stronger than those that pull us apart. By living intentional lives, we continue to make a real contribution to the quality of life for those younger and older than us—to the whole of the planet, for that matter. It seems at times that we don't see each other as much as we used to; just trust that we're still having a lot of fun in our lives, still trying to integrate the personal and the political and trying not to get caught doing it by our mothers!

Love Stories (of a Sort)

If I Could

by Jane Ellen Miles

– 1982 –   *– 1997 –*

If I could,
I'd say no to the boy
who kissed in the strangest
absent-tongued way,
When I'd already discovered
how well your
girl lips fit.

I'd never settle
for third-hour make-out sessions
in the upstairs bathroom,

Risking my adolescent-almost-social-status
by getting caught.

If I could,
I'd learn to say the *L* word
and like it.
I'd tell you, hell, I'd tell me ,
"Yeah, I'm queer."
"And by the way, since you
seem to like
the way I touch you,
you might be too."

You, the girl my brothers
and the others
dreamed of,
If I could, I'd have told them
the reality of you.
For months we told ourselves,
"Just until we have boyfriends."
Why, then,
didn't we stop
when we had them?

The night
I sat upright,
awakened by screams
I couldn't explain...
For once, I could find no words, only
"I can't, I can't."
Guilt persuaded me to stay until morning,
but in a week it was over.
Didn't you feel the strangling isolation?

— If I Could —

I watched you cower,
years later, at the sight of me.
I followed you into Things Remembered,
but without asking, I could tell
you'd chosen to forget.
"Yes, I said, "I have a partner,
she's a woman, and I'm happy."

I waited
for the display case to shatter
under the weight of your fear.
You seemed to want to become part of it,
but couldn't.
Do I remind you that you are real?

Although being real means Feeling,
and that I let you and another
leave me to start again,
empty and nearly undefined,
Strength comes from knowing that
some not-so-small part
has always known
Who I Am.

Clutch As Clutch Can

by Gillian Hanscombe

– *1962* –   – *1997* –

She, Maxine: me, Gill. She taller (six inches), older (two years), stronger (oh—wrestling in the cloakroom…but that came later), faster on the track. Me podgy, clever, lonely—almost a new girl, having been sent a year before to the old-fashioned, run-down girls' school where my mother had gone before me. At my primary school I'd been rough, tough, rude, and crude, having not only bashed up the girls who annoyed me, but also some of the boys: It was thought necessary to make a lady of me.

This was in Melbourne, Australia, where I was born and socialized.

The school no longer exists. Something by the same name on the same site still exists, but the 1990s version is big, prosperous, classy, and coed. In the nineteen-fifties (I have to spell out the times: they seem slightly less ancient that way), the school was called St Michael's Church of England Girls' Grammar School—ST. M.C.E.G.G.S. on our blazer pockets. It was a small, girls-only, fee-based school owned and run by the Sisters of the Church—an order within the Anglican Communion. They've sold out since, and the current version has a headmaster, state-of-the-art buildings and equipment, all things modern and successful. It still has the same uniform, though the boys wear trousers of course; it still allies itself with the Anglican Communion; and it still wouldn't dream of mentioning the word homosexuality in public. Its name these days is St Michael's Grammar School.

When I was at St. Michael's, Melbourne was a mid-century backwater, even by its own standards. Hollywood chose it as the best site for the end of the world, for the filming of *On The Beach*, Nevil Shute's novel about the aftermath of nuclear war. Television came only with the staging of the 1956 Olympic Games. Everyone lived in families where men earned money and women were housewives; everyone lived in suburbs where men mowed their lawns and women went shopping. Divorce was shameful; illegitimacy was scandalous; and abortion wasn't even whispered about. I didn't learn the words homosexual and lesbian until I was well into my third relationship. Maxine fitted no known pattern or stereotype. Not then, anyway—not that I knew of. She was 14 turning 15—mad about sports and very athletic. Straight hair, cut very short (mine was curly); hard wiry muscles from bashing tennis balls at every opportunity (mine were soft and plump); strong, decided opinions (I had none of my own—not yet).

I watched her bashing balls against the brick wall of the assembly hall. There was always a line of girls bashing balls there—the length of the wall could take at once about seven lone rangers wielding racquets. It was a school convention: if you wanted to improve your tennis, you should practice against the wall. Maxine practiced more than anyone and could hit the ball harder and faster than anyone, even the sixth form girls who, although they were older and generally more accomplished, were slowed up by their growing consciousness of feminine elegance and its requirements. The sixth form girls spent all their spare time draping their bared legs over chairs and benches to service the sexy deep tan that was essential to young heterosexual fashion. Dedication to perfecting their tennis was definitely lower down their list of priorities.

Maxine noticed me watching her and seemed pleased. She gave her ball an almighty final belt and came over to talk to me. We said our names. I voiced my admiration. She asked if I'd like to hit up with her on one of the tennis courts. I said I was no good at tennis. She said she'd teach me. Any girl can.

Nothing was more thrilling than to be alone with Maxine. The back tennis courts, two of them, were completely hidden from view by fences and houses adjoining the school. There we both headed at least three times a day, sometimes more: before and after school and in the lunch hours. The school's location was a semiseedy inner suburb called St. Kilda, inhabited by postwar immigrants from Italy, Greece, and the Balkans; by a large Jewish community; and by Melbourne's small but only red-light district. My parents lived in a bayside suburb, so my daily journey to and fro involved a half-hour train ride and walks at each end. It went without saying (though it was said, over and over) that I wasn't to travel after dark. Tennis trysts on the back courts, however, soon meant leaving home earlier and earlier—and getting back later and later. My parents thought I was being rebellious: it never occurred to them that I might have a girlfriend—or boyfriend, either: I'd shown no signs of any interest in that.

As summer turned to autumn and the weather became unreliable, bashing tennis balls at each other was also a less and less reliable activity. What to do instead? The cloakrooms at these early and late hours were dark and empty. We crouched in them talking, talking, when the rain came. Before long talking turned into wrestling. Maxine's family, unlike mine, was working-class; and she was streetwise, though the word didn't then exist. All her mates were boys, and from boys she'd learned to wrestle. She did it well. She could get me in an armlock or a headlock in two minutes flat; or flat on my back while she squatted over me, her knees dug into my biceps and her hands pinning down my own. With frantic pleasure I felt the blood thump in my ears, smelled and felt her breath on my face, saw close-up her fierce and tender eyes.

Tennis and wrestling, insouciant swaggering, having a girl as a boyish best mate—these might be unusual, but were hardly unique: not in a girls-only school, and not in the nineteen-fifties. Other girls, straggling into the cloakroom or seeing if a tennis court was free, might come upon us and giggle a bit—but nothing anyone noticed was cause for sensation or scandal. These were pre–sexual politics days, and if secrecy and shame were at stratospheric heights, so too was ignorance. Crushes on older girls or teachers were normal. In any case, Maxine could sing Elvis Presley songs along with the rest of them; and in girls-only schools, there was status attached to being good at sports. What was remarkable was Maxine's passionate, self-educated interest in poetry. She took from the school library volume after volume, at random, and read through each one: Milton, Tennyson, Shakespeare—whatever dull-covered books, with their cramped double-column print and their long-faded gold tooling, were there. Having read to the end, she then produced wonderfully long pastiches and imitations, which she began to address to me.

This new phase was even more delicious than the wrestling had been. Now I was greeted each early morning with a fat envelope. Inside was a long letter and an even longer poem—in the high style of Miltonic blank verse, or the couplets of Tennyson's Locksley Hall, one of Maxine's particular favorites. I had read none of these works, but my wizened heart leapt at the high-flown language. I couldn't distinguish which was more intoxicating—the physical intensity of harsh, shy, half-embarrassed hugs or the love-language of the letters and poems. Both made the blood thump in my ears and left my flesh burning with unfocused longing.

I kept the letters and poems hidden in a shoebox under my bed, but later, when it all came out, my mother took them and burned them in the incinerator. I still regret not ever having read them with my adult eyes. There was, inevitably, a first kiss (though not with the tongue); a declaration; a frightened acknowledgement that things had passed beyond some shared, vaguely understood barrier or frontier. Now we hardly ever sought the open spaces of the tennis courts; now we chose dark rooms, hidden corners of passages or storerooms, even toilets on railway stations. We kissed and clutched, stroked and hugged, made countless declarations. At weekends she phoned, for an hour, two hours, from a call box, when we knew my parents would be out. We mooned at each other in coffee shops. We held hands in the cinema, in empty churches, and even in the street, pretending no one would notice, or mind. But we didn't, not yet, either of us, take off our clothes.

A term passed; maybe two terms, I can't remember. (School years, then, in Australia, were divided into three terms.) When school holidays were due, Maxine arranged with her mother and stepfather for me to come for a week. Both her parents, unlike mine, had full-time jobs and were out all day. I'd never stayed away from home before that, except with relatives, so it took a lot of nagging and persisting for me to persuade my parents. Who were these people? Would the mother keep a proper eye on things? Maxine was older: would there be boys around? "Boys," sniffed Maxine contemptuously, "are for mates. You don't love them. I love you, Mum, and Stinker," she told me. "That's how it is." Stinker was her dog, a moderate-size Alsatian. I've never been able to cope with dogs, either before or since; but as everyone knows, love conquers all, and I determined to get on fine with Stinker.

Being alone with Maxine in a small terraced house was bliss. Nearly all day we lay in bed cuddling and talking, kissing, patting, and petting. I had hunger pangs by 2 in the afternoon, but cuddling was better any day than eating. At 5 o'clock we got up and dressed, so Maxine could do her chores before her parents came back. Then we ate food: cheese on toast; salami on toast; every day the same. I remember nothing at all about the evenings. There must have been talk of some kind, since working people back then had no television sets, but I remember nothing. It's possible we played in the street with the "mates" until it was dark; or that we walked Stinker around the tight, mean neighborhood;

or that we washed up dishes and vacuumed the floors. All that mattered was being in bed and the unformed expectation at the back of the mind that something further could happen.

Neither of us knew what. It wasn't in Milton or women's magazines or the Bible or anything else available to read. We'd have to invent it; explore; adapt. By about the third day, we managed to work out that touching each other's breasts would be good. Taking off our clothes was immensely daring, and touching breasts was fine. The rest was a matter of writhing and rubbing—by comparison, we were hugely more accomplished at wrestling and tennis. Sex doesn't, that is, come naturally—not all of it, anyway. Back in the fifties there were no sex scenes in films, and parents kept their bedroom doors firmly shut. Standard sex education was a range of booklets—one sort for girls, another for boys—with drawings of wombs and fallopian tubes and penises, and text about babies and happy family life. Occasionally there were talks in church halls—one version for mothers and daughters, another for fathers and sons—and we'd be shown a slide show of the same drawings. No drawings ever included a clitoris, and no text ever mentioned an orgasm. Even tampons were rare: neither Maxine nor I had ever seen one. Given the depth of our ignorance, it isn't surprising that rubbing and writhing was the best conjunction we could invent for ourselves.

Back home again after the holidays, my mother insisted on arranging a return visit—it was polite. Maxine and I weren't very keen on the idea, since my mother was a housewife so all-day bed was out, and I had a younger sister who would notice everything. Maxine came, nonetheless, and joy of joys, we discovered that the house next door was empty. She worked out how to break in without damaging anything, so clutching and kissing went on as usual. Although we didn't dare take off our clothes in this derelict house, the secrecy and daredevilry was massively exciting in itself. I couldn't tell the difference, at that stage, between adrenalin and hormones—it all made the blood thump in my ears.

Nights, of course, were necessarily secret: intense, silent as the grave, full of sighs and whispers. My room had twin beds, and our pattern was to chat and giggle, waiting till the house was dark and quiet so we could creep into one bed to cuddle, kiss, breathe each other's hot breath, load each other's ears with whispered longing…and then, after a long time, we'd unjoin to make sure we slept in our separate beds. On one particular night things went wrong. Maxine awakened me, frightened, holding her belly. She had terrible pains. I got my mother; my mother called the doctor; Maxine was carted off in an ambulance to hospital. She had an about-to-rupture appendix. In my fear and distress, I told my mother everything.

Nothing was the same after that. Nothing could be.

I visited Maxine in the hospital, but my mother came too. My father questioned me about who had touched whom, and where. I was sent to the doctor for chats. The doctor was 40ish, female, unmarried, stern (you'd have thought she'd know better!). She directed me—and my parents—to seek me out more mixed company. How many girls in the fifties had mothers desperate for them to meet boys and more boys! I was sent to ballroom dancing classes (where I met a nice girl) and Church Youth Fellowship (and there, more fascinating than anyone, was one of God's [female] Chosen, already at university). Everyone was careful not to forbid me to see Maxine, but the phone calls and house visits were over. Things cooled. The long summer holidays came. And Maxine had her own mother to deal with, after all.

The new school year began, but the letters and poems dribbled away. Other girls hogged the back tennis courts; and Maxine, having moved up into the lower sixth, was kept busy with senior sports, exam preparation, forced hobnobbing with the giggling Gerties who tanned their legs on the sixth form lunch benches. She had, I knew, one singular aim. She wanted to win the senior tennis championship and go out in a blaze of triumph. It could never be glory, since she wasn't popular, had no friends in her own form, and wasn't one of the sports teacher's favorites. As well, the championship had been won for the previous two years by one shapely, tan-legged Jo (repeating lower sixth)—and if anyone won for three years running, she got to keep the cup. For all these obvious reasons, everyone was rooting for Jo to win. Looking back, I see clearly that the extra, potent, hidden reason wasn't negligible: what group of young ladies, and their teacher-mentors, could possibly root for a wiry butch girl who had no feminine attributes at all?

Maxine won the match, in spite of the one-sided barracking and the clearly frustrated umpiring of the sports teacher, who much preferred lazy, friendly Jo. I was too craven to cheer loudly for Maxine. I felt ashamed about that; just as I would two years later, sitting round the same tennis court, when my own classmates passed around a shocking book wrapped in brown paper covers, and I giggled with them. They giggled knowingly—knowing, it seemed, much more than I did. I managed to borrow the book. It was *The Well of Loneliness.*

Maxine failed her exams and left school. I never saw her again, except once, in town shopping with my mother. She was working as a salesgirl in a large department store. She had an elaborate beehive hair-do, and she wore bright red lipstick and a tight, short skirt wrapped severely round her tough athletic legs. It was my first vision of what someone looks like dressed in drag.

We all greeted each other. Maxine, stiff, embarrassed, self-conscious, said to me only "Have you got a boyfriend yet? I have." Before I could mutter any response, my mother said to her, "Oh, that's nice, Maxine. It's good to see you again." And we passed on.

The teachers and sisters never knew, officially, about Maxine and me. There were no speeches from authority, nor quiet words, nor even a whisper, about crushes, same-sex affairs, or this particular sin. I was 14 at the start of the school year after Maxine left. What lay ahead was a string of minor entanglements, a major romantic tendresse, and a torrid affair, before I finally left school and began all over again at university. Eventually, even in Melbourne, the sixties happened, though it was a good five years later than everywhere else, and I wasn't going to stick around any longer than was necessary. I left for London in 1969. Life became wonderful. There were bookshops, bars, meetings, marches, gay liberation, feminism—and everything finally, suddenly, emphatically, made sense.

I imagine Maxine married someone, had some children, kept playing tennis, got divorced, married someone else, made some money, maybe got divorced again. I imagine she went back to reading books at some stage. I imagine she never had the chance, as I did, to go to university, meet people of her own intellectual weight, escape suburbia, go abroad. I imagine she was helpless prey, being isolated and unsupported, to booze, gambling, suffocating gossip—even battering. But I hope I'm wrong. I hope my imaginings are hopelessly limited. I hope she's sitting somewhere with her middle-aged lesbian partner reading this piece, smiling, remembering with the same affection. Lesbians, after all, are made, not born: we make ourselves out of each other's words, kisses, touch, love. And it was love: That's for sure.

An April Shower: "Tracking" a Path of Self-Discovery Through Poetry and Prose

by Townsand Price-Spratlen

Like most
Queer folks navigating high school
I felt ever alone as I walked and
Danced among the few
The proud
The Children of the Dream that Rev. Dr. King
Stated with grace on an August day in 1963

Now it was nearly twenty years later
And I was a dark spot in a white mass
Sharing in pieces of the dream
The DuBoisian fantasy

The "well-educated leadership pool" of the
Black Middle Class
The youth of the Talented Tenth

Striving to find my silences
Embracing the false protection they provided
And \speak them but
          \\keep them close by
I queered up the margins
Among the racially marginalized
Why can't I tell faggot jokes
Along with the rest of the fellas
With the sincerity I desire so much?
Laughing along with the cool pose' crowd
Not to be
Not to be

I was well-liked
Sometimes
An uppity nigger
Sometimes
A cool brother
Sometimes
An Oreo (Black on the outside, white on the inside)
Sometimes
But never a faggot
Never a fag
God no
Never the cheap discount of so much
Present pain
In three letters or six

It was a tiring dance
And I was ever sure
That I wasn't getting the steps down quite right

But I never stopped trying
To dance the dance
To dance the dance
I thought I knew so well…

I was voted the "Most Spirited Male"
For my senior class and I
\Should have
        \\Would have
                \\\Could have
Won two other "Most/Best" categories for the class
But the voting was jury-rigged a bit
So as to not cause too much attention
I was the most photographed person in my annual
Senior year
We stopped listing in the index at 12 photos
Any more, went the decision, would simply be too many
Too many
Too much

Even for the middle-class Black guy
Coeditor of the annual staff
Cocaptain of the basketball team
Codependent on the need to be liked
The need to be accepted
By the margins and the mainstream
While reeling amid the angst of the Talented Tenth
Living as the best "New Negro"
Being a "Child of the Dream"
Among the white middle class
Pseudosuburbia
Inside the city I know as home
In these hallways
Walked African American young men
Sweet and strong and beautiful

Who galvanized my longing to share
\Succulent desire
\\Erotic warmth
\\\Just good time havin'
And all the in-betweens
With an "other brother" willing to act on
His wants that were somewhere
Close to my own

As the "Most Spirited" member of the track team my junior year
(The first of my two "Most Spirited" high school awards)
Practicing late one April day
I happened upon an image from fiction
That I had seen before in passing
A young brother too beautiful for even a painter's eye
A young brother with all the narrow allure
I could possibly lust for
Long for

I of a darker hue
Was enamored with his
Skin of golden honey
And lanky awkwardness
Just this side of being all arms and legs
I enjoyed
The ease with which he carried his
Erotic immaturity

I had wanted to know Marcus
Since sometime during our sophomore year
In the midst of our junior year track season
On a sunny spring afternoon
I sent Marcus the clearest message
Human eros has yet created

We both practiced late that day
I was practicing my high jump technique
Struggling to get my steps down
Just right
On the approach to the bar
He was running laps around the large field
With the high jump pit at the far west end

We both practiced late that day
I would constantly stop and gaze at his gangly easy stride
Each time that he came around the west bend
Into a line of sight that I could use
While not staring too long too hard
One long lap he ran
Two laps
Three laps
Then four, five, and many more
All the while I pretended to get my steps down

But all I could think about
Was wanting to see Marcus
In the shower
Hoping that no one else would be there
In the shower
I could taste the vision clearly
Nibbling on it once, twice, and more

After many laps
I finally gathered the courage
To speak to him
As he came around the west bend
One more time

"Gettin' all the workout you can handle?" I asked. He nodded yes.

"Me too. I still can't seem to count out these steps right. How many more laps you got to go before you call it a day?" I asked as he turned on his heels and headed away from me. Marcus held up three fingers.

Good, I thought. *Now I can resume my count.* Even I could focus long enough to count to three.

After his second lap, I looked over my shoulder to make sure that he was being true to his three fingers as he once again headed around the edge of the west bend. Suddenly my heart dropped. Instead of continuing down the north side of the cinder track, he headed up the north ramp, away from the oval, away from the field, away from the desire I couldn't help but hold on to much too tightly. The heavy high jump pit had to be put away and locked up, which would take several minutes, and I might miss my opportunity to share my shower alone with Marcus. "Damn!"

I hurriedly dragged the awkward, overstuffed bag that was the high jump practice pit into the holding shed, nearly pulling a muscle in my efforts to move too much weight far too fast. I quickly added the pole standards and the bar itself, and locked them up safely. I started toward the north ramp several yards away, running as fast as I could. Then I looked down at my watch and saw that nearly 20 minutes had passed by then. I was sure I had missed Marcus's shower. Our shower. Together. So I stopped. I stood. And I began to cry. Again. This had been my chance, my one shot at sharing a moment of concealed longing. If only for the five or ten minutes that hot water would be able to pump out of the spigots of the showers that were too old. All because I didn't want to be too obvious to wait for him while stretching down in the off-side gym. To wait for him as he finished his laps. To wait for him to pass a glance my way. Maybe he would even smile at me. I had missed my chance. And the tears would not stop falling.

Once inside the athletic building, as I slowly headed toward the locker room, I heard water running. From a distance, I couldn't tell if it was a toilet flush, a sink faucet, or the shower. It was a long, steady stream. One of the showers was still running! Marcus was still there.

As quickly as I could, I ripped off my practice gear and took off my shoes and socks, and I was buck naked as I approached my locker. In that moment of strong desire, I suddenly could not remember the combination to the locker. But I tried. Once. Twice. Again. Forget it. I hurried over to the towel tray, grabbed a towel and, with the attempted expression of nonchalance, slowly stepped into the shower area. Two steps inside this nearly hollow, tiled space, I saw him, standing with his ass cheeks facing me, the water gently running down his back. I could barely keep myself from running to him, grabbing him, and trying to live out a movie scene of mad passion shared between two lovers. But the images inside my mind did not contain two gay young men of African descent who wanted to want each other. It was time to rewrite the script.

I walked to an adjacent spigot attached to the first of the eight standards that made this open shower area a young gay man's paradise of eye candy. Marcus was at the next spigot over, attached to the same standard. It was like he had been waiting for me. Ripe. Ready. Ripe. He turned toward me without meeting my eyes. He simply closed his, and gently tilted his head back just a bit.

I moved closer to him, and saw that Marcus's eyes were slightly open. Open enough to move still closer to me, to almost touch my thigh against his own. I bent over and took him in my mouth. Hearing his gentle moan, I felt the hum that let me know he too wanted me to do just what I had done. He backed away from the water so I wouldn't drown as the shower spigot continued sending water rushing down the front of his body. Then, just as Marcus began to move to meet my motion—John walked into the shower area! And suddenly both Marcus and I wanted to disappear, to be anyplace else but there.

I quickly stood up, hitting my head on one of the soap dispensers that stuck out from the standards. Marcus grabbed his bar of soap from the tray nearby and began washing himself with his washcloth at a feverish pace. We both turned away from the direction John was walking toward, so as not to further reveal our erotic excitement for each other. My head was moving in many directions at once, trying to decide what to do and how to do it to somehow make this moment disappear. And all the while, in trying to cover up and hide our shared desire, Marcus and I missed the fact that John had simply said, "Hey guys. How's it goin'?" with a wave and had walked right past us without reacting in any visible way to the sexual scenery he was suddenly a part of. Realizing that fact after a few moments helped my heart slow down, if only just a bit.

John was a sophomore, and since Marcus and I were both juniors, the status difference alone allowed us the immediate possibility of denial of circumstance. John was also white. So the folks he was likely to mention anything to would also be white, minimizing the likelihood of a trickle down of rumor to the cool pose' crowd of young brothers who defined my self-worth. The first thought, of course, was what to say — should John choose to mention what he saw to anybody—so as to sustain and perhaps even magnify the myth of my "straightness." I would come up with something and meet with Marcus the next day to confirm a consistent story. That was my decision.

Truth is, no decision was ever necessary. If John ever said anything to anyone, it never got back to me. And for that I was thankful. If it ever got back to Marcus, I would not have known. From that day forward, for sometime thereafter, Marcus maintained a silent distance between us that hurt me endlessly each time we passed each other in the hall or talked among our common friends at lunch. Or showered after track practice. The counting of the steps of my high jump approach had less and less meaning over the remaining weeks of the season. I almost quit the team on more than one occasion, but decided to stick with it so that my jock ego and I could letter in another sport besides basketball.

I didn't run track my senior year. No need to. Not much value in it. Marcus had all but washed his hands of me. And it hurt too much to have to think back to that spring afternoon when he and I had an April shower of shared desire, if only for a moment or two.

The Incomplete Reunion

by Spike Katz

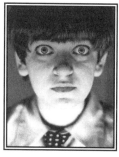 

– *1965* –   – *1997* –

Summer 1995. Carnegie High School 30th Reunion. Pittsburgh, Pennsylvania.

It was a hoot I was not going to miss. True, I had left my hometown in 1965 at a run and had never looked back. In fact, I have increased the distance between us with each subsequent move: 1,000 miles to Boston, 3,000 to San Francisco, 7,000 to the Middle East. Now that I had settled in London for a while, I guess I was slowly approaching home again. I had not been in touch with any old high school friends in 30 years and in the intervening period had been through numerous revolutionary movements, levels of brain damage due to hallucinogenic overuse, love affairs, relocations, career changes, and broken bones.

I had convinced Sarah, my main ex from London, to come along. I signed her up as "spouse" in the prereunion questionnaire from which they were going to produce a mini yearbook. What to wear to ensure an appropriate entrance? She came in her black PVC miniskirt with her low-cut silver bodysuit, accented by rhinestone jewelry. I put my turquoise satin sports jacket over a white ruffled formal shirt and white pants, accessorised with a complementary rhinestone western tie and cufflinks. I was the butchest thing in the room and she the most dazzling knockout. Our unspoken aim was not only to be excessively up-in-your-face, but also to make everyone else eat their hearts out.

As we entered the hotel ballroom, a tall man with a mustache came running up. "Susie Katz! I heard you were coming, and I've been waiting for you to arrive." No one had called me Susie since '65. "It's been 30 years, but I wanted to apologize to you."

I looked at his name tag, which like everyone's was thoughtfully accompanied by the original yearbook picture of the guest, and tried to dredge up some memory attached to the name Peter. "I'm Peter Calber. I was a real pig to you in high school. Since then I've been through a lot of changes, learned a lot from the feminist movement, and I know that I owe you an apology."

Peter Calber. Yeah. He was the anti-Semite who gave me the nickname "nose," the one who used to call me queer.

"Well, that's a good start," Sarah whispered. "Accosted by a repentant man. Could be worse."

"Let's not take it personally," I told her. "It's probably just the requirement of some American recovery program or other."

The evening progressed in a sequence of embraces, my corrupted memory aided by sneaked views of the invaluable photos on the name tags. I was choked up to be reunited with my best friend, Miriam, and then astonished when she confided that she had been screwing my racist brother in his next-door bedroom during our senior year. I was confounded by Dave Golden's claim that we used to snog in between folksinging gigs, and I was amazed by the band. The musical director was the son of the leader of the combo that had played at our prom, so he had access to that original playlist. He was less an imitation than a clone of his naff dad—it was a weird touch to the evening. But Sarah and I, activists in the London queer ballroom and Latin American dance scene, welcomed the admittedly pathetic covers of Chubby Checker and Atlantic Records hits. We were the hottest jivers on the floor.

But where was Janey?

*   *   *

I was 15 in 11th grade when she moved to the neighborhood and joined our class. Janey. Ginger-haired, delicate, modest chin, immodest nose—she was shy and mysterious. Miss Bochichio, spinster extraordinaire, changed my life by asking me to take the new student around.

Janey and I became "best friends," a term which rapidly took on expanded dimensions. Had it not been 1963, but 1863, we would have been romantic friends; had it been 1973, we would have been lovers. But "best friends" worked for us. It meant we could double-date and then go home and have a sleepover. There was, on those occasions, more over than sleep.

Janey dated Elbar, a beautiful boy of black and native American heritage—surely gay in later years. And I dated Langston, the first black president of the student body, the captain of our football team, and a member of our fledgling civil rights group. There was a lot of resistance to such interracial socializing, and I had my ass kicked more than once: by the black girls who resented my taking one of theirs, and by the white boys, led by my brother, who feared their own inadequacies.

Somehow we could deal with the racist reactions to our rather innocent dates, but all hell broke loose when my mother discovered Janey and me, during one of our regular sleepovers, head to foot, so to speak. She called Janey's mother, who came over to jerk her home. My mother closed me into my room with silence.

The next day she told me to dress well, that we had an appointment.

She had contacted the local Jewish welfare agency that provided social services to poor and working-class Jews. I had an appointment with a psychiatrist.

It would take another decade before homosexuality was deleted from the official American medical list of psychotic disorders. It was still the time of aversion therapy, forced psychotherapy, lobotomies, and incarceration. This shrink was a sick man, hungry for the details of our liaison, excited by the minutia of invert lovemaking, thrilled to have a case that apparently supplied fodder for his private wanks. It was hideous, but I was a helpless teenager, dependent on my parents and their compulsion to cure me. None of the adults ever spoke the *L* word or referred to the "problem" directly. My mother just called it "going to the doctor." None of my peers ever knew.

Janey suffered more. Banned from any contact, I only found out days later that she had slit her wrists in such a serious attempt at suicide that she would never again have full use of her left hand. Purely by accident, Elbar found her soaking her mattress red, and her life was saved. While she was being operated on, her mother, in a brutally misguided gesture of "generosity," had a plastic surgeon perform a nose job on her. She awoke from surgery with a reluctance for life and the face of a pug-nosed stranger.

She never returned to finish our last semester at school. During the summer we managed to contrive only a few illicit meetings before I flew off in September to university on the East Coast. Janey remained to work as a salesgirl in a local jewelry shop. We never knew what had hit us, for without language we were unable to form an understanding. The terms queer and lesbian were loaded with evil baggage. The concepts of closet, coming out, and gay liberation were not yet born.

At university I was a stranger in a strange land, a Midwest inner-city hick with a beehive in the midst of sophisticated private-school products, a working-class Jew serving fast-food French fries to my peers who had never had a job, a peacenik among sorority girls. When Janey turned up at my dorm six months later, it was difficult to listen to her. "I've found out what we are. We are lesbians," she told me.

To my shame, I turned her away. "Not me. I'm not a sick psycho. You might be one of those, but I certainly am not." I could not bear being any more different than I already was. She showed uncharacteristic perseverance, getting a job and renting a nearby apartment. Eventually she realized that I couldn't handle it and went back home.

I got a call at the dorm a couple of months later. She was breathless, moaning. "I'm with Langston right now," she told me, "and I wish it were you." There was a rhythm to her breathlessness as if someone were pounding on her chest. "I'm losing my virginity right now. I love you. I love you. I love you." I hung up on her mantra and ran out to spend a week sleeping with a string of men.

*   *   *

The key speaker at the reunion was the present principal of Carnegie High: none other than Langston. He had gone into education, and when the school had disintegrated into massive gang-fighting and vandalism in the '80s, they invited him back to take it in hand. He had turned the school around, using his old contacts with our schoolmates —now the parents of his students—to encourage community involvement. Langston had married the girl he had dumped to go out with me three decades earlier, and she wouldn't look at me or allow him to speak to me throughout the reunion.

Sarah and I were the most interesting phenomenon of the evening. Everyone wanted to buy us drinks, know the history of our relationship, listen to her English accent. The men all asked her to dance; the women all asked me. The men preached testimonies to how I had changed their lives. I asked my old best friend, Miriam, about it. "I don't remember being popular in high school. I remember being utterly out of it, in fact."

"No, you weren't popular. But you were powerful."

Were we an object of titillation or a symbol of freedom to these people? Were their lives the drab ruts we queers too often arrogantly assume of middle-aged straights, or were they truly tuned in? We didn't feel objectified; we felt heartily welcomed. We only wondered where the hell the other gay men and lesbians, were because not a single person came out to us. Perhaps it had never occurred to them to come in the first place.

As for those who did turn up, the men were unrecognizable—after all, at 18 they had still been boys not yet fully grown. The women seemed much more familiar, and all looked like fabulous mature versions of themselves.

Funny that the one person I simply could never forget did not attend. No one knew where Janey was today, and in fact, few remembered her at all. She had always been the comfort in the background, the softness around the edge of any picture.

Throughout out the evening, my inability to put faces to events persisted, and I had to turn to Miriam to fill me in. "Who's that?"

"You must remember her, she was on your majorette team."

One very beautiful woman gushed all over me when I saw her. I had a funny flashback that I had known her, intimately. "Who's that?" I asked Miriam. "I've got a feeling that I've slept with her."

"Oh, for God's sake. That's Eileen Lattle. The homecoming queen. The one with the red Thunderbird convertible. You're just remembering your fantasies—the same ones probably every single man and woman here shared with you in those days. You didn't sleep with her. She was too busy going out with all the most popular boys."

Later in the evening, while Sarah and I were doing the twist with the rest of the crowd, Eileen twisted over in my direction. "Do you remember?" she whispered in my ear. "You taught me how to twist—in your bedroom." She winked and twisted away.

Standing Up for Mr. Peters

by David Garnes

– *1959* –   – *1996* –

The last time I heard about Mr. Peters was one day several years ago during a weekly phone call to my mother. "Didn't you have an English teacher named Mr. Peters?" she asked. "He died down south, in Ormond Beach, Fla. He was 88."

I hadn't thought about Mr. Peters for a long time, and it startled me to realize that he had been almost 90. It was also difficult for me to picture tweed-coated, pipe-smoking Mr. Peters in a tropical retirement community, sitting out his old age in the shade of a palm tree.

The Mr. Peters I knew was a vigorous man of 50 or so, tall and trim with wavy gray hair, horn-rimmed glasses and a vaguely British accent. Mr. Peters was chairman of the English department at the high school

I attended in a middle-sized city in Massachusetts. This was during the late 1950s, *Grease* time, except that at my school no one wanted to look anything like the hoody John Travolta character. Mohair sweaters and flannel pants, white bucks à la Pat Boone, and a Perry Como "continental" haircut defined the look for me and my would-be Ivy League friends.

I was 16 at the beginning of my senior year, quiet and studious. I had skinny arms and legs and on a good day could manage maybe two chin-ups in gym class. I was shy and had difficulty feeling at ease in a crowd. But I was smart, and back in those days being a "brain" at my school carried a definite cachet. Smart, in fact, was the only thing about me that I really liked, yet it wasn't quite enough to compensate for my frequent feelings of isolation.

I had known I was "queer"—not '90s queer, '50s queer—from the age of seven. I am precise about this fact because I can clearly remember the summer between second and third grade when I observed a swimming instructor at camp taking off his clothes. Watching this teenage counselor undress every day is the only memory I have of that vacation. Thus began my life as a boy who knew he liked other boys—and felt different and alone because of it.

My only true sexual experience so far—true in that it felt real to me—had been some experimenting with my best friend, Eddie, when we were in junior high school. But it was evident to me that these sporadic episodes with Eddie were definitely more meaningful for me than they were for him. Eddie and I never discussed our fumblings after the fact, and of course there was no one else I dared talk to, not in an era in which even Liberace was routinely asked in magazine interviews to describe the type of girl he wanted to marry—and obligingly did so.

As I began the 12th grade, I was happy with my schedule, especially my class with Mr. Peters. We were going to be studying classical influences on English literature, beginning with the ancient Greeks. Mr. Peters's classes were reputed to be like college seminars, and I anticipated a happy experience. I knew I was just the kind of serious student a good teacher like Mr. Peters would appreciate.

Even better, I had been assigned boys' patrol duty at a desk right outside Mr. Peters's classroom during the period immediately following English. I should explain about boys' patrol. During study periods, some students were asked to sit at portable desks at various locations around the school. We were expected to monitor whatever infrequent activity occurred in the corridors during classes. The year before I had happily occupied a location at the entrance to the boys' bathroom, where, by carefully maneuvering my desk, I was able to watch whoever was standing at the long marble urinal that ran the length of one side of the room. Shy I might have been in real life, but in my other, secret world I was already an accomplished voyeur.

One particular day after Mr. Peters's class I had taken my usual post in the quiet corridor near his room. Mr. Peters was free that hour too, and we had already had a few conversations. Soon he emerged for what I suspected was a midmorning smoke and coffee break in the teachers' lounge. Mr. Peters intimidated me a bit—all male adults did—but I was beginning to look forward to this daily routine.

When Mr. Peters returned a few minutes later, he paused as usual to speak to me. He stood close enough to my chair so that I was aware of his Old Spice aftershave and the whiff of his tweed coat, a nutty mix of tobacco smoke and wool. (Years later this combination of male smells continued to take me in an instant back to that school corridor.) Mr. Peters asked me if I was enjoying the Homer we were reading in class. He had a habit of gazing into the distance when he spoke, avoiding eye contact and smiling in a distracted way.

Mr. Peters then suggested that I read a recent book by Mary Renault called *The Last of the Wine,* which, he said, gave an excellent depiction of ancient Greece. He returned to his room to bring me his copy, and when he came back I stood up to thank him. As he gave me the book, Mr. Peters put his other hand around my shoulder and lightly traced a line down my back with his finger. He then held his open hand at the base of my spine. The only other movement I recall was the regular rising and falling of Mr. Peters's prominent Adam's apple, half visible at the top of his shirt collar. After several seconds, he moved away and returned to his room.

This pattern was repeated nearly every day for the next several weeks. Each morning I rose to attention as Mr. Peters walked down the corridor toward me, the tap-tap of the soles of his leather loafers echoing down the long hallway. Gradually Mr. Peters grew bolder in his gropings, although these corridor encounters never lasted more than a few seconds and I was never invited into his empty classroom. Mr. Peters continued to avoid looking at me during these moments. Sometimes he maintained a casual conversation, usually about what we had been reading that day in class.

Not surprisingly, I found myself increasingly preoccupied with thoughts of Mr. Peters, especially after I got home from school. At night in my bedroom I read Mr. Peters's copy of *The Last of the Wine*. I was transported to the Athens of Socrates and Plato and imagined myself as Alexis, the main character, who was in love with his wise and noble mentor, Lysis. I don't remember being physically attracted to Mr. Peters, however, not in the way I was to Mr. White, who taught physics and coached the football team. But Mr. White and I had no daily contact, and so my fantasies regarding him were similar to those I had of movie stars like Alan Ladd and Robert Taylor (interestingly, both older actors at the time): vivid and intense, but safe. Mr. Peters, on the other hand, was having quite a bit of contact with me every day, and consequently our situation began to dominate my thoughts and influence my behavior.

One night I looked up Mr. Peters's telephone number in the phone book, and while my parents were in the living room watching Milton Berle dressed up as Carmen Miranda, I dialed his house. I listened while he said hello several times before I carefully placed the telephone back on the receiver. If Mr. Peters's wife answered, I hung up. I made this phone call many times over the next few weeks.

Who knows how long this singular relationship might have continued or where it might have led? As it happened, one day a couple of months into our corridor encounters, things rapidly and irrevocably unwound.

I had just finished a particularly grueling gym class. The exercise that morning involved the dreaded climbing ropes, and I had managed to make it hand-over-hand about ten feet off the ground before sliding back down. Still, this was a real accomplishment for me. I was aware, however, of the barely concealed scorn of Mr. Valley, our local athlete-turned-gym teacher, and my hands had already started to hurt from rope burn.

As I sat dressed in the locker room, I became jittery and preoccupied. I began to think of my upcoming class with Mr. Peters. Lately I'd find myself slouching down in my chair, hoping he wouldn't call on me, waiting for the bell to ring. I hardly ever raised my hand anymore. Did I detect a slight smirk this particular day when my friend Wally said, "See you in Mr. Peters's class" as he left the locker room? I remember that my hands were shaking as I rolled up my wet towel.

A few minutes later I eased myself into my back-row seat just as the bell rang and Mr. Peters closed his classroom door. We were discussing Plato's *Symposium,* probably a letdown for most of the class after the earlier adventures of Odysseus. No one-eyed monsters or enticing sirens here, just a bunch of boring men lounging around the dinner table and talking endlessly about philosophical matters of one kind or another.

But I had read *The Last of the Wine,* and I knew what was really going on. These were the kinds of intimate evenings the young Athenians Alexis and Lysis spent together with their friends. When these men discussed the meaning of friendship and love, they were talking about themselves. And by extension, they were also talking about me. I was nervous about how Mr. Peters would proceed that day.

"So, who is this dinner guest Alcibiades?" Mr. Peters began. "Who would like to tell us something about him?" It was not unusual for Mr. Peters to call on me first thing. I hoped he would choose someone else today, but this was not to be the case.

"David?"

I didn't look up, and I felt my face turn scarlet. Mr. Peters had asked me about Alcibiades, the beautiful symbol of Greek manhood, the lover of Socrates, the object of everyone's rapt attention after he arrives late at the dinner party. I gripped the sides of the desk. "I can't," I replied, my voice barely audible.

"I'm not sure I understand," said Mr. Peters.

"I didn't do the assignment," I finally croaked. "I didn't read it. I don't know who he was."

I don't remember the rest of the class, except that Mr. Peters quickly called on someone else. What I do recall is that when the bell rang I raced to the boys' room and was violently sick.

I knew Mr. Peters would have left for his break by the time I got back to my patrol post. I considered going to the nurse and telling her I needed to go home, but I had never done anything like that before. Besides, even that effort seemed more than I could manage. Instead, I slumped down in my hallway desk and awaited the inevitable.

I heard the sound of Mr. Peters's footsteps as he approached. Maybe he expected me to stand up as usual that day, but I didn't. For a moment I wanted to. I wanted to tell him that I wasn't stupid and that I had done my assignment and that I did know who Alcibiades was. But I didn't, and when he reached down and touched my shoulder, I backed off with such force that the desk almost tipped over. Mr. Peters turned and walked quickly into his classroom.

It was easy the next morning to convince my mother that I was still sick, since I had gone to my room as soon as I arrived home the previous afternoon. I spent most of the day planning my strategy. I knew I could never go into Mr. Peters's classroom again. I had acted like a fool. I had appeared stupid in front of the whole class. And the idea of having to face Mr. Peters was out of the question. He must think I was an idiot too, and I had made things even worse by pushing him away in the corridor. But I don't remember feeling angry at him.

By the following morning I had it all worked out. I went to see the school counselor. I told her I finally agreed with her that it would be better for me to have another science class instead of the history elective I had chosen that year. Was it too late to switch?

And so ended my time with Mr. Peters. My boys' patrol duty got changed to the afternoon, to another floor near a rear emergency exit.

The school building was big and rambling, and I saw Mr. Peters only a couple of times a month. At first he nodded to me when we passed in the hallway and I responded in kind, but as the year progressed we stopped acknowledging each other altogether.

Looking back, I realize Mr. Peters was probably relieved at this tepid outcome of our risky and potentially disastrous encounters. Perhaps he had been worried that I would reveal what had been going on. Of course, I never even considered telling on Mr. Peters, because that would have meant telling on me too. In fact, I didn't talk about Mr. Peters to anyone for a very long time.

I did not come out fully as a gay man until several years later, when I moved to New York after college to do graduate work in English. During the first week of classes at Columbia, in the checkout line at Salter's Bookstore on Broadway, I met someone I'll call Max. Max was a middle-aged instructor at Barnard, and he took me back to his apartment on 115th Street that afternoon.

I'm sure that at some point in our relationship I must have told Max about Mr. Peters, and we probably laughed at the fact that Max taught English, too. I do know that by then I had ceased judging Mr. Peters's behavior, and I chose instead to believe that perhaps he had sensed in me a younger version of himself. I like to think that Mr. Peters introduced me to *The Last of the Wine* to make me comfortable with a world that no one had revealed to him as a young man. In this respect, he succeeded.

Survivors

Home

by Michael Floeck
Dedicated to Jeffrey Laham

My head is sort of swimming, I am thinking of that seventh grade picture of me and it looms out, enlarges with those young flushed cheeks, neatly combed hair and white shirt, with those eyes looking out of that picture so quiet, so white bread and quiet bred on Lassie and Lucy wanting laughter and adventure, but never venturing far away from home, never too many friends to stray me. Always with my own agenda, and that was to get away by myself, keep a heavy coat on, keep myself from the pain my mother and grandmother fought about. My mother drank and gambled, and drank some more to fuel herself for more gambling, and I took another step inside away, and yet I was her shield. Let me run defense, let me live my childhood through your anguish if that's what you need, and you said and I said and the anguish bled under the floor like blood in a Stanley Kubrick film, and when I couldn't stomach any more I got sick or whittled away my time counting records, putting them in order of my favorites, or sitting on my stairs above the traffic masturbating, rubbing myself in my pants at the top of the stairs in the daylight, waiting for my mother who never came home. And I was quiet, so quiet unless she was hurt, and then I rose to defend. I want to throw up my life thinking about those times caught inside me and my childhood lost to the blank walls, the neatly decorated living room walls, lost moving every two years, people asking me why I went to so many schools. I couldn't say because my mother couldn't pay the rent, I couldn't say because my grandmother hated each apartment and it became another "hole" she had to endure, and so I had to endure, another year, another moment of my life lived wondering if the rent was going to be paid the next time it was due, wondering if my mother had lost the rent money gambling.

I grew up in the same Los Angeles streets as both my mother and father and even went to the same elementary school, but whereas that may have been the only elementary school they each went to, I went to six different ones. We moved apartments in that neighborhood all around the house my grandmother once owned where she raised her family, and for three years in junior high school I went to just one school, but moved all around it. And I was shy, quiet as a student, and in my PE class was diagnosed with a spinal sway as many of us new recruits were. There were medical words I had never heard used to describe a variety of spinal malformations we didn't even know we had until we were told. I didn't know my lower back swayed and I don't know what they did to correct the diagnosis except brand us, moving us to a "special" PE class where the misfits assembled. I was walking in a world I didn't understand that I didn't know anything about. I had never climbed a rope to the ceiling and somehow never had boy friends to play sport games with. I didn't know what soccer was and there was no one to show me. I didn't have a father, he was dead, and I lived in the specter of his glorious shadow. I didn't think of how he let me down by his death, didn't think about my mother convincing him to go back to war to make a living killing. I didn't think why, I just accepted my fate and tried to swallow my life with whatever childhood amusements I could, but I had no socialization skills, and the older bully boys with a more mature knowledge, with crazy leers on their faces and hair on their dicks because they were bigger, although they didn't know anything they knew to tease me. They somehow got my clothes out of my gym locker one day and threw them up to the ceiling pipes, as if I was raised in my incapacity for more humiliation. So I was quiet, I didn't know anything about what was going on and why it didn't make much sense, I just endured like my heart would break if I thought about it, and no one told me to just exercise, to get physical. Of course at home, they didn't know how I felt and didn't take time to care, I was always in the way. My grandmother wished I wasn't there and spent the day in her slippers and robe, with rotting Kleenex bits trailing after her, while she clutched the sink, her dentures in a cup, and took a swig of port wine from the upper cabinet, and my mother was gone somewhere. It wasn't much of a life to grow up in to naturally unfold my creative talents, but just survive.

After I graduated junior high school my mother married a blackjack dealer and we moved to Las Vegas where I started high school and lived for the first time in a family structure with two parents. Summer came and my mother went somewhere, back to California maybe, and left her husband and me living together in a motel room. One night he tried to molest me and then blackmail me so I wouldn't tell her, as if I could tell her about his mouth on my dick. The next morning there was nowhere else to go; I took the bus to my grandmother's in Los Angeles and we lived together for a time in a small house my mother rented for us, but she wasn't there at all. I remember the Stones' song "(I Can't Get No) Satisfaction" on the radio; it was 1964. A black man tried to pick me up one afternoon as I walked alone on the street to school. My cousin had bleached her hair and experimented on mine and made a mess; it was a strange strawberry blond and I felt very different, odd in the difference, and must've looked very queer, that was how I felt in my near-virgin adolescence on that hot-summer Los Angeles street. It was a new experience being cruised by this man in his slow-moving car; I didn't know I could have wanted him. I feared the unknown and certainly couldn't allow myself to take the ride. Summer ended and we moved and moved again, kept moving in some household combination of my mother, grandmother, and aunt in Los Angeles or my mother in Hawaii, living by myself in Hawaii, and then back to Los Angeles and finally back to Las Vegas. Eight high schools later, back to the first high school I had attended, where after the difficulty with residency they finally allowed me to graduate. Somehow throughout the changes I had maintained a GPA that got me into UCLA and moved out on my own just as I turned 17.

I thought freedom was something outside of myself, and I just wanted to get away. Nobody was there to care when I was growing up; it felt like everything that I was expected to know was assumed would just happen. I guess it's no wonder I never wanted to know what I was thinking. For years afterward I plunged like a child naked and dazed out of focus, parts of myself disoriented, chose freely to wander sabotaged, and searching men seemed an adventure. Some were wonderful new experiences, exciting or tender, while others were a mistake from the onset, but still I kept on seeking men stripped to the flesh to hold. Half naked in shadows of adult movie theaters, my mind overactive and exhausted from days of methedrine and cocaine, I never found what I wanted, I never wanted to stop to wonder what I wanted. I didn't want to think, just follow the drug drifting, the ocean tides, midnight rides; and side road fucks under the stars were sweet, to have found somebody to be there with for a moment, unraveling sexual intensity and the passion of strangers touching just once, just one more time, and I never formulated any other plans, couldn't motivate any desires, so when the time came I got sober and my sex life just stopped; that was 1989.

I never wanted to know what I was thinking until now. It makes sense; there was no reason to be anywhere with the adults I had to defend making their way around me, what could I know walling my heart in with dead bodies and sexual parts caught set adrift in a sea of loneliness flooding me, coming from and becoming me. Now the walls are not up in force as much as they are thinned, and my spirit is flapping about wanting to be free, because time has come I am faced with a part of myself I had stopped recognizing, parts of myself coming back for me to reclaim, drifting toward me in spontaneous reattachment, my wings, the few stray feathers that lighten my hold connect, and from a bed of unconscious skins I emerge intact.

Confrontation

By Robert Brown

I

To this day I don't understand how the game of "bombardment" can pass for physical education. It seemed that every time it rained during my sophomore year at Blacksburg High School, Coach decided that it was a good day to play bombardment. I recall distinctly how a knot would form in the pit of my stomach whenever he brought out the large mesh bag of ammunition. He dumped the rubber balls unto the floor, and the frontline bombardiers would rush to grab up the slightly deflated ones (these, as I recollect, produced more sting upon impact). Coach then divided us up into two teams, and we took our respective places on either side of the center line. The object of the game was rather straightforward: Ream the other team. If you were hit, you were "out." You then had to wait on the sideline until someone on your team caught a ball, thus allowing you to reenter the game.

Bombardment was the perfect outlet for the sadistic tendencies of adolescent boys. The structure of the game allowed for personalized assaults: A boy on one team could single out another on the opposing team for torture. A few kids, though, were not even safe from their own team members. I remember seeing one kid catch a stray shot in the back of the head. Accident? I didn't bother to ask the boys laughing behind him.

Fate would have it that my archnemesis always ended up on the other team. So, I spent the period watching the clock out of one eye and his movements out of the other. My enemy, however, was unpredictable. Some days he would seek me out for abuse, while other days he seemed not to notice me at all. Undoubtedly, his inconsistency made him even more effective as a bully. I never knew when to be afraid and when not to; consequently, I remained in a constant state of anxiety during gym class that year.

Even if I did make it through the game of bombardment unscathed, I still couldn't count myself home free. The severest trial was yet to come. At the end of the period we were given ten minutes to change back into our school clothes. (I think the state of Virginia mandated that there be enough time for kids to take showers. This was not our custom, however. And I am thankful.) It took only about half that time to put our clothes on, so until the bell rang we were free. Having long since accepted the maxim "boys will be boys," Coach left us to entertain ourselves.

During those idle minutes we would gather outside under an overhang where the buses unloaded. It was here that one day my bully confronted me. I was by myself, leaning against the brick wall when he approached. He swaggered over and planted himself squarely before me. He flashed a menacing grin: "What are you looking at?" Instantly, my body tensed, and my heart rate shot up. Terrified though I was, I tried to look calm, and I didn't dare say anything back. He repeated the question, this time punctuating it with a light tap on my shoulder. Again, I did nothing. He pushed me again, harder. I pressed my back flatter against the brick wall and braced myself for what I feared was coming.

At the time, I suppose, I was dimly aware of other people around us closing in anticipation of a fight. His friends were probably egging him on and taunting me with jeers, but nothing was comprehensible to me. The rush of adrenaline had warped my perception. The only thought in my mind was what I was going to do if he threw a punch. *Will I hit him back?* Clang. I was saved. When the bell sounded the circle of blood lust broke. I heard a few groans of disappointment as the boys dispersed. My bully took a step back, looked me up and down, and laughed: "I knew you were a faggot." Someone standing near him grabbed him in a headlock and gave him a noogie. I looked after them as they rounded the corner of the building out of sight. The threat had passed.

Suddenly I started to feel empty and cold. Sweat that had broken out over my body was beginning to cool in the morning air. As the flow of adrenaline ebbed, my higher-order thinking began to return. A new emotion rushed in to fill the cavity fear had left behind. Shame. It would be at least seven more hours before I could cry, and by then the urge would have passed. So, instead, I let myself go numb, completely numb. I picked up my books and made my way toward my second period class.

II

As an adult gay man looking back on the experience ten years ago, I wonder if I should have stuck up for myself. From a purely practical standpoint, I probably did the right thing in backing down. I had never been in a fight before in my life, and I'm sure I would have made a poor show of it had I decided to make this my first. No one could charge him, though, with picking on someone less than his size. By appearances, I had the clear advantage of height over my bully (I must have been at least a head taller). But in this case, my height would have done me little good. He was a thick, strong boy, and I was not. He would have beaten me up anyway, and I would have looked like a long, lanky goon. But as it turned out, I did not even have the satisfaction of looking like a goon, only a coward because I had refused to fight. A red-blooded boy would have defended himself when he was wronged, but instead, I was yellow and cowered. I was a failure to my gender, right? As woefully unenlightened as this reasoning appears to me now, it still manages to haunt me to some degree, and at the time of the confrontation with my bully, it consumed my thoughts.

The year I missed my chance to prove myself a man was also the year I lost my two best male friends. I never got so emotionally close to other boys in high school hereafter. I became increasingly aware of feeling different from other boys: I felt uncomfortable around them and did not speak their language. In their presence I felt too self-conscious of the way I talked, the way I carried myself. I did not attribute this sense of being different from other boys to any identifiable cause. Strictly speaking, I had no sexual identity at this time in my life. Although my homosexuality was present, it was tightly confined to the realm of fantasy, barred from entering my conscious mind by a denial so reflexive as to seldom even register in my thoughts. When I did think of my sexuality, I wondered if I lacked a sexual drive entirely, if somehow I was born to be asexual. In order to escape the discomfort of feeling different around boys, more and more I sought the company of girls.

Making friends with girls was comparatively effortless for me. I felt at ease around them; I could giggle and camp it up without having to worry about drawing their scorn. I was perfectly content just being one of the girls, yet when one of my girlfriends once told me something to this effect, I deeply resented it. The notion that my gender identity might be fuzzy confused and upset me; I was in no way ready at that time to reconsider my concept of masculinity. Instead, what I realized was that girls were as cognizant of the criteria of appropriate masculine behavior as were boys, and my girlfriend was not going to let me forget it.

When I got to college the situation remained much the same. My closest friends were female, and I continued to feel threatened and alienated by certain males. The days of overt physical intimidation had ended, but I still had to be on my guard. Though burdened with a sense of inferiority, I had by this time learned coping mechanisms for dealing with overbearing, macho types. I had taught myself how to feign a degree of poise and self-confidence even when I was not feeling it inside.

Another way I coped was to withdraw from the social scene. I concentrated my energy on my schoolwork and spent less time worrying about trying to fit in. Through observation and introspection I learned more about the kind of person I was and the kind of person I wanted to project to the world. I decided that I would have to invent new standards by which to judge my masculinity. As a gay man I would never be a real man, at least not by the commonly held definition. My homosexuality disqualified my masculinity, though it did not release me from having to measure up to those same standards. People would always judge me as a man, even though I would prove to be less than a man in their eyes if they suspected the truth of my sexuality. Unraveling this knotty double bind required that I redefine manhood in a way that made sense to me. Most important, I had to overcome the destructive notion that a man who loves other men forfeits his masculinity. Or, more to the crux of the matter, that gay men permit themselves to be feminized. Herein, I discovered, lies a vicious battle for gay men, to fight against men's general contempt of femininity: to be homosexual entails conscription into the campaign against sexism. This, I learned, was simply one of the trials of growing up gay. What remained for me to see, however, was how effectively I could overturn the gender indoctrination of my own childhood.

III

Recently, I dreamed about the confrontation with my bully. In the dream I decided to correct the error of the past and stand up to my aggressor. This time I arrived on the scene with an adult's understanding of the brutality and stupidity of the situation, and I was prepared to disarm him with my words. Yet when I opened my mouth to speak, I could find no words for my feelings. As I lost my ability to articulate, I lost all self-control. All I could manage was to sputter curses at him. My voice was not that of a man, but of an hysterical child. I continued to squeak my rage between fitful sobs until I had calmed to the point where I began to rue my outburst. I looked around me, and everyone in the circle was laughing at me. It was at this point in the dream that I woke up. Immediately the former feeling of self-loathing set in. In the moments before the dream sensation melted completely away I knew that I had lost again, this time without even the meager satisfaction of having grimly forborne. This time the feeling of humiliation was worse because the bully had defeated the man, not the boy. The pain of the memory brought to life in my dream was as fresh as the day I lived it. When the experience replayed itself, it resembled nothing like the noble act of perseverance I had constructed from later reflection on the event. Even though I tried to fight back in the dream, my weapons were useless, my words bore no barbs. All my fine rationalizations were futile in a situation where rational arguments were precluded. It seems apparent to me that my bully still lurks in my unconscious as the specter of all the intolerant heterosexual males I have lived in fear of. It is a fear I have not yet completely overcome. Reflecting on this dream summons up uncertainties about the security of my self-made gender identity. I know that am not impervious to disdain expressed through a half-guarded facial expression or an inflection of voice. I may have overcome my own shame of being gay, but I haven't yet acquired the self-assurance to brush off the censure of others. As it is, I find that I am still confronting my bully.

The Diary of "Anne Moore": Why I Was a Prepubescent Punching Bag

by Michele Spring-Moore

The summer I turned nine, just before I entered fourth grade, my family moved to a new neighborhood where my peers, both boys and girls, tormented me at school and especially on the afternoon school bus. They had tacit permission, if not outright encouragement, from the driver, whom my mother labeled "ignorant," her code word for the crude, ill-mannered, and often the working-class. His opinion of me became clear the afternoon my torturers, keen on getting me into trouble, told him that the girl who lived next door and I were whispering about him; the other kids were disappointed when he only sneered at us in the rearview mirror and said, "I don't care what those little fairies are sayin' about me!"

I was shocked; my father cursed and had been generally verbally abusive all my life, but none of the adults I knew called children names. Our neighborhood had a code of conduct in keeping with the residents' expectations of the suburbs. Most of these families of second- or third-generation Italian-, Polish-, Irish-, English-, and German-Americans, and a few African-Americans, had left the city behind, bought a house and three quarters of an acre in this new subdivision, and gotten busy making their way from the working class into the lower middle class. Even if they didn't like their neighbors, they would be civil.

But they couldn't keep their children from beating up others when the kids were out of sight. My classmates began abusing me as soon as I started fourth grade. The girls shoved me around at the lunch table and approached me as I worked at my desk, asking in distorted cartoon-character voices, "Are you a *queer*?" The whispering and name-calling often escalated into physical assault in junior high, where I committed ever-more-blatant gender crimes—carrying my books like a boy (held under one hand, both arms down at the sides of the body) instead of a girl (held in the crook of one arm, in front of the chest, as if cradling something precious), and wearing jeans, a zippered sweatshirt with a hood, and T-shirts printed with the likenesses of my heroes, such as Baretta, a tough working-class private detective played by Robert Blake on the TV cop show of the same name. I also committed geeky infractions such as reading chemistry books and writing in my journal on the bus, which earned me the moniker "Anne Moore" from high school boys who had to read *The Diary of Anne Frank* for English classes. That sort of teasing was relatively harmless, unaccompanied by physical attack. But kids my age punched and slapped me, and a couple of boys whacked me over the head with thick five-pound textbooks so often, some afternoons I wondered if I'd go home with a concussion. My mother advised me to develop a "thicker skin," and called other children's mothers to complain when the assaults got out of hand and I ended up at the breakfast table in tears, afraid to go to school.

All of this mystified me—why had these kids singled me out? I had a sense of myself as different, but in my school in 1972, *queer* meant weird, and I felt attracted only to boys' activities and privileges, not to any particular gender. This didn't change until I developed a crush on my physical education teacher when I was a high school sophomore, but even then I was so out of touch with my sexuality that I noticed only that I enjoyed watching her walk across the gym, and when I asked myself why, the closest I got to an answer was, "She's cool. She's just really cool."

I fought my peers' abuse with whatever weapons I could muster, especially when I sensed that my enemy was weaker than I. In one case I used racial prejudice—I called the stout brown-skinned Sicilian kid who used to slap me around before math class a "greaser." When a younger boy even nerdier than I began to ride the junior-senior high bus, I picked on him in the vain hope that it would make me look tougher and the other kids would leave me alone. A year or two later he tried to kill himself by overdosing on aspirin; his ambulance ride to the hospital to have his stomach pumped was the talk of the neighborhood for weeks. (I'm certain I had this in the back of my mind when I made an identical suicide attempt in my first year of college.)

I continued to escape through books, but I also became slightly more athletic. When I was a young child, my mother spent hours in conferences with my gym teacher, who was worried that I seemed so uncoordinated and was convinced that intelligence and academic achievement were closely linked to physical prowess; Mom informed her repeatedly that my reading scores were among the highest in my class. I remained physically slow for years, then suddenly developed an interest in baseball. For my 12th birthday my great aunt gave me a softball and my mother bought me a bat. I never joined or started a game with the serious neighborhood players, all boys, nor even learned the rules, but I spent many contented hours tossing the ball into the air and swinging at it or throwing it against the front steps, pretending to be Catfish Hunter, a pitcher who endorsed products advertised in my younger brother's *Boy's Life* magazines. My biggest surprise was that gym classes had suddenly changed from torturous to enjoyable. For some reason most of the other girls had stopped trying to do anything at all in PE, and the teacher began to compliment me after class on my soccer and basketball playing, which was still mediocre.

I didn't understand how I'd become a jock overnight; years later I made jokes about the other girls being "afraid to break a fingernail if they played." Only recently did I realize their sudden disinterest in sports was part of the passivity the overwhelming majority of girls began to learn to display at that age: Boys won't like you unless you give up what you've been all your life. With the onset of puberty, my friends stopped talking about which boys had cooties and began devising methods of "catching guys." Even then I wondered at this language, as if liking us was some sort of game we had to trick boys into playing. I ignored, and much of the time simply didn't comprehend, these new messages from my female peers, so although I was used to ostracization from those I considered enemies, I was stunned when my friends turned on me. As a preteen I loved slumber parties because we got to eat pizza and stay up till the wee hours to watch *Saturday Night Live* and old Doris Day movies on TV, but as we approached adolescence even these playgrounds became battlefields for me. At one party at my best friend's house, she and the other girls crowded around her vanity table for hours, applying makeup and gossiping about boys. I was bored, so I found my usual refuge in reading, starting the latest Stephen King horror novel. Then they decided that I needed to be made-up and descended upon me with mascara and a Maybelline eye shadow kit. I declined, they insisted, I refused, and they pinned me down on the bed where I lay with my hands pressed tightly over my closed eyes, shouting "No!" until one of my friends said, "Oh, let her go if she's going to be such a baby about it." I cried quietly while they resumed their posts at the mirror.

My usual enemies last attacked a year later, on Freshman Friday, a Churchville-Chili High School hazing tradition in which sophomores, juniors, and seniors lobbed eggs and rotten tomatoes at first-year students at the end of the first week in September. The gang of neighborhood kids who'd shoved me around for the past five years had gleefully warned me for months, "Just wait till Freshman Friday," so I was expecting at least a few mushy vegetables to sail my way, but nothing prepared me for what they'd cooked up. On the morning bus they threw eggs at my head; I didn't bother showering during the day because I expected another assault at any moment. I still remember the sight of thousands of minuscule bits of dried yolk falling out of my hair and making spiky patterns on my desktops in various classrooms.

On the afternoon bus, kids of all ages spent the 45-minute ride home covering me with shaving cream, more eggs, baby lotion, and a foul-smelling dark concoction; they loudly enumerated the ingredients, but the only one I recall now is dog shit. After I'd sat in my seat (I had a good portion of the bus to myself because no one else wanted to be baptized in goo) and taken this for a while, it occurred to me that I really had nothing to lose. For some reason, three of my nastiest torturers of the previous few years had worn dressy black clothes that day. As they approached for another round of smashing eggs, shrieking, and hitting me, I smeared them with the glop. They seemed shocked; apparently they hadn't expected meek Michele to fight back. They stepped up the attack, but by then I no longer cared—when you're dripping a salad-dressing-and-dog-shit mix, things can't get much worse. The driver got into trouble that evening for returning to the garage with a filthy vehicle, so he reported the kids to the administration. They sat in their usual spots in the back of the bus and screeched "Narc!" at him for the next couple of months, but they also pretty much left me alone until we graduated.

The "Why me?" mystery was solved after high school. I came out to my friends that summer and started college in the fall at a small school in a suburb on the wealthier side of the county. In October I attended my first Lesbian Resource Center meeting at the Gay Alliance office in the city. Afterward some of the women took me to my first lesbian bar where, standing in the lurid red dance floor light, I saw the chief tormentor of my youth. I was as afraid as I'd been on the school bus when I was 12 and she 13, but when I walked back to the bar and told my new acquaintances that someone from my high school was there, they asked if I'd said hi to her. It hadn't occurred to me that our statuses had changed, but when the young woman saw me later on the dance floor, she was quite friendly.

She was only the first. Nearly all of the kids who had slapped, punched, and insulted me showed up during my college years at that or another gay bar—the guy who'd made snotty comments in front of my friends in high school about my hair, makeup, and wardrobe, the girl who'd missed no opportunity to make me miserable in fifth grade, the boy I'd called a greaser. Encountering these former classmates inspired in me a wary sense of solidarity—I knew intellectually that now that we were grown-up and gay, we had in common at least the coming-out process that had led us to this particular watering hole. But I couldn't forget their having picked on me for the preceding ten years, and every time I saw another of them in the bars, I understood a little more that they had taken out on me what the culture had dumped on them. My pubescent peers saw their problems with gender and sexuality clearly written on my body, and did their best to scrawl their own graffiti, with and without dog feces.

Hearing Voices

by David Ortmann

– 1982 –   *– 1997 –*

Seventh period—chemistry. Only eighth period gym class after this and then—home—to my precious books. Reading became my life when other worlds proved unsatisfactory at 15 years old. A mousy-haired, effeminate boy, whose voice had not yet changed and whose body had not yet caught up with the growth spurts of his other limbs, I had already realized that I could survive better in worlds of my own creation.

I had been called "fag," "queer," "pansy," "cocksucker," and countless other names for as long as I could remember. I bore them all in silence, knowing that life would be better once I reached the end of adolescence. Then I would lift weights, race cars, date girls, and get my secret revenge on anyone who had ever used names and boots and fists to re-mind me that I was different from other boys. This did not come to pass; not even a simple attraction to girls which, for this lonely boy growing up in New Jersey and attending John F. Kennedy Memorial High School, was the most important thing in the world for acceptance by his peers.

For me, chemistry class was the worst because the teacher, Ms. Frico, was always late. This allowed for plenty of social time, which led to talking, which led to "fag" jokes, which led, always, to me.

Joe Clayton, who wore jeans so tight that I couldn't help but find myself staring at his gorgeous legs and buttocks, was laughing with Denise Katrina, a cheerleader with breasts of mammoth proportions, about the purported gay sexual orientation of a classmate. "So Denise, do you think he's a fag?"

"I dunno." Denise sucked away at a Hershey bar she'd just bought from Frank Catalano to support JFK's wrestling team.

Joe turned to wink at me in a way that made me hate him and hate myself more for noticing how beautiful his blue eyes were. "No, really, Denise, what do you think?"

The door opened and the teacher, Ms. Frico, entered. Thank God. No more jokes—just chemistry where everything had a "yes" or "no" answer and none of the indefinites I was forced to deal with in the out-side world. In this respect, once called to order, class was a safe haven for me. Unbeknownst to Joe and Denise, Ms. Frico overheard half of their conversation. "Yeah, Denise what do you think?" she ask as she crossed the room to her desk smiling.

"I dunno." Denise threw back her mop of dyed blond hair and laughed at being caught discussing a topic that was "taboo."

Ms. Frico looked directly at me, smiled, and said, "Joe, why don't you just ask Mr. Ortmann. He should know. He's a fag."

For a moment there was unbelieving silence and then the next minute half the kids in class were laughing, pounding on their desks, and spilling out of their seats into the aisle. The rest of the class con-tinued to stare, disbelieving. At that moment I instantly understood the term "fire in the belly," and this was years before reading Robert Bly. My gut burned. My spine tightened and cracked. My throat immediately went dry. Flushing crimson, beads of sweat broke out on my brow. I dared not move as I felt like I could cry, puke, shit, and piss all at once. I wanted to run. Run home. Run somewhere…anywhere but here. But I just sat there, unbelieving…

This is not supposed to happen!!! A teacher can't say that!

But she did. She said it and everyone heard. The next 45 minutes of chemistry class loomed ahead of me like a doctor's needle must loom to a feverish toddler. I could not contemplate how terrible eighth period gym was going to be for me once word got out in the halls that Ms. Frico called David Ortmann a fag in front of the whole class and he just sat there.

*   *   *

It has been ten years since I graduated from JFK High School. Aside from the incident I described above, I had been told many times, directly and indirectly, by students and teachers alike that the world would never accept me. The singular rationale for this rejection was that I had always been labeled "the fag."

I was personally physically and verbally bashed by both students and teachers countless times throughout my four long years at JFK. At the time I had no clear idea of what being gay meant, with the exception of stereotypical comic relief characters on television shows like *Soap,* in bad Eddie Murphy films, and in jokes that filled playgrounds, living rooms, and hallways. I just knew that I was different from other kids, and "faggot" was the name attributed to me for as long as I could remember.

In June of 1987 I was handed my high school diploma from my senior class adviser. She said sarcastically, "I doubt you'll really get anywhere…but good luck anyway." Ten years later I am happy to report that life could not be more wonderful or fulfilling. After completing my undergraduate degree with honors and working as an educator and conflict specialist in the beautiful and rich Czech Republic, I embarked on a three-year commercial and theatrical acting career in Washington, D.C. Although successful, I felt I was somehow being called to work with disenfranchised youth. I have recently relocated to California's Bay Area to begin my graduate degree and work in social intervention with youth and persons with AIDS.

Since JFK was a place where I could not be who I am without the threat of physical and verbal violence from staff and students alike, it is impossible for me to attribute my eventual success to the school—although I often wish I could say otherwise.

I still hear Ms. Frico's voice and the voices of the many others who have tried to discourage me, shame me, or stop me throughout the years. These voices that used to make me cry and pray at night never to wake again have become the same voices that propel me forward. They remind me of where I've been and what I endured there. I continue to work toward a future where everyone, regardless of sexual orientation, physical ability, race, religion, gender, and socioeconomic condition, is afforded equal opportunity and treated with the respect due all human beings. This is as it should, and will, be. In retrospect, I guess I did learn some important lessons at JFK—in spite of, not because of, the school.

Ready to Try

by Scott A. Giordano

The cold New England wind blew on my face as I sat by the railroad tracks deciding whether my life was worth living. I was just 16 years old—only a boy—yet I was faced with such intense loneliness, isolation, and misunderstanding. So many memories rushed through my head.

I took out Sean's picture and clenched it to my heart.

Sean was one of Walpole High School's top hockey players. He was tall and slim with pale white skin, jet-black hair and ice-blue eyes. I had met him through a mutual friend who was my next-door neighbor at the time. I spoke to him a few times, and we even spent a few nights together as friends, but I never truly got to know him as a person.

Rather, I quickly developed my own image of him in my mind. I saw the person I wanted him to be, not the person he truly was.

Having known him for little more than one month, I wrote Sean a long letter telling him how much I admired and loved him as a friend. The next day, my letter was the hottest gossip among my classmates. I was ridiculed at every corner of the school halls and in every classroom. I even remember one of my teachers holding back his laughter one day when he overheard a group of students verbally harassing me. Other teachers simply ignored my emotional abuse, leading me to believe they didn't care.

Periodically, the verbal abuse would turn physical, but not very often. The worst torture of all was my broken heart when Sean became one of tormentors. His insults cut through my heart like a knife and left me feeling alone and abused.

"Gay away from me you fudgepacker! Homo! Fairy! Faggot!"

I went to school every day listening to these words from Sean and all my other classmates, and they were all coming back to me as I sat alone by the tracks.

"What purpose is there to live if I can't love someone openly?" I asked myself. "How can I change this side of me when I've tried for so long and the feelings just won't go away? Does God love me this way? Would my family love me if they knew? Who can understand what I am going through? What do I have to look forward to in my life?"

So many questions and so few answers. Then the tears started to fall as I looked at Sean's picture before me and held it to my broken heart. I knew he could never be with me. Who would want to be with me? I had so few friends because I was the object of such ridicule everywhere I went, and I had such low self-respect. I started to believe all the negative remarks that were made about me. Maybe I was better off alone, or maybe I was better off dead.

The light beyond the tunnel turned green. The train was on its way. My heart was pounding with fear.

I held Sean's picture close to me one last time, and then I tore it to pieces and let it go, watching the bits blow with the New England wind. The tears filling my eyes, the train became more of a blur as I saw it speed closer. I stepped onto the tracks. I was prepared to die.

The train's whistle blew a deafening sound as it got near me. Then I jumped to the side of the tracks and watched the train speed by me with full force. All I could feel was the sharp wind blowing the tears off my face.

I just sat there alone and cried for what seemed to be a lifetime. No one was there to witness my pain or see how close I came to death. It was the love I had for my family that kept me alive, and the little self-respect I could find in myself.

At that moment, I realized that the question to ask myself was not "Is this how I want to die?" but "Is this how I want to live?"

So I became determined to take control of my own life. The shy and vulnerable little boy was all cried out, and now he was ready to become a man.

Today I am a gay man who is proud, but I'm still struggling to be happy. My high school experiences have left me with a distrust of people and a lack of social skills that still haunt me. Furthermore, I have spent far too much precious time being on the defensive and trying to prove myself to others rather than just enjoying the simple things in life.

Growing up without any friends, my only escape from my loneliness and pain seemed to be when I sat alone in my room and listened to the music of Madonna. She represented what I was striving to become: an independent, strong, and outspoken person. Through Madonna's indirect example, that is the person I eventually learned to be.

However, my time alone had some very serious side effects. Most notably, it kept me out touch with those around me, so I never learned how to socialize and interact with others.

The saying is true that "Children learn what they live." In high school I learned to survive by keeping to myself. As an adult, that is what I am so desperately trying to unlearn.

Consequently, I have never had the one thing in life I desire most: a loving relationship.

To this day, I have not found the courage to approach other men I am interested in, and the few times I have managed to approach men, I have failed to spark their interest.

I believe their lack of interest isn't due to my physical appearances, because many men have expressed a physical interest in me. My problem is my inability to carry on a casual conversation. I either try hard and come off as too strong and straightforward, or I will try too little and the men think I am not interested at all.

Although I do have many friends today, all of my friendships are with people I knew for a long time before we became friends: people I met in the gay student group at my college and coworkers from my previous jobs. All of my friends tell me they thought I was on the defensive when they first met me, and they are all right because that is what I learned from my high school experiences.

For years, my high school experiences also prevented me from trusting others. I would trust my friends with secrets, but not with my heart. I was always afraid of what they were really thinking of me, and I always felt a need to prove I was worthy of their friendship

I recently have grown to realize that true friends will love me for who I am, not what I do, and true friends will stand by me through all my life changes. They are the friends who matter. I also have begun to break out of my social shell, and I am finally finding true happiness— that comes from within.

But nothing can change the years I've wasted by myself.

I didn't attend my five-year high school reunion because I still hadn't let go of my anger at my former classmates, but I'm planning to attend my ten-year reunion in 1999.

Who knows, maybe I'll make a friend?

I think I'm finally ready to try.

Unexpected Allies in Alabama

by Randy Fair

Growing up in Weaver, Ala., was a lonely experience for a gay boy in the 1970s. Weaver is a town of about 2,000 people with one red light at the center of the town. On the four corners of this center point are the Baptist church, the Methodist church, a produce stand, and a gas station. Rarely did I ever travel outside the general area surrounding this town. It was definitely not a diverse town in any sense. We had two black students at our school. I don't think I ever met an Asian or Latino person until I went to college. I certainly had never heard of anyone who was gay, and I virtually never heard the subject mentioned. But two instances, both of which happened at school, gave me hope.

One took place in the eighth grade. The town was so small that students went directly from elementary school to high school. The high school included grades seven through 12. Most of the teachers had been there since the high school was first built in the early '70s, but when I was in eighth grade the school hired a new social studies teacher.

In a town of 2,000, anyone new generates a great deal of interest, but Mr. Fincher created even more because he rarely talked about any personal history. One thing that everyone did know was that he was in his 30s, extremely handsome, and unmarried. Quickly the students at school and the people of the town filled in his personal history with rumors. One of the rumors involved his alleged affair with the home economics teacher. Another rumor was that he was gay.

I heard both of these rumors and didn't really believe either one of them. Still, in the back of my mind, I hoped that he might be gay. I already knew that I was gay, but I thought that I might be the only gay person in my town. The idea that this might be someone like me made me feel less isolated. This man was the sponsor of the student council, so I quickly decided to run for student council representative. I was thrilled when I found out that I had won the election, not because I wanted to represent the school, but because I wanted to be around Mr. Fincher as much as possible.

I hung on every word Mr. Fincher uttered in class. I never missed a student council meeting, even though attending them meant I couldn't ride the bus, and I would have to walk two miles home. But the greatest moment of my eighth grade school year was finding out that the end-of-the-year party for student council members would be held at Mr. Fincher's house. I wanted to know every detail about his life. Was he gay? Was he happy? Did he have a lover? I hoped seeing his home would give me some clues.

I went to the party, but I didn't find out any answers to my questions. I did notice that, like me, Mr. Fincher loved to read. There were books everywhere. I don't think I talked to anyone all night long. I looked around the house and watched as my teacher spent most of his time with the president of the student council. This boy was extreme-ly handsome, and I remember being jealous that my teacher lavished so much attention on him. I wondered if they might be lovers. On the one hand, I hoped that they were because this would mean Mr. Finch-er was gay. On the other hand, I hoped they weren't because my crush on Mr. Fincher was growing stronger every day.

As it turned out, I never would get the chance to find out if this man was gay. He didn't return after summer break. Everyone at school was sad to see him go, but no one was sadder than I was. I still wonder whether or not he was gay and wonder if he left because life in a small town in Alabama was too unbearable for a gay man. Whether he was gay or not, in the back of my mind I always wanted to believe he was. It gave me hope.

The only other time the subject of sexual orientation came up in my high school career was in my tenth grade English class. My English teacher was an anomaly for our small town. Mrs. Williams was young—early 30s. She was the talk of the school. Rumor had it that the reason she always wore sunglasses on Monday was because she had been smoking pot and drinking all through the weekends. She was known to hang out at the bar in the neighboring town, and rumored to have won the wet T-shirt contest there.

She was known for her beauty, but her radical ideas were her greatest asset. Her class was the highlight of the school day. Students could count on her saying something that would generate discussion during class and provoke thought throughout the day. I will never forget one class when the subject of homosexuality came up. It was during the reading of *Julius Caesar*. Because the characters called each other "thy lover," someone asked if they were gay. I can remember my face turning red and feeling very uncomfortable as the discussion began. She told us that Caesar and most of the others in the play were bisexual. She handled the discussion, just as she handled every discussion, with a matter-of-fact honesty that let us all know that no subject was off-limits in her classroom. Still, while the discussion was going on, I remember staring at my desk, refusing to raise my head up. I could feel my face growing hot and red.

When students asked her if she thought homosexuality was a sin or was sickening or gross, she turned the questions back on the students. She asked them why they believed those things. After a few minutes of discussion on the subject, she told the class that her roommate during her college days at Auburn was a lesbian. Students in the class asked her many questions about her roommate, and she answered them all openly and honestly. The question that still stands out most to me today was when a football player and a friend of mine asked her if she hadn't been afraid to undress in front of this woman.

Her answer was, "Why would I have been afraid?" "Well, because she might have been looking at you and thinking about you sexually," he said. She replied, "Look, I am comfortable with my sexuality. I know that I am heterosexual, so why would I worry what anyone else thought? If she looked at my body and admired it, I would have been just as flattered as if anyone else had." This was without a doubt the first time I had ever known of someone who wasn't afraid or disgusted by homosexuality. Her honesty and openness took great courage for someone who taught in Weaver, Ala., in 1978. I don't know how many times I have reflected on this class discussion throughout my life, but I know that it was definitely a turning point for me.

After this discussion, I looked forward to going to her class more than ever before. Even now I can recall almost every classroom discussion we ever had. This is when I first started to seriously think about a career in teaching. I began to think that maybe I could become like Mr. Fincher and be a role model for kids who felt isolated and afraid. I thought maybe I could be a teacher like Mrs. Williams and have candid, honest classroom discussions with students. Now that I am a teacher, I try to remember what these wonderful people did for me, and I try to do the same for my students.

Unlike many gay and lesbian teens, I never tried to commit suicide or drop out of school. I'm sure one of the reasons I never did was because these two wonderful human beings gave me something that every child must have to succeed, hope. Both of these teachers, without knowing it, threw me a lifeline. The first teacher gave me hope that I

About the Contributors

Donna E. Arzt is a professor at Syracuse University School of Law, specializing in international human rights. She is the author of *Refugees Into Citizens: Palestinians and the End of the Arab-Israeli Conflict.* The first draft of "Barbie Doll Dropout" was written for a 1975 college course in autobiography, a good 15 years before the author's coming out as a lesbian.

Jon Barrett grew up in Boise, Ida. A former editor at the *Idaho Press-Tribune* and Chicago's *Windy City Times,* he now lives in Los Angeles, where he is an editor at *The Advocate.*

Warren J. Blumenfeld is coauthor (with Diane Raymond) of *Looking at Gay and Lesbian Life* and editor of *Homophobia: How We All Pay the Price.* He facilitates diversity workshops for educational, business, religious, and community organizations. In 1971 he founded the National Gay Students Center for the National Student Association, Washington, D.C. Today, this organization exists as the Lesbian, Gay, and Bisexual Student Caucus of the United States Student Association.

Ed Brock grew up outside of Philadelphia. Since graduating with honors from Brown University in 1995, Ed has been teaching history to eighth, ninth, and tenth graders at a private school in the Bronx. He currently lives in Manhattan, and is on the steering committee for the New York Metro chapter of the Gay, Lesbian, and Straight Education Network.

Robert Brown grew up in Blacksburg, Va. He is currently a Ph.D. candidate in the English program at the University of Virginia.

Patricia Pomerleau Chávez lives in Santa Rosa, Calif. She has published under the name Pomerleau, but has recently taken the name Chávez in honor of Cesar Chávez and in solidarity with Mexican people in California and the rest of the United States.

Randy Clark lives in San Francisco, where he writes software documentation. He has also published articles, photographs, and poetry related to gay issues, and in the '80s contributed to a gay radio show, *Closet Free Radio,* in Santa Cruz. He is an active member of the Gay and Lesbian Historical Society of Northern California.

John Di Carlo was born in 1965 and lives in New York City. He teaches at Greenwich Academy and is a graduate student at Columbia University. He is also a freelance writer.

Peter Dell is a writer and former school teacher living in Los Angeles. His writing has appeared in *Ten Percent,* UCLA's *Queer Newsmagazine, Campus Circle Newspaper,* and *The Pink Sheet.* He is now looking for someone to publish his first novel.

Larry Duplechan is the author of four novels, including *Captain Swing.* He is currently at work on a nonfiction book about long-term male couples.

Randy Fair teaches at Milton High School in Alpharetta, Ga. He received his undergraduate degree from Jacksonville State University and received his master's and specialist degrees from Georgia State University.

Michael Floeck did his first poetry chapbook 32 years ago and has since published poetry, music reviews, and photographs. He watercolors and teaches painting. He has yet to travel abroad, and lives in Los Angeles, where he was born.

David Garnes is a longtime academic reference librarian specializing in the health sciences. In an earlier career he taught English at the secondary school level. His work has appeared in a number of publications, including *A Loving Testimony: Remembering Loved Ones Lost to AIDS; Gay & Lesbian Biography; Answers: The Magazine for Adult Children of Aging Parents; Connecticut Poets on AIDS: A Cross Culture Collection; Liberating Minds: The Stories and Professional Lives of Gay, Lesbian, and Bisexual Librarians and Their Advocates;* and *Gay & Lesbian Literature, Volume II.*

Sally Miller Gearhart is a lesbian-feminist writer, activist, and teacher who has recently stepped off of the cliff of materialism into abyss of New Age metaphysics. She is the author of *The Wanderground: Stories of Hill Women* and coauthor (with Susan Rennie) of *A Feminist Tarot*, and she was one of the interviewees in *The Times of Harvey Milk*. She now lives in Northern California in the company of multitudinous contradictions, many cats, birds, deer, and the memory of a remarkable pit bull companion.

Scott A. Giordano is a 1989 graduate of Walpole High School and a 1993 graduate of the University of Florida. He received his bachelor's degree in journalism and worked as a staff reporter for the *Philadelphia Gay News* and an associate editor for *The Weekly News* in Miami. He currently is a freelance writer based in Massachusetts.

Susan Gorrell is growing into middle age, living in Nashville, Tenn., with a wonderful community of friends and three exceptional cats: Hazel, Basil, and Leo. Her day job is managing prevention programs for a mental health agency. Everything she knows about writing she learned in 15 years at Womenwrites, a lesbian writers' conference held every spring in Georgia.

Kathryn Hamm is a counselor at Maret School, a master's candidate in the School of Social Service at Catholic University, and a cochair of the metropolitan Washington, D.C., chapter of GLSEN. Her passions include playing and coaching soccer, mountain biking, and her partner of four years (but not necessarily in that order). Although she is now a grown-up and has a real job, she still proudly shows off her Nancy McKeon Fan Club memorabilia (circa 1982) and her Bionic Woman lunch box (circa 1979) to all who visit her home in Arlington, Va.

Gillian Hanscombe was born and educated in Melbourne, has lived in England since 1969, has worked in education, commerce, and publishing, has been a feminist activist in a range of roles, and now lives and writes in rural Devon. She has published poems, fiction, articles, and essays in anthologies and collections in Britain, the United States, Canada, and Australia, in addition to her own books. Her collaboration with Suniti Namjoshi, which began with the verse sequence *Flesh and Paper,* includes further articles and *Kaliyug: Circles of Paradise,* a full-length theater piece for two principals, singer, and chorus.

Loraine Hutchins helped organize the National Network of Runaway and Youth Services and has worked in her hometown, Washington, D.C., on youth advocacy issues for many years. She coedited *Bi Any Other Name: Bisexual People Speak Out,* the anthology credited with catalyzing the national bisexual movement, and cofounded Washington, D.C.'s Alliance of Multi-Cultural Bisexuals as well as BiNet USA: The National Bisexual Network. She has contributed to many subsequent books on bisexuality and is now working on her doctorate in sexual healing.

A native of North Carolina, **Kevin Jennings** received his BA in history from Harvard University in 1985 and was a high school teacher in Massachusetts and Rhode Island for ten years. After receiving his MA from Columbia University in 1994, Kevin became the founding executive director of the Gay, Lesbian, and Straight Teachers Network (now Gay, Lesbian, and Straight Education Network), the first national organization working to end antigay bias in K-12 schools. He continues to serve as GLSEN's executive director while pursuing an MBA at New York University.

Jaron (Caroline) Kanegson attended Baker Elementary School and Brookline High School in Brookline, Mass., and graduated from the University of California, Berkeley with a BA in women's studies. Jaron is now earning an MA in English and creative writing at San Francisco State University and works as educational services coordinator at the Lavender Youth Recreation and Information Center (LYRIC), a non-profit organization in San Francisco for lesbian, gay, bisexual, transgender, and questioning youth.

Spike Katz has written journalism and fiction for queer, feminist, and left political periodicals and anthologies since the '60s. She has lived many lives on three continents, ranging from 20 years as a tae kwon do master to her present job as manager of a charity in the U.K. She is presently working as coeditor on an anthology called *Lusty Autumn* about lesbians and sex after 50.

Michael Kozuch graduated from Northeastern University in 1993 with a BS in Human Resources. He has been involved in Queer Nation and the No on 9 campaign in Portland, Ore., and also worked for Senator Edward M. Kennedy on education and AIDS issues as well as the gays in the military debate. He is currently working for the Massachusetts Department of Education's Safe Schools Program for Gay and Lesbian Student. He holds a master's degree from the Harvard Graduate School of Education.

Kerry Lindemann-Schaefer lives in a small southern town and greatly enjoys the nonurban lifestyle. She has held a wide range of jobs, all the way from crew on a schooner to health professional. An amateur science-fiction writer who has yet to sell a novel, she survived her first half century of life and is looking forward with enthusiasm to whatever lies ahead.

Jane Ellen Miles has been teaching in private and public elementary schools in the St. Louis area since 1989. Having earned her MA in professional counseling in 1998, she hopes to continue providing therapy with research on the particular needs of women and gay youth. Her interests include writing poetry, singing, doing advocacy work through both GLSEN and PFLAG, and spending time with her seven nieces and nephews. She is thankful to be part of a supportive family, a loving group of friends, and a progressive catholic church.

Michael Mitchell lives in New York City, where he is an executive producer of the Gay/Lesbian American Music Awards (GLAMA), which he helped create in 1995. As a community activist, he has worked extensively in AIDS education and prevention and HIV vaccine research. "Toughskins" is Michael's first short story to be published and is for David, who became a dentist; Casey, who did time for stealing cattle; Frog, who couldn't have become a greater brother, but did anyway; and Kent, because he rocks. Finally, it's for Kelly De Hill, my high school English teacher, who showed through example that being exactly who you are carries its own brilliance.

Merril Mushroom is a "'50s Butch Dyke" who grew up in Florida and now lives in Tennessee. She has written many articles and stories about gay and lesbian life in the '50s.

David Ortmann is an artist, actor, activist, writer, educator, and a proud gay man. He loves trees, books, music, sleeping, animals, and most people. He lives in San Francisco.

Grant Peterson completed 35 years of employment in the California public schools, where he worked as a teacher, a counselor, and a site and district office administrator. Now in his eighth year of retirement, he has served two years as chair of the Alameda County Human Relations Commission and presided over two nonprofit organizations, We Care Bay Area and the Bay Area Network of Gay and Lesbian Educators, which, under his leadership, is now a chapter of GLSEN, on whose national board of directors he also serves. He is currently heavily involved in conducting school staff development workshops that promote awareness of the needs of gay, lesbian, bisexual, and transgendered youth. He lives in Hayward, Calif.

Born in São Paulo, Brazil, **Marcelo F. Pinto** first came to the United States as an AFS exchange student in 1978. He earned a Ph.D. in social psychology from the University of Texas at Dallas in 1996 and currently conducts educational research involving at-risk children in the Dallas public schools. Marcelo lives in Dallas. He has two sons, Gustavo, age ten, and Mauricio, age eight.

Townsand Price-Spratlen was born in Bellingham, Wash., and raised in Seattle, Wash. He has been writing poetry and short stories while striving to complete his novel-in-progress for quite a while now. He strives to stay happy, living and working in Columbus, Ohio, where he is an assistant professor of sociology at Ohio State University.

Matt Rottnek is the former assistant to the director of the Center for Lesbian and Gay Studies at the City University of New York Graduate School, where he also studied philosophy. He is the editor of the forthcoming book *Sissies and Tomboys: Gender "Nonconformity" in Childhood* and is pursuing a career as a writer. He lives in New York City with his boyfriend, Jeff, and their three dogs, Norma, Waldo, and Rufus.

Ken Rus Schmoll founded Sensibel Avhängighets Teater in 1996 with a production of the collaboratively created *The Uncertain Jane Eyre*. He currently teaches in the Creative Arts Program at Watkinson School in Hartford, Conn.

John R. Selig lives in Dallas and earns his living doing marketing and advertising in the restaurant industry. He raised his 19-year-old son, Nathaniel, and was married for 13 years before coming out. During his free time he is an activist, photographer, and writer.

Michele Spring-Moore grew up in the suburbs of Rochester, N.Y., and has lived in Boulder, Colo., where she earned her MA in creative writing at the University of Colorado. Her work has been published in journals including *Hanging Loose, Bay Windows, Fireweed: A Feminist Quarterly, Many Mountains Moving,* and the anthology *Plural Desires: Writing Bisexual Women's Realities* from Sister Vision Press in Toronto. She's a former editor of *Empty Closet,* New York State's oldest lesbian and gay newspaper, and a cofounder of Rochester Bisexual Women's Network and Boulder Bisexual Women's Voice.

Before moving to Burlington, Vt., **Janet Stambolian** lived for 17 years in Los Angeles, where she worked as a carpenter in a women-owned construction company and as a construction manager at Cedars-Sinai Medical Center. Now director of business development for a health care architecture firm, she also acts, sings, and aspires to be a writer. A lifelong lesbian, Janet has dedicated herself to enhancing intergenerational communication and understanding, ardently believes that the personal is political, and plans to build communities for aging baby boomers and their friends.

Carter Wilson was born and raised in Washington, D.C. He is the author of four novels, including *Treasures on Earth* and *Crazy February: Death and Life in the Mayan Highlands.* He wrote narration for two Oscar-winning documentaries, *The Times of Harvey Milk* and *Common Threads,* and received the Ruth Benedict Prize for his 1995 non-fiction book, *Hidden in the Blood: A Personal Investigation of AIDS in the Yucatan.*